D1518703

GOMEZ
Tyrant of the Andes

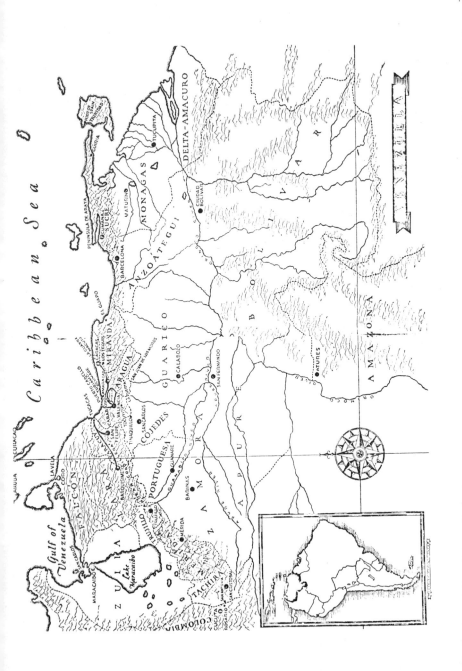

PIMENTEL MAKES GÓMEZ LAUGH

GÓMEZ

Tyrant of the Andes

by

Thomas Rourke

GREENWOOD PRESS, PUBLISHERS
NEW YORK

Los pueblos de nuestra América caerán en manos de vulgares tiranuelos.

SIMÓN BOLÍVAR.

CONTENTS

viii CONTENTS

ILLUSTRATIONS

ACKNOWLEDGMENTS

❖

THERE are many people to whom I owe thanks for helping me in the collection of material for this book. The full list would be very long but these I must name.

Mr. Rudolph Dolge permitted me the use of his very comprehensive library, one of the most complete in existence, in Venezoliana. Mr. Dolge is one of the oldest American residents of Venezuela and he has earned the respect and affection of the people.

Señor Don Lorenzo Mercado provided me with many facts of Gómez's early career out of his great store of personal memories. Don Lorenzo is a fine gentleman and his long, amazing life, lived with dash and humor, makes the invented tales of romantic fiction taste like rapadura. I hope he will write it some day.

Others who helped me in many ways are, Mr. E. E. Boylan, Mr. F. I. Martin, Mr. Gilbert Cover, Señor Porras Bello, Señor Manuel Flores Cabrera, Señor Pedro José Muñoz and the students of the Universidad Central who are employed at the Biblioteca Nacional.

THOMAS ROURKE.

PREFACE

❖

THE writing of a book which sets out to be the personal story of a man who has died within the past few months becomes, of necessity, the recording of contemporary history. And that is always a difficult and thankless task: difficult, because it is impossible to get an entirely dispassionate opinion on any single event, and thankless, because, in the end, you are bound to offend practically everyone involved as well as all of his wives, aunts, uncles, children and grandchildren.

Nevertheless, I shall attempt it, for it is a story that clamors to be told. Furthermore, I have been boring my friends with it for so long, that, perhaps by writing it and going in for some wholesale boring, I shall get it out of my system.

For some reason, completely obscure to me, there is an amazing lack of interest in the United States in Latin-American affairs. Before leaving the States for Venezuela shortly after the death of General Gómez in December, 1935, I was certain that there was trouble brewing and I asked my agent to get in touch with the various news services in New York with a view to securing free cable privileges should I come across anything of interest. There was no question of contract or payment of money, simply the right to send cables collect. Complete apathy, lack of interest. No news value in the political affairs of Venezuela.

Four days after I arrived in Caracas, nearly two hundred men, women and children were mowed down without warning by government soldiers in the Plaza Bolívar in the center of the city.

The newspapers are not to blame. Had the two hundred been two thousand, the interest, or disinterest, of the American public, would scarcely have warranted more than a modest front-page article.

I know, for I have tried it, if you ask any ten Americans who live in the States, whether Venezuela is in Central America or South America, you will get two correct answers, four wrong ones, and four uncertain ones. And Venezuela is a country of over three million people. In 1928 it was second in the world in the production of petroleum. There are hundreds of millions of American dollars invested there. It is the birthplace of Simón Bolívar and was the scene of most of his battles against the Spaniards that won independence for the whole northern part of South America. Bolívar is regarded by all South Americans as a greater man than Washington.

In order to explain the difficulties involved in collecting authentic data relating to Juan Vicente Gómez, I shall have to anticipate my story somewhat and describe conditions as I found them in Venezuela after the General's death. The years I had spent in the country prior to that had created in me a great interest in the man and it seemed that, with his death, I should be able to obtain, at last, documentary proof of all the things I had known of him through association with some of his admirers and with certain "enemies of the Cause."

For a period of twenty-seven years the printed history of Venezuela is an absolutely blank page. During all those years of Gómez's dictatorship, there was not one line of free, unsubsidized opinion set up in type and preserved in public archives, nor indeed one word of free opinion uttered in public. To be sure there were, among the more gallant and foolhardy of the "periodístas" and civilian patriots, individuals, from time to time, who burst the bonds of self-restraint and spoke their minds. They sealed their own doom. Their words were quickly muffled, their presses confiscated and the type scattered and the gallant ones themselves sent to the prisons to die or go mad.

It is difficult to imagine, in these times. Twenty-seven years of the history of a whole nation completely unchronicled, or worse, written falsely to the glorification of a conceited and power-mad tyrant: the whole artistic expression of a people stopped at the fountain-head, the poets condemned to sing false and sickly paeans or remain mute, the painters to ennobling the features of the despot and all his kin and all their works, or flee the country.

So, in the National Library today, one cannot find a single printed line of unbiased truth. Plenty of saccharine adulatory slime written by well-rewarded panderers. Plenty of that. But it would not mislead a lad of ten, none of it.

Then, in December, 1935, the Dictator died. A flood of exiles poured back into the country, some five thousand of them, among them newspapermen, poets and novelists, many of them with ankles and wrists distorted by the chains they had worn in Venezuelan prisons. Speech, the press, the air waves, were free. Free, after twenty-seven years. And the exiled ones made the most of it.

The presses hummed. The air waves throbbed. A tidal wave of hate, diatribe, odium, all the feces of twenty-seven years of emotional constipation, spewed out upon the Gómez tribe, upon anything that looked like Gómez or smelled like Gómez. The newspapers ran special editions and vied for the personal stories of the victims and gave them front-page spreads, the cartoonists worked all night to draw the things they had sketched in secret on bits of paper for so many years. All of this in passion, in hate. Not for the historian. All of it had the virtue of sincerity and some of it of truth.

And where, between these two extremes of what should be legitimate sources of information, does the calm historian get off? The answer is he doesn't get off. He wanders his uncertain way through the mess, trying to pick up the threads of the story he so confidently started out to write.

A cultured, middle-aged Venezuelan lady said to me once, "Tomás, te digo una cosa. Nunca vivía, nunca vivirá, un hombre tan cruel como Gómez." "Thomas, I tell you one thing. There never lived and there never will live a man so cruel as Gómez."

On the other hand, the National Library is full of volumes by such worthies as V. Márquez Bustillos, Nemesio García Naranjo and Aurelio de Vivanco y Villegas, which paint the man as white as a lily, as the saint of saints, the savior of his people, the ultimate in all human virtues.

Somewhere between these two opinions, leaning rather heavily toward the lady's side, lies the truth.

The lady's opinion was disinterested. Neither she nor any of her immediate kinsmen had suffered particularly at the hands of Gómez; not any more so than the average citizen of Venezuela. She was intellectually incapable of making a more profound psychological classification of the man, but she was sincere.

As for the others, the writing gentlemen, they are liars.

The dictatorship of Juan Vicente Gómez in Venezuela is unique in modern times. There is no parallel for it. It is unique not only for its many years' duration but also for its perfection, its smoothness of operation, its ruthlessness, and, above all, its stealth. It was carried on so quietly, that, in these times of radio and air travel and talking pictures, scarcely anyone outside of Venezuela knew of its existence. It was so perfect that nothing but death availed against it—natural death, death from old age—and even death would have been defeated if Gómez had had any luck in the sons his women bore him.

It has been compared to the dictatorships of Mussolini, Hitler and, perhaps with more reason, to those of Porfirio Díaz in Mexico and Machado in Cuba. But these comparisons are futile.

Gómez built his machine by force of arms and maintained it by terror. He instilled in his people blind, unholy fear. The peons called him brujo, witch-doctor. He built his machine and maintained it against the will of the people and not with its co-operation as did the European dictators. The power of those worthies rests in the delusion of their peoples and was established by oratory, spell-binding, appealing to racial prejudices and all the other puerile instincts that exist in all of us, by the mumbo-jumbo of patriotic cant and martial trappings—the same methods that built up the Ku Klux Klan in the United States.

Gómez never made a speech in his life. Even his literacy has been questioned. He wouldn't have understood an "ism" if anyone had bothered to explain one to him. It is rather significant that, in quite a few years of living in various parts of Venezuela, I never met a person, not directly employed in some function of the Dictator's machine, who, once his confidence was won and his fears allayed, did not damn his soul.

Díaz and Machado were seduced by foreign capital. They sold out their people and used the funds to maintain their power. No one ever seduced Gómez. He got funds from foreign interests, it is true, but he drove hard, legal bargains and those funds were in the nature of legitimate income for the Nation, and the fact that he was able to direct them into his own pocket is evidence of the efficiency of the governmental machine he developed and not of under-the-table negotiations with exploiters.

No, the dictatorship of Gómez was something different. It was something more primitive. It goes back further than Díaz and perhaps further than the later Czars. It harks back to medieval times. It was the iron rule of the caciques, the tribal chiefs of the Andean Indians. It carried a faint odor of witchcraft and mysticism.

In the preparation of this book, I have received help from sincere, disinterested people who will perhaps find many of my opinions at variance with theirs. I wish to apologize to them beforehand and ask their indulgence. I wish to point out that I have sought other opinions also and my conclusions have been based upon the truth as I have been able to see it. I will quote the trite but pertinent example of the seven witnesses to a street accident, none of whose stories jibed in essential details, and point out that for me the problem was further complicated by the fact that some of my witnesses were men who had been hung up by their testicles in Gómez's prisons.

To the others, the interested ones, they have fed at the Gómez trough, and I make no apology at all.

T. R.

Caracas, February, 1936.

PART ONE

THE LAND AND THE RACE

Chapter I

A BIT OF GEOGRAPHY AND HISTORY

❖

THE road from Cúcuta to San Antonio was a foot-trail in those days. The distance is only twelve miles but there is a range of mountains, the Táchira River and the Colombia-Venezuela border along the route.

The trail was narrow, between steep rock walls. In the early morning the cold mists billowed up from the ravines, rolling in lazy surges along the mountain sides, clinging to the tapering peaks till they reached the sunlight high up, hanging there like glistening white halos. Down in the passes along the trail, it was cold, with the damp cold of rocky places where water trickles, and the long, slanting rays of the low sun on the peaks above was a promise of only a brief warmth at mid-day when they would stand erect like bright lances, piercing the deep, shadowed places. The woman tightened the folds of the blanket under the baby's rump at her hip.

She prodded the pack-mule with a stick. "Mu-u-lá!" she called. The breath came white from her mouth. Her sharp voice and the delicate, uneven clopping of the animal's hoofs on the rocky trail echoed among the quiet gullies.

It was hard going, afoot. The steep trails were worn into twisting stairways of low steps made by all the hoofs that had followed them for three hundred years. The mule found the steps nicely placed for him and he trod

3

them surely and daintily but the woman jolted along in awkward pace, long strides and short ones, finding footing, the wide, woolen skirts swinging free, the bare, sandaled feet shuffling over the smooth stones. The little boy toddled beside her, silent with the cold. His stubby brown fist was twisted in his mother's skirt.

At the crossing of the Táchira there was a clearing with a thatched hut and a corn-field. The ferryman set about taking the packs from the mule's back and the woman and little boy went to the hut. They squatted outside and the ferryman's wife brought them black, bitter coffee and half-gourds of steaming caldo, seasoned with onion and salt. The woman nursed the baby girl under the blanket.

"When do you return to Cúcuta, little daughter?" the older woman asked.

"I don't return, old woman. I stay there on the other side."

"Por dios! Then you leave Evaristo?"

"I leave him."

"Do you think you do well? Evaristo is a wealthy man. Pedro is poor."

"I tired of Evaristo. Pedro pleases me."

The ferryman piled the packs into a dugout, tied the halter of the mule to a thwart and pushed the boat into the stream. He sat in the stern with a paddle and urged the animal into the water behind him. The mule stepped cautiously into the cold river. He lost footing, submerged and came up, swimming. The man paddled across the current, the animal, snorting, his neck stretched out, following the narrow boat.

On the other side of the Táchira the ferryman tied the mule, replaced the packs and returned to bring the woman and her children across.

The day was warmer now and the woman folded the blanket into a flat strip and hung it on her shoulder.

She prodded the mule up the trail and waved to the old woman standing by her hut across the river.

"Mu-u-lá!" she cried and the boy repeated, "Mu-u-lá!" He gathered pebbles and tossed them at the animal's rump.

It was nearly noon when they reached the village of San Antonio. The sun was bright on the little town in its high valley. The low, adobe houses were silent in the brilliant warmth and dogs slept in the middle of the dusty streets.

Pedro was waiting in the shade of a ceiba tree beside the plaza. There were two saddle-mules tethered beside him. He leaned against his animal's flank, smiling a little to himself, watching the woman who came toward him. A fine woman. She walked with a fine stride, the long, full skirt swinging. Her skin was the color of burnished copper, her hair shining black, smoothed back and plaited down her back. Her eyes flashed under the wide felt hat. She carried the baby astride her hip. The youngster beside her trotted along on sturdy legs.

"You came in good time," Pedro said.

"I hurried."

"Are you tired? I brought an animal for you. You can ride now."

The woman laughed. "Tired? I?"

"No, I suppose not," Pedro said. "The youngster doesn't seem tired either."

"Not that one. He's a tiger for walking."

"Did you have trouble there, with Evaristo?"

The woman shrugged. "Men do not make trouble for me," she said. "One has yet to put the halter."

Pedro laughed. "I believe it. And to me will pass the same thing when the time comes."

"Maybe not," the woman said.

Pedro untethered the riding animals and held the baby while the woman mounted. Then he tied the

halter of the pack-mule to his own saddle, lifted the
boy to the animal's back and mounted in front of him.

He reined away and they moved off toward his farm,
the woman at his side, sitting side-saddle, holding the
baby, the boy behind him, clinging to his waist with his
stubby fingers.

The man was Pedro Cornelio Gómez and the woman
was Hermenegilda Chacón. The boy was four years old
and his name was Juan Vicente. All his life he called
himself Gómez, but his name should have been García,
after his real father, or legally, Chacón, his mother's
name, for he was a bastard. The exact date of his birth
is unknown. The year was 1857.

If any man ever was the product of the race that bore
him and the land that fed him it was this man. So, to
know this man we will have to know a little of that
race and that land and we shall try to learn something
of them as briefly and painlessly as possible.

It will be a strange land in many ways to most of us,
and a stranger race.

It is a land very close to the equator. We are accustomed to think of it as no more nor less than an expanse of steaming jungle. In reality, it is nearly one-
third high, cool plateaus and chilly mountain peaks and
nearly one-half, rolling plains of waving grass with
scarcely a proper-sized bush appearing in days of travel.
It is a land that has fine, modern cities, that had thousands of permanent European inhabitants a hundred
years before the Pilgrims landed, that had a university
two hundred miles back among the peaks of the Andes
fifty years before Harvard was founded and yet today
has one hundred and thirty thousand completely un-
civilized Indians inside its boundaries and over one-
third of its adult population illiterate.

As late as last year, young American and European

engineers and geologists doing their regular tasks in the bush were fired upon by six-foot arrows from the bows of Indians of whom no white man has ever had more than a fleeting glimpse, and in the last ten years quite a few of those young men have been killed.

It is a country that enjoys the most solid economic standing of any country on earth, with no internal nor external debt and a substantial balance in the national treasury, and yet the average money value of all the earthly possessions of most of its citizens does not exceed twenty-five dollars. It will be a strange land to most of us.

The Andes rise out of the sea at the southern tip of South America and march northward the whole length of the continent, following the western coast, peak after peak, a ragged file of bayonets marching northward, piercing the clouds, glistening cold in the sun. It is a wandering, straggling file, bunching in places, but mostly it keeps its line of march until it nears the northern coast, till it reaches the southwestern corner of Venezuela where it touches Colombia. Then the file divides. The main column continues northward across Colombia. A wing deploys northeastward in a slow arc across Venezuela, reaches the coast on a line of tangent, and tapers off into the sea at La Guayra. That wing, that curved file of marching mountain peaks, is very important to us in coming to know Juan Vicente Gómez and it was very important, too, in the history of the whole of South America. In the Y that is formed when the wing swings northeastward and the main column goes on, lies the great Lake of Maracaibo, and that is important, too, for it is one of the richest oil fields in the world.

So, with that curved range of mountains established as the dominant topographic feature of our country, we'll forget the rest of South America and look at the map of Venezuela to see what the other parts of it are like.

A range of lesser mountains borders the northern coast along its whole length. Along the sea are wide strips of flat, sandy salina [1] and little pockets and valleys of hot jungle between the hills, shut off from any breeze, and inland, behind the range, is more jungle, all hot and low and thick, a band of it about forty miles through. And then, to the south, the great basin of the Orinoco-Apure River System, about two-thirds of the whole area of Venezuela. And this, too, all low and hot. Here and there, toward the east, in the States of Guárico and Anzoátegui, rise some table-lands where the breezes sweep fresh and cool, but it is low, for the most part, and hot. Not jungle though. Llanos. Rolling, grassy prairie, miles of it, sloping gently southward and eastward toward the Orinoco. These llanos are important, too. We'd better look at them some more.

We'll have to look at them in two different seasons of the year for they are utterly different in those seasons.

The rainy season first, or, rather, just after the rainy season. The llanos are covered with tall, waving grass, as high as your head, green, the color of young pea sprouts. The sandy soil beneath is hard-packed and moist. There are sunken places here and there, marked by the dark green clumps of chaparro trees and the tall, waving fronds of moriche palm, lagunas, mirrors of clear, still water with bulrushes and reeds and clouds of water-fowl. Egrets, thousands of them, white and blue and red, herons, ducks, and maybe a flamingo or two. There may be a few small deer grazing under the trees. There may be a large land-turtle and some armadillos but not much else. There isn't the game you'd expect on the llanos.

[1] Salty place. Particularly, the wide coastal flats of sand and salt formed by evaporation of the seasonal lagoons.

Away off somewhere there'll be a dark green line of chaparro and that marks a river. There are many rivers in the llanos. Now, they will be full and flowing— smooth, muddy water, down in deep gorges eaten into the soft soil. They all flow to the Orinoco and the Orinoco is full now, too. At Ciudad Bolívar, the principal port on the river, the average difference in height of water between seasons is forty-five feet. In the strip of thick jungle along the banks there may be wild pig, called váquira, and, burrowing into the banks, huge, pig-like amphibians called chigüire. You can eat them. The váquira is very good. You can eat the big land-turtles, too, and the big lizards, iguanas, that live in the branches of the trees.

At the end of the dry season the llanos are quite different. The grass is brown and brittle, the fuzzy tops blowing about. Or the grass is burned off. Miles of charred, black waste, the sandy soil powder-dry, mixed with black ash. The lagunas are dried up. The bottom is hard, baked clay, checkered with cracks. The birds and animals are gone, all but some buzzards that perch in the skeletons of the chaparros over the carcass of a deer.

The rivers are deep scars in the earth. The banks are chalky white or red palisades, the beds, dry gravel. Bone-dry, most of the rivers. Some of them, though, have a trickle of clear, sparkling water, rippling over the gravel, away off, down in the gorge.

Those are the llanos, the cattle country.

Near its mouth, the Orinoco River has built up a great, flat area of swampy land and finds its way to the sea through it in hundreds of twisting, narrow channels called caños. This is the Delta Amacuro. It is low, thick, mangrove jungle, damp and hot.

In the southeastern corner of Venezuela, south of the Orinoco, is the largest area of real jungle land in the

country. It lies in the State of Bolívar and used to be
called Guayana. It extends to the border of British
Guiana and the northern border of Brazil. This is real
jungle, the jungle of great, tall trees and tangled lianas.
There is little dry season here. Plenty of rainfall. It is
rough country, hilly. There are great waterfalls and
rocky gorges and rising mists. There are brilliant birds,
macaws and parrots and toucans and bell-birds and
there are monkeys and boas and big tapirs that swim
the streams and crash through the jungle at night. It is
the "Green Mansion" country of W. H. Hudson. It is
the gold country of the old Spanish legends. It still produces gold and diamonds and wild rubber. This is all
hot country, too.

That pretty well covers the map of Venezuela.

Going over it, we'll find that there are principally
only two kinds of country—high country and low country. The low country is divided up considerably, into
llanos and delta and jungle and coastal salina but it is
all low country. And the high country is that curve of
mountain range that swings along the west and northwest, only about a third of the whole area of the country. High country and low country, cool country and
hot country, for that's what it amounts to, generally
speaking.

Your temperature gauge here is vertical. Latitude and
season don't enter to any extent, the only element is
altitude, with proximity to the sea a small factor where
there are no hills to shut off the southeast trade winds.
That is no original observation, certainly, in a book on
tropical country, but it needs repeating here.

What we're getting around to, in our peculiar way,
is people.

The original inhabitants of this country, the Indians,
are so strongly marked in physical and mental traits by
the climatic conditions of their particular regions that

those traits are apparent after centuries of infiltration of foreign bloods, in the Venezuelan of today, the mestizo, almost a racial type now, more completely developed in Venezuela than in any other so-called Latin-American country. Fernándo González, the Colombian writer, defines the type: 45% White, 45% Indian, 10% Negro. The 10% Negro seems rather too high for the Venezuelan type taken as a whole. At any rate, it is the Indian element that differed originally and makes for the differences today in the mestizo type of different parts of Venezuela. That is the reason for the rather lengthy dissertation on the geography of the country that we have just waded through.

The Venezuelan aborigine racially belongs to the Caribe group, the widespread and one-time numerous race that inhabited all the shores and islands of the Caribbean Sea. Caribe means flesh-eater. Tribally, they are split up into innumerable small bands scattered over the country, each band entirely independent, having its own dialect, customs, religion, favorite locale, dress or undress, but in all these things bearing a certain similarity one to the other. In all the tribes the chief is known as cacique, pronounced kah-sée-kay.

The tribes of the highlands, of that Cordillera of the Andes in the northwestern part, have always been vastly superior to the lowland tribes of the rest of the country. They have always been comparatively large, healthy and strong, hard workers, shrewd and war-like. That is easily explainable, of course. Their high, cold mountain country made them that way. There were no insects to give them fevers. The water was pure and flowing. The cold nights kept their blood thick and their energy alive and the steep, rocky trails kept their muscles hard. So the Táchiras and Mombunes and Oracás and Jirajaras and all the other Andean tribes have always possessed the strongest qualities of all the Venezuelan Indians though

not always the best qualities from the social point of
view.

The lowland Indians are a different story. They have
always been small, degenerate physically, slow-witted
and pacific. The Delta tribes live along the mosquito-
ridden caños. Their principal food is fish and they grow
a little corn. They are rickety, they have bad teeth and
pot-bellies. The Indians of Lake Maracaibo are much
the same. They live in villages built on stilts in the
water of the lake or in the swamps along the shore. The
llanos Indians are somewhat better off, possibly, especially those of the mesa districts around Cantaura, but
they, too, have suffered from the heat and lack of proper
food and water during the long dry seasons.

While the tribes of the Cordillera itself have become
completely civilized, it is significant that, among the un-
civilized Indians in Venezuela today, the only war-like
ones are of the high country. There have been reports
of strange, hostile tribes far back in the Guayana country but nothing definite has ever been learned of them
and they are probably a myth. On the other hand, the
Motilones are no myth. They are the lads who have
been sending the six-foot arrows flying from the bush
into the American and European geologists working for
the oil companies. They live on the slopes of the main
Andean range along the Colombia border west of Lake
Maracaibo. And the other mean ones, the Goajiras, live
in the mountains on the peninsula called by the same
name, Goajira. They're not really hostile, but they're
strong-willed, independent people.

The coast of Venezuela was the first land of the South
American continent seen by Christopher Columbus. It
was on his third voyage, in 1498, and the land was the
Peninsula of Paria, in the extreme eastern part. Columbus entered the Gulf of Paria and sailed along the coast
of the Orinoco delta but he didn't establish a colony

anywhere. The next year an expedition under Alonzo de Ojeda and Amerigo Vespucci followed along the whole northern coast, leaving shore parties here and there, and finally entered Lake Maracaibo at the western end of what is now Venezuela. Ojeda found the Indians living in their grass huts built on stilts in the water, paddling around among them in dugout canoes, the same as they do today, and he called the place "Venezuela" which is Spanish for "Little Venice."

After that, colonization went on pretty rapidly. The Spanish were at the height of their mad era and this long, mountainous coast-line looked good to all the wild young dons with their bright, new swords. They swarmed all along its length. In 1521, they established the first permanent colony at Cumaná. They worked inland here and there along the eastern part of the north coast, crossed the thin range of low mountains, and were disappointed in the low jungle country they found beyond. Some missionaries went in, even to the llanos, and established posts, but this wasn't the country the dons were looking for and the trend was westward along the coast.

At La Guayra the mountains reared higher. They looked more inviting to the dons, more promising of what they were after, more worthy of cradling those golden-castellated cities of which they dreamed. So, in they went, working their way back among the peaks, swarms of young dons, Díaz Moreno, Juan de Villegas, Juan Rodrígues Suárez, Juan de Maldonado, helmets and breastplates and swords burnished, looking for gold and hoping for dragons.

The Spaniards were pleased to find that here, the mountains weren't just a thin strip that died away into low jungle. Instead, they swung off to the southwest, peak after peak, growing higher, table-lands and high valleys, very inviting. The dons went in, further and

further, in breathless haste, over the rough, chill, mountain country.

Diego de Losado founded the city of Caracas and in
1550 the territory was made a captain-generalcy of
Spain. In eight years' time five cities were founded
along the Andean Cordillera, one of them more than
five thousand feet above sea-level, and one of them four
hundred and fifty miles inland from the coast. And
they were cities. They had cathedrals, fine mansions for
the captains, fortifications, well-laid-out streets, away
back in the mountains, just a foot-trail between them,
Valencia, Barquisimeto, Mérida, San Cristóbal. It is a
good, rough week's journey by car today from Caracas
to San Cristóbal along the so-called Transandean Highway that follows the old Spanish route along the
Cordillera.

These Spaniards were of the finest blood of Spain in
her heroic era. They were strong-willed, venturesome,
fighting men. And they bred with the sturdiest Indians
of Venezuela.

In Venezuela the Conquistadores were more gracious
than they were in Mexico and other places for they
established peaceful relations with the Indians from the
start. They put them to work, but they also taught them
to plant new products and brought them cattle and
horses and won their friendship.

The Spaniards came here to stay but they didn't bring
many women. So, they planted their seed in the strong-
limbed daughters of the Andean caciques. And they
bred a race along the Cordillera that influenced the
whole history of South America and that, even today,
influences the history of Venezuela.

Later, other Spaniards drifted into the lowlands of
the country and founded other cities and mixed their
blood with other Indians, but the Indians were of a
different breed. And that was later. The Andean race

had over a hundred years start and was bred upon stronger blood. Barcelona was founded in 1671 and of the inland cities, Maturín in 1710, Calabozo in 1695, Ciudad Bolívar in 1764—all more than a century later.

The Negroes came in as slaves to the Spaniards. Some of them went into the highlands with their masters and added a trace of their blood in the race that evolved there. But mostly, both as slaves and, later, as freemen, they kept to the coast and to the low, inland country. As slaves, they weren't needed in the mountains, for the Spaniards found the Indians there better suited to the altitude and climate and as freemen, their own tastes kept them to the warm, low places with the easier ways of life, to the coast regions with their movement and color and contact with the world.

The Cordillera of Venezuela became the home of a race of feudal lords. They were condors, all of them, with nests in the high table-lands. They ruled over their Indian peons in the manner of the old caciques but they raised their families in the tradition of the Spanish dons. The wealthier ones sent their sons and daughters to Europe to study the culture and graces of the old world. Their Indians were armed retainers. They were politically-minded and fanatically acquisitive. They waged wars among each other over their lands and herds of cattle and over questions of state.

This Andean race produced the great poet, Andrés Bello, the painter, Michelena, thousands of caudillos, the egotistic, uncompromising little generals that have been the curse of the country for centuries, the great warriors, Miranda and Páez, and the Liberator, Simón Bolívar. It produced, too, in our own time, Juan Vicente Gómez.

Chapter II

SIMÓN BOLÍVAR, THE LIBERATOR AND THOSE WHO FULFILLED HIS PROPHECIES

❖

AFTER the colonization period in northern South America there is nothing of interest to us particularly until Bolívar appears like a bursting rocket in a tropic night.

To treat of this man here in our brief way would be little short of blasphemy, meriting the fancier forms of torment of the Gómez Rotunda. We shan't attempt it. But we shall repeat a little of his career in an effort to arouse interest to further study in other volumes. There are innumerable fine books about him. Besides, we must know something of Venezuela's greatest man and of those who came after him in order to understand the political and social traditions that had been established when Juan Vicente Gómez was born.

Into Bolívar's short life was crowded one of the most amazing records of victories and defeats and triumphs and tragedies in all of history. He fought over two hundred bloody battles. He achieved independence from Spain for six countries. He was given the title, Liberator, by all six congresses, he marched through arches of flowers in all the capitals and they wanted to crown him emperor; but he was driven from those capitals and he lived to see all his works crashing about him, almost before they were accomplished. He lived to see the imprisonment of one of his staunchest comrades,

Miranda, the banishment of another, Santander, the treason of another, Páez, and the murder of another, Sucre.

A man of puzzling contrasts in his traits of character and in his luck. He was an idealist to the point of fanaticism, yet he issued a proclamation of "War to the Death" and he ordered eight hundred and eighty-six Spanish prisoners executed in one lot. He devoted his whole life to republicanism and to overthrowing the tyranny of Spanish rule, yet he toyed with the idea of becoming emperor and he stated very forcibly many times that "an able despotism" was the only form of government possible for his people. He was an aristocrat and very proud of his noble blood, yet he forced one of his nieces, Felicia, to marry one of his generals, Laurencio Silva, a Negro. Felicia bore the Negro many children and when she was an old woman and Bolívar was dead, she cursed him "por haberme casado con este Negro."

A man of puzzling contrasts, physically, too. He was small of stature, very delicate, and had been raised in luxury, yet he performed amazing feats of physical endurance. He burned himself out and he died at forty-seven, penniless and almost friendless.

Bolívar accomplished one of the greatest exploits in military history. He marched a ragged, starving army of two thousand, five hundred men, dragging cannon and munitions, from the steaming, flooded llanos of Venezuela over the bitter cold, barren, trackless heights of the Andes into Colombia. A march of nearly a thousand miles. With only three days' preparation, he engaged the main Spanish army of five thousand men and defeated it decisively to break the hold of Spain on Colombia for all time. This was the Battle of Boyacá, August 7, 1819.

Bolívar was born in Caracas on July 24, 1783. He was

of the mantuanos, that is, of the class whose women wore the mantilla of Spain. His father was Juan Vicente Bolívar, a pure Spaniard of noble blood, and his mother was Maria de la Concepción Palacios y Blanco, of older Venezuelan blood, mainly Spanish, too, but with some mixture of Indian.

So, by blood, Simón Bolívar was not wholly of our Cordillera race but by tradition and background he was. And he was its foremost interpreter in his writings and words. He understood it as no one else ever has, saw its weaknesses and its strengths. He berated it, counseled it, warned it, planned for it, tried to lead it along the way of political dignity, loved it. He died, despairing of it.

Whatever differences of opinion there may be of Bolívar's qualities as a military leader, there are none as to his ability as a political and social observer. He was the wisest of his time. No one has ever written with clearer understanding of his people nor with a more precise analysis of their political needs. He watched the whole world scene during the revolutionary era of the late eighteenth and early nineteenth centuries, studied the political forms evolved in various countries and the psychological traits of the peoples, measured them to his own problems, selecting and rejecting, bit by bit, with rare foresight, constructing a code of political principles and a form of government which would fit exactly his wayward people and bind them into the great, united South American Republic of which he dreamed.

Bolívar died, saying, "I have plowed in the sea." He said, "Our America will fall into the hands of vulgar tyrants." He said, "Only an able despotism can rule America." As a political prophet he was unsurpassed even by George Washington.

The subsequent history of Venezuela up to modern

times is the story of the fulfillment of the prophecies of Bolívar.

It began before he died, first, with the treason of Páez, the plotting of Santander and the withdrawal of his own country, Venezuela, from the Federal State of Colombia which Bolívar had founded. Venezuela had declared its independence from Spain on July 14, 1811. After ten years of fighting, the power of Spain was broken and the Federation was formed, including Colombia, Venezuela and Ecuador. In 1829, a year before Bolívar died, Páez seized the power in Venezuela and broke away from the Federation and Venezuela has been an independent nation ever since. That was the end of Bolívar's dream and he lived to see it.

After Bolívar, there were three important figures in Venezuelan history—Páez, Guzmán Blanco and Juan Vicente Gómez—and there were some sixteen presidents of minor importance. We must look at them briefly, for our man, Gómez, was the culmination of the political traditions which these others built up.

José Antonio Páez was born in 1790 in the village of Curpa in the foot-hills of the Andean Cordillera where they slope southeastward to the llanos. As a boy he was a peon on a cattle ranch. He became a famous horseman and he was called The Centaur. He looked the part. He was all shoulders and head, no neck and short, spindly legs. His head was large and square, the forehead high, the hair fine and light-colored and wavy. He was mestizo but the white blood dominated.

The Spanish settlers in the llanos had brought horses with them. The race that developed there from the mixture of Spanish, Indian and Negro bloods became cattle-raisers and horsemen. In the war of independence, the Spanish butcher, Boves, won the loyalty of the llaneros and organized them into a bloody band of cut-throats that became the terror of Venezuela. They fought on

horseback with long lances. They defeated Bolívar's
army twice and entered the city of Caracas and massa-
cred three thousand, five hundred refugees who had fled
the city to Aragua. So, when Boves was killed at the
battle of Urica, Páez gathered up the remnants of the
band and won them over to the revolutionary cause.

Bolívar had suffered reverses at the hands of the
Spaniards and had taken refuge at Angostura, now
Ciudad Bolívar, on the banks of the Orinoco. Páez
joined him there with his horsemen and put new heart
into the revolution. His first exploit was typical and
spectacular. The Spanish gun-boats were lying at anchor
in the river and one night Páez took to the water with
his horses, swam them to the gun-boats, boarded the
vessels and captured them after bloody hand-to-hand
fighting.

Páez was given full command of the revolutionary
forces in the llanos and he cleaned out the Spanish in
short order, using much the same tactics as his prede-
cessor, Boves. He was left in full charge of the llanos
when Bolívar crossed the Andes into Colombia and it
was then that he began to plot against the Liberator.

Bolívar was in Colombia and Perú for two years and
during this time Páez had entered Caracas and virtually made himself dictator. And he had been seduced
by flattery and society and the fine living of the capital.
He was a peon who had never learned to use a knife
and fork. He had always been avaricious. He had had
his little business with his llaneros from the beginning.
The soldiers got their pay in the form of credit slips
on the treasury of the new government of Gran Colombia and Páez bought these from them at a ridiculous
price and with them, bought from the State, the great
estate of a Spanish marquis. The little business made
him rich.

In the capital he stole everything in sight and Bolívar

had to return from Perú to correct his abuses. Páez could be very engaging when he wanted to and he patched things up with Bolívar and Bolívar returned to Colombia to put down the uprising headed by Santander.

Bolívar never returned to Venezuela. In 1829 he sent General Sucre to Caracas to take over the presidency but Páez refused to let Sucre pass the border, declaring himself president and Venezuela independent of the Gran Colombia.

There are a lot of precedents set in all this that we'll do well to remember.

Páez played up to the mantuanos, the men whose wives had the exclusive right to wear the mantilla, and to the caudillos, the little generals from the Cordillera who were resentful of Bolívar's liberalism, and supported Páez to a man. Páez built up a strong, autocratic machine that maintained its power for sixteen years, from 1830 to 1846. He was the first Venezuelan dictator.

Páez ruled the country with a firm hand. He created monopolies for himself and his friends and lived a gay, easy life in the capital. He liked to gamble and he was epileptic. He was a genial soul when he wanted to be and he liked the foreign diplomats and became intrigued with the culture of foreign countries. He learned rapidly and even developed literary aspirations and wrote his memoires. But he loved only two things— to acquire money and to kill his enemies. Remember this. We'll find those dominating traits in another man, later.

There was a revolt against Páez in Caracas and all the leaders were executed. In 1836 a man named Farfán raised a revolt in the llanos and Páez went out in person to put it down. He bottled up the rebels in a place called Payara and he killed so many of them with his own sword that his arm became almost paralyzed. They called him The Lion of Payara after that and later, Guzmán Blanco said, "Páez was a murdering tiger in the hills of Payara and a tame sheep in the salons of adulation."

A caudillo named Luciano Mendoza, of the town of Petare on the outskirts of Caracas, began a series of raids on the Páez forces among the hills around the capital. Páez sent out a party to subdue him. Mendoza ambushed them, wiped them out, and the leader, Torres, was so fearful of the consequences that awaited him at the hands of Páez that he committed suicide. Páez went out himself, then, and defeated Mendoza. He entered the town of Petare and found there, in their houses, the bodies of all the mantuanos. Their genitals had been cut off and stuffed into their mouths. Páez ordered his prisoners put to death.

He had married a rich woman named Dominga Ortiz in his early days. She bore him many sons and went with him everywhere, even onto the battle-fields. As dictator, he abandoned her and took a mulatto mistress, Barbarita Nieves, an intelligent, beautiful woman, who had a taste for political intrigue. She also bore him sons and these were sent to the United States to be educated. Páez went to the United States himself later, and he died there.

On two occasions Páez turned the presidency over to other men while he held control with his militia from his hacienda at San Pablo. He chose men whom he could trust, mantuanos, both of them, by birth, idealists by nature, and therefore harmless, as Páez well knew. The first, Dr. José María Vargas, was a physician, a man of learning, almost an ascetic, of great popularity among the common people. He is known as The Father of Medicine in Venezuela and established hospitals and scientific institutions. He was a ridiculous figure as president. When Páez wanted to name him president for another term he refused and left the country in disgust. He died in New York.

The second, General Soublette, was a more practical man but an idealist, too, though his ideals were political rather than social. Under the surveillance of Páez he was a good administrator and maintained peace and order but alone he would probably have been ineffectual. His principal achievement was securing the recognition of the independence of the Venezuelan Republic by the governments of France and Spain.

In 1846, Barbarita Nieves, the mulatto mistress of Páez, died. The dictator had come to depend too much upon her political wisdom and his power died with her. He made the mistake of backing General José Tadeo Monagas for president.

Monagas was leader of those llanos horsemen who had brought Páez to power and whom Páez had come to dominate through the mantuanos of Caracas and the caudillos of the Cordillera. Páez apparently didn't suspect the resentment that lurked among the llaneros for his selling them out.

Monagas was a fierce, tall, thin man of Jewish, Spanish and mulatto blood. He was a superb horseman, intelligent, educated, and a fanatic for the cause of the llaneros. He carried his "machete clean" they said, that is, unsheathed, ready for action.

Elected president by the mantuanos and caudillos through the influence of Páez, he went to work at once to clean them all out. He dissolved the congress by force, assassinating some of the members in the process, and a reign of terror began, the pueblo, that is, the common people, against the mantuanos. The public treasury was ruined, commerce demoralized. There were revolutions everywhere. The caudillos were in action all over the Cordillera. Two brothers and a cousin, the Belisarios, attacked the house of Monagas in Caracas and they were driven off and fled to the llanos. Monagas sent one, Sotillo, after them. He caught them, cut off the heads of one of the brothers and the cousin, put the heads in a sack and forced the other brother to carry the sack to Caracas to his chief, Monagas. The man went mad during the journey.

Páez himself raised two revolutions against Monagas but they were put down easily. In the second, Páez was taken prisoner. He was held for a while in the prison at Cumaná and then ordered from the country.

Monagas passed the power to his brother, José Gregorio, for one term of four years and then he took over again himself. In all, he ruled for ten years, from 1847 to 1857. His one noble act was a decree made in 1845 freeing the slaves.

We come now to a period of thirteen years during which there were nine different presidents. The little generals were swarming all over the country in those years and most of the people, going about their work in the cane fields and corn patches, couldn't tell you who was president on any particular day. The buzzards of the Andean peaks and the chaparro trees on the llanos grew fat.

A revolution formed by a coalition of all parties overthrew Monagas and General Julian Castro was made provisional president. No sooner was he named than the conservative group broke away, imprisoned Castro and named Manuel Felipe Tovar, a wealthy, educated gentleman, to succeed him. Tovar lasted one year, 1860. The guerrillas were in arms all over the country, and, while Tovar defeated and killed the worst of them, Zamora, his own troops were beaten by Febres Cordero. His party recalled old Páez from exile to take charge of the government forces. Páez came back and, as you might expect, immediately began plotting to take over

THE OFFICERS OF THE RESTAURACIÓN
CASTRO TOP CENTER, GÓMEZ TO THE LEFT

the supreme power. Tovar, disgusted, resigned in favor
of Don Pedro Gual.

Gual was a fine old man of eighty years. He was easy
for Páez. He lasted nearly a year and then Páez threw
him into prison and took over.

This come-back of the old Centaur lasted only for
two years. The old stamina was gone and Barbarita was
gone and he couldn't cope with all the little generals.
The people laughed at him on the streets of Caracas.
In the midst of general revolution he left the country
for the United States where he died. The old federal
party, favoring the defunct union of Gran Colombia,
triumphed and General Juan Crístomo Falcón became
president.

Falcón was a good, strong man and he remained in
power four years, from 1863 to 1867, in constant warfare. He issued a decree of guarantees to the defeated
but there were never any defeated; there were only
dead. He divided Venezuela into the twenty states that
exist today. His own party revolted against him and he
resigned in favor of Bruzual.

Bruzual lasted a year. He was an honest, gentle person, much too good. He rode through the streets on
horseback and asked the people, "Why do you make
war against me, who am a gentleman?" Old José Tadeo
Monagas formed a union between the caudillos and the
liberals and instituted a movement known as the "Blue
Revolution" which took Caracas. Bruzual was wounded
by a cannon-ball and went to Curaçao to die.

Old Monagas died and left things in a bad state. The
caudillos had been rampant for thirteen years and nothing had been accomplished but destruction. Monagas's
son Ruperto was president and then Guillermo Tel
Villegas and Esteban Palacios in quick succession. Weak
men, all of them, they couldn't last, here. Bolívar's
prophecy, again. The country was ready for another

strong man and he was there. His name was Antonio
Guzmán Blanco and he lasted for eighteen years.

The necessity for this recording of apparently ir-
relevant history may be obscure to some of us but there
are good reasons for it. You cannot pass any sort of fair
judgment upon a man until you know something about
the atmosphere he breathed and the things that went
before him and formed the ways of thought that governed his actions; and we do, sincerely, want to be fair
with this man when we come to him. And we shall
come to him presently but there is still a bit more
which must be told first.

Guzmán Blanco was the tropic Latin-American aristocrat in full flower. Elegant, proud, military in all
thought processes, pathetically addicted to French culture, the French language, French perfume, everything
French. Always a little bit ridiculous and always in bad
taste and always serenely unaware of it out of his
sublime egotism. Always money-mad. He erected statues
of himself and saw nothing fatuous in using the title,
The Illustrious American.

Physically, he was a fine figure. Robust, rather tall in
his Prince Albert coat. He was swarthy of color and his
eyes were gray. He had a thin, curved nose, a fine high
forehead and a beautiful, black, wavy beard.

His father had been a sort of secretary to Bolívar and
a confidential messenger to Páez and other generals
when the Liberator was in Colombia and Perú. It was
he who first proposed a crown for Bolívar and he carried
the conviction to his grave that Bolívar as emperor
would have solved all the problems of his country. His
mother was of Bolívar's own family, a daughter of his
sister, Maria Antonia. So Guzmán Blanco inherited the
mantuano tradition and the caudillo tradition. He was
almost the culmination of the caudillo tradition and he
gained the supreme power by a practically unanimous

coalition of all the little generals of the Cordillera, a thing that had never happened before.

Guzmán Blanco had been secretary to General Juan Falcón and when Falcón became president he made Blanco vice-president. Blanco had great talents for taking advantage of his public offices. As vice-president he got away with a million dollars before Falcón's administration cracked up. The Blue Revolution was on and the country in a state of anarchy and Blanco took his million to Curaçao.

In the Dutch island of Curaçao, he made the plans for a revolutionary movement that was to set a new style for such actions. With his million and more money from two Jewish bankers (they were paid off later out of the Venezuelan public treasury) he bought a sizeable lot of munitions of war. He sent an American named Pyle who had been minister in Caracas to scour the Antilles for boats. Pyle returned with fifty-two vessels of every description. There were decrepit paddle-wheel steamers and sail-boats, sloops and schooners and square-riggers and boats of undefinable rig such as you can only find in those waters. Blanco paid cash for everything. He hired men to man the boats, loaded his munitions and sailed for the Venezuelan coast. He landed on the shores of Coro and raised an army of eighteen thousand men. He established a large training camp and all the little generals flocked to join him. He paid cash. In a forced march of three days he reached Caracas, took the city and overthrew the government of Esteban Palacio. This was in 1870 and Blanco was forty-two years old.

Guzmán Blanco was an able administrator. He gave all the caudillos good jobs, made them vice-presidents and cabinet ministers and paid them well and kept them satisfied. He shot one for insubordination. He reorganized the treasury and paid the interest on the public debt and made himself a rich man at the same time. He built up a personal fortune of eight million dollars which he invested safely in France. To do it, of course, he taxed the people tremendously and sold out the country to foreign interests.

He had a mania for France. He built theaters and fountains in rococo French style, put ornamental French façades on old public buildings, made the study of French obligatory in the public schools. As a French liberal of the time, he closed the convents and expelled the bishops.

One of his daughters married the Duc de Morny and another the Marquis de Noé and both of these worthies profited handsomely by way of Venezuelan concessions granted to them or their business associates. He bought a palace in Paris for himself and his plans were to go there and live permanently, governing his country by remote control. He did go several times but he found he couldn't stay there and keep his job. He went first in 1877 and left the presidential duties in the hands of General Francisco Linares Alcántara, one of the caudillos who had been with him in the drive on the capital.

Alcántara was an engaging lad. He was completely worthless and admitted it. He was a tall, handsome mulatto, a great dancer, a devil with the ladies. Someone asked him what his political program was and he said, "Mount to the tower of the cathedral and toss gold pieces to everyone who passes." And he did almost that. He helped himself to the Treasury and he helped his friends, handing out all manner of expensive gifts. He killed his enemies. Ordering them shot, he would say, smiling, "And you, my friend, I have a gift for you, too. I shall give you a buzzard for a breast-pin." He established his mistresses all over the country. He did absolutely nothing for the country. Someone tried to interest him in some business or other and he said, "Don't be a damned fool, fellow. I've got the best business in the world, the National Treasury."

He couldn't stand the pace and died in two years. A bastard brother took over his office until Guzmán Blanco came hurrying back from France to straighten things out.

Blanco stayed home for five years, from 1879 to 1884, and then he was off to France again and left the executive power in the hands of General Joaquín Crespo.

Crespo had been Blanco's ablest general in the military action of the drive on Caracas and in the uprisings that took place from time to time afterwards. He was a cavalryman by profession. He was a thoroughly honest gentleman and, much more rare, a very moral man. His administration was a complete failure. Everyone robbed the treasury, even his relatives, right under his nose, and he was unaware of it. He looked exactly like General U. S. Grant and he was like him in his traits of character and in his career. He was an able, calm, colorless general who was an utter incompetent as a political executive.

With his enemies he was completely, coldly, self-righteously ruthless. He killed all the little generals who raised their heads. He killed "Chingo" Machado, Solórzano, and he went down into Apure where the remnants of the old Blue Revolution had taken refuge and killed or scattered all of them. He served from 1884 to 1886 and then Blanco came back again. Blanco stayed only a few months though and then returned to France, leaving Hermógenes López in power during the year 1887.

López was a fat, stupid man whom the people called "the sow of Nagua-Nagua." Blanco removed him at the end of a year and had elected in his place, Dr. Juan Pablo Rojas Paúl.

With this man terminated the dictatorship of Guzmán Blanco. An educated gentleman, a lawyer, a man of peace, Blanco considered him another handy instrument for the long-distance type of government which he had established. Blanco was wrong. No sooner was Paúl in office than he set about making things over to suit his own ideas. He repudiated all of Blanco's foreign contracts, the railways, sewers of Caracas, bank-loans, land-grants, in so far as he was able, freed all political prisoners, established freedom of the press and conducted himself generally in a manner to draw roars of rage from the dictator in his palace in Paris.

General Crespo had broken with Blanco and gone to the West Indies to organize a revolution against him. Now, his plans ready, and considering Paúl the tool of Guzmán Blanco, he left Curaçao for the coast of Coro, employing the revolutionary style that Blanco himself had set. But Paúl intercepted his vessels on the sea, took Crespo prisoner and had him brought to Caracas and put into the famous Rotunda. This man Paúl was clever. When Crespo reached his cell, he found it beautifully furnished. There were soft sofas and pictures on the wall and even a reception room for guests. Paúl visited his prisoner there, talked to him for hours, convinced him that he was in reaction against Blanco and won him over. He got Crespo's word that he would behave himself and he set him free. A good man, Paúl.

Unfortunately he only lasted two years. He was sixty-two when he took office. He became infatuated with an Italian opera-singer and had a violent affair with her that weakened him so that he had to retire from active life. He left in his place Dr. Raimundo Andrueza Palacio.

And now history repeats itself. The power of the strong man broken, the country again fell into the hands of the caudillos and went into a period of disorganization that paved the way for the dictatorship of Castro-Gómez.

During nine years there were three presidents, Palacio, Crespo and Ignacio Andrade and the little generals were in constant action all over the country, particularly along the Cordillera.

So, from the time of Bolívar and the winning of independence, Venezuela saw two long periods of dictatorship, that of Páez and that of Guzmán Blanco, and after each there were years of disintegration with many rulers succeeding each other rapidly, all of them setting certain styles of procedure and precedents in political behavior that influenced those who came after. It saw the firm establishment of the military tradition in politics and the domination of the Andean race over the rest of the country.

PART TWO

THE PEACEFUL YEARS

1857–1899

Chapter III

THE CONDOR'S NEST

❖

WHEN Gómez became dictator of Venezuela he had a false entry made in the birth records of the church at San Antonio fixing the date of his birth as July 24 so that it would coincide with the birthday of the Liberator, Bolívar, and the place as San Antonio. The fact is, he was born in Colombia and it is doubtful if either he or his mother ever knew the real date of his birth. He had that false entry photographed and published in the Caracas newspapers.

Hermenegilda Chacón was of Indian blood. She was a spirited, handsome woman and Evaristo García took her to Cúcuta across the Colombian border and established her as his mistress. García was an educated gentleman of Spanish blood, a brother of Dr. José Rosario García, one of Cúcuta's leading citizens.

Hermenegilda bore García two children, a boy and a girl. When the boy was four years old she tired of the man and went to San Antonio to become the mistress of Pedro Cornelio Gómez, taking her children with her.

The farm lay among the highlands a few miles from the town. There were some rich valleys with good grass and some shaded slopes, already cleared of undergrowth and planted with coffee. There were a few head of cattle grazing in the valleys and a few mules in the corral. That was all La Mulera amounted to when Hermenegilda went there. The house was of adobe with palm thatch, of one story, two rooms in the front for the

Gómez family and a wing on one side for the vaqueros and their families.

Pedro was little more than a peon himself so that there was no manifestation of caste in his establishment and everyone, owner and vaquero, lived together on terms of equality. They took their caldo [1] from the common pot, all squatting together in the patio formed by the main house and the wing, drinking from wooden totumos.[2] The men shared the work in the corral and pastures and the women, in the house.

He was a kindly, ordinary Andean farmer, but he had the wit to appreciate the woman he'd taken and he permitted her to dominate the whole hacienda and himself as well. He could neither read nor write but that was nothing to remark in that region. He harbored not only the children that Hermenegilda brought him and those she bore him, but the illegitimate children of his brother as well. And all these lived together and used his name and grew up as one family without a thought of the real blood relationships among them.

He worked hard. His woman saw to that. And the farm expanded to meet the needs of the growing family. There were more cattle in the valleys and there were fields of corn and cane and yucca. It was a hard life and a brutal one in many ways. All the cattlemen were really bands of half-wild Indians, cattle-stealing was considered a fairly legitimate business and the only real law was the law of the güinche which was their way of saying winchester, a general term they used for rifle. It was hot working in the fields during the day and it was cold at night and in the early morning among the valleys. Pedro Gómez guarded his lands and his herd

---

[1] Broth. Sometimes only of water, onion, salt and pepper, and sometimes having a meat stock base.

[2] Gourd. Particularly the half of a certain type of round gourd, hollowed out to a thin shell and used as cup, platter, soup-plate and basin.

and built up a strong, numerous tribe. He lived under
the dread that Hermenegilda would tire of him as she
had of García but she stayed with him till he died, bearing him a child each year for their nine years together.

It is not known what Pedro Cornelio Gómez died of.
It was probably pneumonia for that is the illness most
common to the Andes, especially among the cattlemen
who endure the violent changes in temperature, sometimes spending nights among the peaks with their
blankets still wet from a sudden storm or from fording
streams. It is known that before he died he said to
Hermenegilda, "I want to leave everything to Juan
Vicente for he is the smartest." And Juan Vicente was
not his own son.

There were thirteen children at La Mulera when
Pedro Gómez died, nine of them his own by Hermenegilda, two of them Hermenegilda's by Evaristo García,
and two of them his brother's by a woman named Prato.
Juan Vicente was the eldest and he was only fourteen.
He had never been to any school whatever and a peon
had taught him to write his name in the sand with a
stick. The management of the hacienda fell upon him
and his mother.

The first thing he did was to teach himself to read
and write and add and subtract a little and then he
applied a crude sort of book-keeping system to the
cattle business.

It was Sunday morning. A few peons lay in their hammocks in the patio, smoking. Small, brown, naked children played on the bare earth floor. Hermenegilda and
the grown girls had left early for San Antonio to attend
Mass. Most of the boys had gone in early, too, or they
had gone in the night before and not returned.

Juan Vicente rode in from the fields, dismounted at
the corral gate, removed the bars and led his mule

inside. He took off the saddle, put it on the corral fence and turned the animal loose. He went into the patio.

"Who took the gray mule?" he asked.

"Eustóquio rode her to town," a peon said.

"Sin vergüenza! Why didn't he walk? He knows the animals are to rest on Sunday."

He went to a small coop near the corral, reached inside and brought out a fighting-cock, holding it tightly in his left hand. He set off down the trail, carrying the bird under his arm.

It was a clear, bright morning. There were no clouds anywhere, no mists hanging about the peaks. Away off to the northeast the snowy tops of the peaks of Mérida glistened white and gold in the sunlight, hanging suspended in the blue sky, inverted cones, completely detached from the rest of the earth. To the south the Páramo de Tamá rose like a gray trunk and the peak of El Cristo towered above it. As the boy came down the rocky trail toward the town, the clatter of the church bells rose from below to make discord with the bird songs that came from the wooded hillsides. Wild doves spoke their hollow mutterings and quail sent clear notes across the valleys.

San Antonio was a small cluster of huts down below, a little square of green that was the plaza lying in the center, the towers of the old Spanish church standing high and pink in the clear air.

Dark-skinned men lolled about the plaza and the botaquín [3] at the corner. Some boys played a sort of bowling game with large round stones in the dust of the street. Old women and young women and young girls in black lace mantillas or in the wide straw hats of the Indians moved about the entrance to the church.

Juan Vicente passed the plaza and made his way to a

[3] A small public house. The cantina of Mexico and other Caribbean countries.

courtyard behind the botaquín. There was a crowd of
men gathered there and the fights were already started.
The boy pushed his way in close to the pit. He was
taller than the others and they fell back to let him
through.

Deadly serious, this crowd of mountain Indians. There
was none of the noise and confusion of the cock-fights
in the lowlands, none of the loud betting, the laughter,
the boasting and the cheering. Here, the dark, sweating
faces were calm masks, the bets were made in short,
muttered phrases. The birds in the pit fought in almost
dead silence, their own flutterings and shufflings sound-
ing above the hoarse, low-spoken encouragement of
their squatting handlers.

The boy from La Mulera stood watching, his bird
under his arm. He was about nineteen then, fully
grown, and he stood higher than most men of the region
and he was built solidly. He stood five feet ten inches
and weighed one hundred and sixty-five pounds. His
skin was dark but he was a shade lighter than the
Indians of purer blood around him. His dress was much
the same as theirs. He wore a wide straw hat, a dark
blue woolen "ruana" that fell over his shoulders front
and back with a hole for his head like a poncho, cotton
shirt and trousers and leather-soled sandals of hand-
woven cotton yarn.

The fights went on and the boy watched and bickered
with others over a match for his bird. Occasionally he
bet a few coins on the fights. When he won he put the
money into his pouch without a word and when he lost
he scowled and cursed under his breath.

A match was finally arranged and he left the pit,
going to the space behind the on-lookers to prepare his
cock. He drew a cloth pouch from his belt and spilled
out a handful of spurs. They were horn spurs, taken
from larger cocks of less fighting spirit, long and curved

and wicked-looking. He held his bird and tried all the spurs, very patiently, one by one, selecting and rejecting, slipping them over the natural spurs till he found a set that satisfied him. Then he took a stone from the pouch and rubbed the horn points down to needle-sharpness. He bound the spurs to the cock's legs with strong, fine palm fiber. When the time came, he carried his bird to the pit.

They tried the birds for courage by holding them in both hands and thrusting them at each other. Then they tossed them together and they rose into a fluttering column in the center of the pit.

They were an ugly sight, these birds, for whatever of natural beauty they possessed had been shorn from them. Their curving tail-feathers had been plucked and all the feathers of their necks removed, leaving red, raw, scrawny flesh like the neck of a buzzard. They fought with quiet fury. The two men squatted on opposite sides of the pit, their black eyes darting with the quick, almost indiscernible flashes of the deadly spurs.

The fight was over quickly. There was no stalling on the part of either bird. They fought from the instant they were released, a darting, moving mass of feather and beak and spur and the end had to come soon. One fluttering assault, a lightning stroke of spur against an ugly, hard, red head and one bird went down, stone dead, his feet in the air, his neck laid open from comb to shoulder. Juan Vicente snatched his bird from the pit while it was still drawing up its chest to give its cry of victory.

He moved to the open space behind the watchers. Then he plunged the whole raw, red head and neck of his bird into his mouth. He rolled his tongue around, slobbering saliva well over it. Then he held the bird to the ground and squeezed the juice of a half-lime into all the wounds and scratches about its body. He tucked

the bird under his arm, collected some coins from the
loser and pushed his way out of the crowd.

He found Eustóquio playing at the bowling game in
the street.

"Sin vergüenza!" Juan Vicente said. "Where is the
gray mule?"

"In the corral at the house of Emilio."

"The animals are to rest on Sunday."

"I know but you were in the fields and I am to carry
those heavy iron things home. I had no opportunity to
ask you."

"No matter. You shall go back on foot and you shall
carry the iron things on your back and this bird as well.
I shall take the mule back myself." He gave the fighting-
cock to the boy and went on his way.

Near the outskirts of the village a small, poor hut
stood by the side of the road. A peon of middle age
squatted at the door. Juan Vicente approached the
house and greeted the man.

"Is Elena here?" he asked.

"Yes, compadre, she is waiting for you. You are in
your house."

"Where is Doña María?"

"She is in the village."

The man walked away down the road and Juan
Vicente went into the house, closing the door after him.

It was late afternoon and the sun was beginning to
set when he came out again. Clouds were forming, black
around the mountain peaks. Elena came to the door
with him. She was a pretty young Indian girl.

"It will rain before you get home," she said. "Won't
you stay till morning? I'll wake you early."

"I have work to do tonight."

"Very well. When will you come again?"

"I can't say. Perhaps next Sunday. And about the
child. You are sure he is mine?"

"Of course, Juan. You know he couldn't be of anyone else. You have been the only one."

"Well, we shall see when he is born. If he is mine, I shall look after him."

The girl put her arms around his shoulders and kissed the side of his cheek but he was watching the clouds forming in the sky.

He went to the corral behind the house of Emilio where Eustóquio had left the gray mule. He saddled the mule, took her by the halter and led her out into the road.

The rain came when he was well along the trail. It was dark then and the skies opened, pouring a fierce torrent of bitter cold rain over the highlands of the Andes. The boy drew the soaking folds of the ruana about his body. He climbed along the rocky trail toward La Mulera in the dark, leading the mule by the halter.

Chapter IV

THE CACIQUE

❖

IT was a wild and conglomerate family that grew up at La Mulera under the dominance of Juan Vicente Gómez. After the death of Pedro Cornelio, Hermenegilda bore two children to a man named Matute, so that there were fifteen children in all under her roof. Then, as the boys grew up, they brought their own children into the household, children born of any neighboring peon girls who took their fancies. These children were raised as criados, some of them acting as servants and some treated as equals.

The men of the Gómez clan had come to be regarded with considerable fear throughout the region and there were few peon girls who dared to resist them. Juan Vicente had many children by many different girls in the district of Capacho. Just how many, no one knows and it is probable that he never knew himself. Those whom he believed to be his beyond any doubt were taken into his house or were cared for in other ways.

La Mulera grew and prospered. A new house took the place of the old one, this one with tiled roof and stone floor. The corrals were expanded, new out-buildings of adobe and thatch were put up for the growing clan, drying-sheds for hides, store-houses for coffee, butchering sheds. Juan Vicente, with his small knowledge of figures and his extraordinary business cunning and acquisitiveness, was the director of all enterprises and the other boys carried out the action. This action

43

was sometimes in the dead of night and these enterprises sometimes rather mysterious. The Gómez herds increased astonishingly. The Gómez brand appeared in most distorted form on the rumps of steers that bore amazing resemblance to steers that had borne other brands.

The sloping mountainsides were cleared of underbrush and coffee was planted in the shade of the taller trees. Juan Vicente drove good bargains, got good prices for his products in San Antonio or San Cristóbal or across the border in Cúcuta. He was a quiet, slow-moving, rather heavy man with heavy-lidded, sleepy eyes. The peons said that he knew what you were thinking. His own brothers and sisters were in awe of him.

With prosperity and expansion, life had not changed much at the hacienda. The ruanas and alpargatas[1] of the Indians were still the common style of dress for everyone, the food was still prepared over an open fire and eaten from totumos, the vaqueros still squatted in the patio. There were fiestas in the village that meant wild drinking bouts for the men of the Gómez tribe, dancing the joropo to the tiple[2] and marracas.[3] Juan Vicente tolerated these debaucheries of his younger brothers but he took no part himself. He drank nothing at all, ever, he rose at four in the morning and he worked till dark. His one unrestrained appetite was sexual indulgence, which was nothing remarkable in the region—indeed, abstinence would have been much more so—but he practiced such indulgence in the complete

[1] Sandals. In Venezuela they are hand-woven of cotton yarn with soles of leather or palm fiber and are the shoes worn throughout Venezuela by the peon class.

[2] Pronounced *tee*-play. A stringed instrument, native to Venezuela, resembling the ukulele.

[3] Rattles. Made of round gourds filled with dried peas. They are an indispensable part of a Venezuelan orchestra and differ slightly from the Cuban and Mexican marracas more familiar to Americans.

detachment and naturalness of the animals that roamed his pastures. He never gave anything of himself in his affairs with women. He took them into his hammock at night and he sent them away at daybreak.

Even in these early days Juan Vicente showed the dominating trait that was always characteristic of him— absolute singleness of purpose. And that purpose was acquisition. Now, it was the acquisition of money and power through the exploitation of La Mulera and later the acquisition of money and power through the exploitation of the nation. The purpose was always the same, only the instruments and methods differed.

The type of man who would develop in these surroundings would almost certainly come to possess habits of direct action, a disregard for suffering and callousness to scenes of brutality. The only exception would be some unlucky individual born into them cursed with an extreme sensitivity through a capricious hereditary prank; and he would not survive. For this life of the Andean ranges brought one very close, constantly, to brutality and bloodshed. The work involved the castration and branding and birthing and butchering of animals, the taming of horses and mules and the constant holding by force of arms of your own against the encroachment of your friendly neighbors and the pastimes quite often ran to knifings and machetazos and shootings.

Juan Vicente was always the director and observer. His brothers were his machetes, particularly Juancho and Eustóquio.

During these years of his youth, Gómez took no part in the political warfare that raged along the Cordillera, all around him, among the caudillos. He and his tribe confined their activities to protecting their lands, adding to them by sharp dealing, building up their resources. By caste, he was not of the caudillo element, for the little generals were descendants of landed families, more or less educated men whose haciendas, having been established for generations, didn't need their active direction, so leaving them free to indulge in their favorite pastimes. Gómez, on the other hand, had inherited a small, undeveloped property as well as a large family to support so that his concern was with other things. By blood, however, he was of them. He alone, of the Gómez tribe, through the aristocratic blood of his father, García—the others being of purer Indian peon stock on both sides—had the two racial elements of the true Andean feudal lord type. It is true that the others, all of them, by virtue of the qualities of their mother, Hermenegilda, possessed strong, individual traits of character, extraordinary in the nearly pure Indian peon. It may be that Hermenegilda came of old chieftain stock. Nevertheless, had Juan Vicente been really born of Pedro Cornelio instead of Evaristo García, without the leavening of Spanish blood that gave his character balance and intelligence and qualities of leadership, he would never have become a great figure and the Gómez tribe would have been simply another wild, marauding, mountain clan that would have been exterminated sooner or later by some caudillo.

These were the years following the fall of the Guzmán Blanco dictatorship. The nation was in one of its periods of upheaval—presidents coming and going, the little generals active everywhere, along the Cordillera and over the llanos. It is interesting to look briefly at the methods of these guerrillas in their chosen pursuits. There were very definite traditions, rules of the game, strictly adhered to by all of them.

Here was none of the wanton pillaging, burning, butchering of the Mexican bandits, for the most part. The leaders were gentlemen, mostly of old families, often blood-relations of their opponents; and through the years a code had been established. There was a certain respect for private property, a spirit of camaraderie, often exchanges of courtesies in terms of polite, ironic humor. When cattle were stolen, a message would be sent to the owner to the effect that it was deplored, but necessary for the good of the cause. The little bands followed the mountain trails, the leaders assuming little eccentricities of personal conduct to maintain their dignity, such as carrying a silver spoon to eat with or a mustache cup, but otherwise living the life of their Indian peons, sharing their meals, sharing their hammocks at night with sturdy young Indian girls. They straggled along, men, women and children, driving mules and burros and goats, carrying blankets and cooking utensils, the animals loaded with crates of chickens, large discs of casabe wrapped in banana leaves, loaves of white goat cheese. Perhaps there would be two or three workable güinches and a hundred rounds of ammunition among the whole caravan. Approaching the hacienda of a rival leader, a party would be sent ahead to learn if the man and his "army" were about. If not, the party would advance boldly to the house and make camp in the yard and settle down for a nice rest. The leader would go inside, greet the womenfolk, ask after all the kin, relate whatever news or gossip he brought from other parts and sit down to a good meal. It is told that, during the Guzmán Blanco revolution in 1870, two rival generals sent messengers to each other to arrange a meeting in the town of La Vela. They rode into the village alone, met at the posada [4] and had a nice meal and a chat. Then, they agreed upon the time and place and other details of the coming battle, embraced each other, commended the care of their respective families one to the other in case one were killed and rode off.

[4] Wayside inn. Usually the private home of a peon who will accommodate travelers overnight.

There was another side to it, of course. In the midst of these picnicky little wars and martial pleasantries would come, suddenly, word of a bloody atrocity, carried out with fiendish, cold ingenuity and probably, a grisly humor. A strange race, the Venezuelan mestizo, to most of us.

The largest town known to Juan Vicente Gómez at this time was San Cristóbal, capital and principal village of the state of Táchira. Its population was perhaps six thousand. Until he was forty-two years old he never knew a larger city. An old Spanish settlement with the usual churches, adobe houses, three or four streets, a plaza, it was like all the others of the Cordillera, an accumulation of people of a very primitive way of life dressed in an illusion of a little European civilization because of the building mania of the Spaniards for a brief period centuries before.

Gómez went to San Cristóbal occasionally, riding the eighteen miles of mountain trail from San Antonio on mule-back, carrying his sacks of coffee beans for the market on burros or driving a few head of cattle. On one of his trips there he saw the wife of an Italian merchant, a woman named Dionisia Bello.

He was twenty-eight years old. He had had many women and numerous children but he had never taken a woman into his home. Now, perhaps because he found this woman particularly attractive or because he had come to desire a more permanent sort of feminine companionship but more probably still because he saw in her a worthier vehicle for producing his children, he carried her off with him to La Mulera. There is no record of the reaction of the Italian husband but the chances are there was no reaction at all. By this time the reputation of Juan Vicente's brothers, Eustóquio and Juancho and Santos Matute, was pretty well-known over the state of Táchira.

Dionisia Bello was the established mistress of Juan Vicente Gómez for many years. She lived with him in the same house, but she never shared his room nor his life. He lived the life of a bachelor with a mistress, sending for her when he wanted her, never permitting her presence in his house to interfere with affairs with other women, never surrendering any of his ego. At La Mulera she bore him four children which he "recognized" by registration with the public authorities at San Antonio, thereby making them legitimate and his legal heirs according to the Venezuelan law. Subsequently he recognized the later children born to Dionisia, seven in all, and they were the only ones among all his off-spring so honored. Whether he considered this brood of Dionisia Bello more worthy than his begettings by other women no one can say. Those born at La Mulera and recognized at San Antonio were; a girl, Josefa María, on December 15, 1886, a boy, José Vicente, on April 15, 1888, another girl, Flor de María, on July 5, 1890, and another boy, Augusto Alí, on March 27, 1892. José Vicente was always known as Vicentico and Augusto Alí as Alí.

When Rojas Paúl was forced to resign the presidency in 1890 because of a break-down in health, he left in his place a man of straw, Dr. Raimundo Andueza Palacio.

Palacio was a stout, elegant mulatto with beautiful mustaches and a neat, curly imperial. He was an orator, a great orator, and nothing more. He sipped whiskey all day long and relished lingeringly the sonorous phrases that began way down in his stout, Prince Albert-covered middle and came out from his mustaches in deep, rich tones. His white-palmed hands made slow, graceful gestures. His geniality and stirring words won and held the common people for a while, but the little generals saw the man for the easy one that he was and got their heads together.

Palacio did nothing for the country. He instituted what came to be known as La Cajita, the little box, a pretty little ornamented casket which was always beside him and from which he drew gold coins for his friends with delightful movements of those graceful hands. He freed the political prisoners and tried to buy their loyalty as he bought the press. The national revenues fell off.

His mentor, Paúl, became disgusted with his behavior and left the country. General Joaquín Crespo, who had promised Paúl to be a good boy, now felt that he was released from his promise and went to his hacienda, Totumo, in the state of Guárico, issued a manifesto of revolution, and formed a coalition with the guerrillas who were already in arms throughout the country.

In Guayana there was a fierce fighting man, a revolutionist by nature, a psychologic non-conformist, named José Manuel Hernández. He was called El Mocho [5] by the people, in affection. In the central part of the country General Ramón Guerra rose against Palacio and declared for Crespo. In the Cordillera states of Trujillo and Táchira, Generals Eliseo Araujo and Espíritu Santo Morales also declared for him.

Juan Vicente Gómez was thirty-five years old at this time. He had spent all those years of his early life quietly building up his cattle and coffee business, completely oblivious to the skirmishings of the caudillos, apparently unconcerned with national politics. Now, however, he was a large landowner and wealthy, according to Andean standards, and political policies, with questions of land taxes and property rights, were be-

[5] Mocho means maimed or crippled. Hernández was known, affectionately, as El Mocho or The Crippled One, because he had been left slightly crippled from wounds received in battle.

THE CACIQUE 51

ginning to touch him. Then, too, this new action along
the Cordillera was quite formidable and striking close
to home, and even, perhaps, interfering in some way
or other with his own business activities. It is reason-
ably certain that he was quite unconcerned and even
uninformed about national problems. In that remote
section of the Andes there was probably little knowledge of or interest in the behavior of Palacio in the
metropolis of Caracas. The motives that governed the
course of action which Gómez now took must have been
purely personal ones. Perhaps his ambition was beginning to tempt him to wider horizons. Perhaps his blood
inheritance for conquering by the sword was asserting
itself at last.

Chapter V

THE CONDOR MOVES HIS NEST

❖

THE Gómez clan at La Mulera now comprised quite a formidable body of men with all their peons and criados. What was more important still, at this time, they had money. The commander of the government forces in Táchira, General José María González, approached Gómez with an offer to make him Chief Commissary with rank of colonel, promising certain other rewards when the rebels had been put down, in exchange for his services and contribution of funds. Gómez accepted the proposition.

He rode out from the hacienda with his henchmen, formally under arms for the first time, and joined González in action against the revolutionists in Táchira.

On March 28, 1892, a battle was fought at Topón between a force of four hundred government soldiers and a much greater force of rebels under Araujo. The government forces were victorious in spite of the odds against them. Araujo had to retire and there were several months of comparative inaction during which both sides recuperated. Then, on May 14 and 15, a large force under Morales met González at Táriba in two days of fierce fighting, much of it hand-to-hand with machete, and the revolutionists were again defeated by the much smaller government force. In the meantime, General Cipriano Castro had defeated the revolutionists in Trujillo so that the whole Crespo movement was squashed along the Cordillera.

All of this action had taken place among Gómez's own peaks and valleys, within a dozen miles of La Mulera. He himself had had very little to do with the actual fighting, having been occupied with his duties as Commissary, maintaining a service of supplies for the troops by pack-train from his hacienda. Nevertheless, he had seen some very able guerrilla generals in action and had learned a lot about supporting an army in the field. And he had come in contact with a man who was to become quite a figure in his career, General Cipriano Castro.

The Crespo revolution had been defeated in the Cordillera but over the rest of the country it had been highly successful. "El Mocho" Hernández in the east and Ramón Guerra in the center had completely scattered the government forces and opened a way to the capital city, Caracas. Andueza Palacio fled the country. In October, after seven months of warfare, Joaquín Crespo rode into the city to receive a great welcome from the people. He threw out the old Congress, named a new one, and had himself elected president. It would be well to mention here that the Venezuelan Constitution, in all the changes that it has gone through, has never provided for any other form of presidential election than by the Congress assembled and the naming of the members of Congress has always been a function of the executive, thus providing an easy, legal method for the establishing of a dictatorship.

So, in his first military venture, Juan Vicente Gómez had chosen the wrong side. While his party had been successful in the Andean states, it had been defeated throughout the rest of Venezuela. As a national organization it had been destroyed, its leader, Palacio, had been driven out of the country.

Crespo assembled all his victorious forces for a big drive on the Cordillera to clean up the remnants of the

Palacio troops and there was nothing for Gómez and Castro to do in the face of the odds against them but to flee to Colombia as Palacio had done. Fortunately, the back way into Colombia was handy, just across the Táchira, the trail to Cúcuta. Fortunately, too, there was plenty of time, for it would require quite a few weeks for a military expedition to work its way from Caracas to that remote section of the Andes.

The evacuation of the Gómez clan as well as of Castro and the other Palacio partisans from Táchira across into Colombia was carried out with great order and thoroughness. There remained to the force a considerable park [1] of military supplies, guns and ammunition, and this was under the immediate charge of Gómez, the Commissary. With the aid of some of his brothers, he contrived to cache it all secretly in a spot close to the Táchira, known only to themselves.

La Mulera was stripped of everything of value. All the furniture and implements and even the hewn timbers of the buildings were packed on animals. The cattle were driven in from the ranges, the mules and goats herded and the exodus began. Crespo had come into power in October and on the 8th of November, 1892, the Gómez caravan crossed the Táchira into Colombia. All the tribe, the Garcías and Pratos and Matutes, all the peons and their women and children, driving their cattle and pack-animals and household goods, followed along the same rocky, mountain trail toward Cúcuta that Hermenegilda Chacón had followed thirty-one years before when she went to meet Cornelio and found the Gómez clan at La Mulera. Hermenegilda went back along that trail now and Dionisia Bello went along, taking the four young children of Juan Vicente.

He decided upon a spot down in the wide valley of

[1] A space occupied by assembled military supplies; also, the objects themselves; as a *park* of artillery.

the river near Rosario in the Department of Cúcuta, just a few miles from the border. He took up a piece of land there and called it Buenos Aires. He could look up to the east and see plainly the peaks around La Mulera. One day he looked up and saw a column of smoke rising from the peaks, yellow against the dark gray of mountain and cloud. His enemies had come and were burning what was left of the old hacienda.

Gómez was thirty-six years old, the head of a large tribe in a new country, and he was penniless. He had his land and his cattle but he had put ten thousand bolívars, all the money he had had, into supplies for the González troops. A bad state of affairs for one whose only concern was the acquisition of money and power. He set to work immediately to remedy the situation.

The high valleys of Táchira were just across the river and those valleys were the grazing land for many herds of cattle. Gómez knew those valleys like the palm of his hand. He knew, too, many dark, untraveled passes that crossed the frontier and carried to those valleys. There was the Venezuelan frontier, there was the deliberately uncurious market at Cúcuta, there were his idle, venturesome brothers, Juancho and Eustóquio.

He sold all the cattle, handled the funds, directed the operations, as he had always done before. Bland, soft-spoken, a little shrewd, perhaps, but a most enterprising and honorable young haciendado of humble origin. Most honorable, at his home at "Buenos Aires" and at the cattle markets of Cúcuta. But dark figures of horsemen rode those lonely passes on moonlight nights, muffled in ruanas against the mountain chill. The clattering of many hoofs and the soft lowing of cattle echoed among the rocky walls.

Gómez lived at Buenos Aires for seven years. In that time he acquired more capital than he had had before at La Mulera. He came to be a wealthy man for those regions, with credit at the banks in Cúcuta and cash on deposit of thirty thousand bolívars, about six thousand dollars.

He is at his prime, now. Still the ruana, wide hat and sandals. He speaks seldom and then in monosyllables that are almost grunts. He uses the ungrammatic, colloquial phrases of the mountain Indians. He can read and write but he knows nothing but his mountains and his business and men. He knows men instinctively as an animal knows them. He is addicted to the diminutive suffix, "ito," and he uses it in a faintly ironic way. He has his hair clipped close to his skull all over and has long black mustaches.

He is heavily built. His hands are much too small and delicate and he is never seen without gloves. He wears his gloves even when eating. No one knows why. Some say that he is afraid of contracting a skin disease. Some say that he has a skin disease, some kind of eczema, and some say that he is ashamed of the weakness of his hands.

He has the slow energy of the animals of the cat family, of snakes and bull-fighters. Heavy-lidded eyes, almost asleep, face and body immobile; then suddenly, lightning action; the whole body in action in one swift, sudden, graceful movement, almost too quick for the eye; and then repose again, lethargy, and there is nothing there but the results. The results and your own pounding heart and the memory of something which you aren't quite sure you saw, something beautiful and fearful and not human.

The Indians say that he reads your mind. They whisper that he is brujo, witch-doctor. They tell of how he remembers everything, how he remembers every man and animal that he ever saw. They tell of the time a neighbor rancher, driving a thousand steers to Cúcuta, kept them for the night in the Gómez corrals and in

GÓMEZ, STANDING, CASTRO, THE PRESI-
DENT, SEATED. THE BUTT OF CASTRO'S
REVOLVER SHOWS FROM HIS BREAST
POCKET

the morning when the owner said that two had strayed, Gómez looked over the herd and said, "Yes, two are gone, the crumpled-horned one and the one-eyed one." They tell of his disregard for the priests and the Mass, his contempt for religion. They tell of his preoccupation with numbers and dates—how he carries a little paper with numbers written on it that he is forever studying, how he watches the moon and stars and makes all his plans according to dates. How he is obsessed by the number thirteen.

At "Buenos Aires" Dionisia Bello bore him three more children and these were recognized at El Rosario. There were two girls, Graciela and Servilia, born September 22, 1895, and January 13, 1897, and a boy, Gonzalo, born January 10, 1899.

At Buenos Aires, too, he became closely acquainted with his fellow-exile, General Cipriano Castro.

Gómez had never known a man of Castro's type and class. Castro had settled in the same section of Colombia and he often came to visit at the hacienda. Gómez would sit by the hour, listening to the words of this man, studying him, absorbing him, measuring him, watching him with his narrow, heavy-lidded, half-closed eyes. He had nothing whatever in common with him. It is certain that he found little to admire in him and later events indicate that he had contempt for him. The only reason that seems plausible for his association with him—which began now and lasted many years—is that the germ of broader ambitions had begun to grow and he saw in Castro an instrument for attaining them. He saw the capabilities of the man and he saw his weaknesses. Castro had plenty of both.

He was a lawyer, educated, dashing. A slight, elegant man, impulsive, daring, superficially brilliant. He was passionately devoted to politics, capricious and shallow in his political beliefs.

He talked constantly and Gómez listened. Gómez knew that he could learn much from him. Castro was always informed of what was going on in the capitals of both Colombia and Venezuela through the secret and intricate channels that politicians of his type always have. Through him a new world opened up for the ignorant hillman. They talked together of the things that were taking place in their homeland. Castro, on his part, knew of the military stores that Gómez had cached away across the border and he knew of the thirty thousand bolívars.

Joaquín Crespo remained in the presidency for six years after the revolution that had put him into power and that had driven Gómez and Castro from the country. His administration was simply a repetition of the two years he had been in power before, or even worse. He was victimized by everyone. He created new debts for the nation, ruined the foreign credit of the merchants. To pay the debts of the railroad, he borrowed fifty million bolívars from Germany but most of the money found its way into the pockets of his friends, many of whom became rich and left the country. Nevertheless, he himself was an honest man and the people knew it and he maintained his power until his term expired in 1898 and then he put in his place a dummy figure, Ignacio Andrade.

The two generals who had won the presidency for Crespo were El Mocho Hernández and Ramón Guerra. During the six years of their leader's term, both remained calm, awaiting the reward which they felt was coming to them. Crespo sent Hernández to the United States as minister, but that wasn't what he really wanted. When the time came for a new president, he returned, expecting to be given the post by Crespo.

Hernández was a Caraqueño, of liberal political tendencies, a great figure with the pueblo. He had a large

following in the llanos of the state of Bolívar and from
there he had raised a revolution against Guzmán Blanco
and later against Palacio. In the United States he had
learned about popular elections with political campaigns, newspaper propaganda, and all that goes with
them. So, when he saw that not he, but Andrade, was
to be Crespo's man for president, he brought pressure
to bear on Crespo and finally got him to permit an
election à la Yankee. Hernández set out on a speech-
making tour, talking to the people, explaining the details of this new thing, buying up space in the newspapers, having a fine, Yankee time for himself. He
wasn't interfered with by Crespo in any way. However,
when election day came around and the people appeared at the little tables in front of the jefeturas where
they were supposed to register their choice between
Hernández and Andrade, they found Indians there
armed with machetes and they were only permitted to
vote if their choice happened to be Andrade. So,
Andrade was elected unanimously, although many of
the ballots were marked El Mocho Andrade. The real
Mocho, Hernández, was furious. He left Caracas for
his old haunts in the llanos, raised an army and declared himself in revolt against Andrade. His old friend,
Crespo, now retired from the presidency but still Commander of the Army, went out into the llanos to meet
him.

Hernández hid his army in a little wooded spot called
Mata Carmelera and waited for the government troops.
As they drew near, he sallied out onto the llanos to meet
him.

This Hernández did things in a colorful way. He had
a flair for the theatrical. His men had the trappings of
proper soldiers. There were flags and trumpets and
flashing sabers and the picture they made charging out
upon the sun-drenched plains proved the end of Crespo.

It was too much for the old war-horse. He sniffed the air and rushed out to meet the enemy at the head of his men and was killed in the first charge.

Andrade, the man of straw, was having his troubles in Caracas. The other caudillo, Ramón Guerra, was showing signs of making trouble. So, to appease him, he made him Commander of the Army in Crespo's place, and now Guerra went out against his old comrade. There were a series of battles and then Hernández was taken prisoner. He was put into prison at Maracaibo. There had been one hundred and five days of this revolution and one hundred bloody skirmishes.

And more trouble for Andrade. Confronted with naming the various state presidents, he made every mistake possible. He named Guerra president of Guárico and General Lorenzo Guevara revolted. Andrade, seeing everything crashing, tried to win over Hernández again by turning him loose and bringing him back to Caracas. Then Guerra revolted. General Guevara was at the gates of Caracas. It was too much for poor Andrade and he left in a steamer for Colombia, turning the power over to General Victor Rodríguez. This was in October, 1899. In eighteen months of his office, there had been nothing but fighting. The country was in a frightful state.

At Buenos Aires, back in the mountains across the Colombian border, the restless caudillo, Castro, and the Indian brujo sat watching all these things and talking them over.

PART THREE

THE FIGHTING YEARS

1899–1908

Chapter VI

THE CONDOR SWOOPS

❖

THE germ of wider ambitions was sprouting in him. There is no other explanation for it. He had never been nationally-minded, scarcely knew anything about the rest of his country or its problems, had never seen a city and certainly had no sympathy for cities. And Castro had not converted him to patriotic thinking. No one ever converted him to anything. He converted others, by one way or another.

He was not a gambler either. There was nothing sporting about him now, nor before nor after. In his cock-fighting and during his whole military career, he always played safe and sure, never giving the other fellow a chance, never gambling except when the straits were desperate. And yet, he put up his thirty thousand bolívars, everything he had. And he was a man to whom money had always meant more than anything in the world.

It must have been ambition. The prize that he saw must have been large and he must have been very sure of winning it, very sure indeed. And that prize was so very far away, so many years away, for an Andean peon. How sure he was of himself, how far ahead he looked, how patient he was. He was brujo, witch-doctor.

He looked at his tables of dates, studied his little papers with the numbers written on them, and on the 13th of May called together his tribe.

There were sixty men in all, mustered there at

Buenos Aires for the drive across the frontier. La
Sesenta, the Sixty, they were always called afterward.
They represented the full fighting strength of the
Gómez clan. Castro was in command. The others were
the family, kinsmen, criados and peons of Gómez. They
were a wild, illiterate lot of mountain Indians. As an
indication of the close blood-ties that bound them, there
were, among the sixty, seven men who bore the name
of Gómez, seven by the name of Nieto, six, Ruiz, four,
Gámez, ten, Sánchez and at least two of all the others.
By marriage and by illicit unions not involving names,
they were all related. Juancho Gómez, the steadiest of
the older brothers, was left behind to look after things
at the hacienda. Aníbal, Eustóquio, Ovidio, Evaristo,
Hernán and Canuto went along with Juan Vicente.

Again, the rocky trail across the Táchira, across the
Venezuelan frontier toward San Antonio. Sixty men
now, the full harvest of Hermenegilda Chacón, all the
power of her body and her strong will and strong mind
reproduced by union with the males she had selected,
pouring back into the country to make it theirs, the
rocky valleys repeating their shouts and wild laughter
and curses. One of them riding a white mule, silent,
calm, as though he were riding to market, almost as
though he were asleep.

Castro had made his plans well. He had also used his
secret channels in Venezuela. When La Sesenta crossed
the Táchira, their old comrade of the Palacio forces,
General González, was waiting to join them with two
hundred men. The munitions that Gómez had cached
seven years before were unearthed. Rifles, cartridges and
machetes were distributed among the men and, while
they joyfully fitted the rifles to their shoulders and
studied their action and swung the machetes through
the air, severing the heads of multitudes of imaginary
enemies, the leaders held a war council. General

Cipriano Castro was chosen Commander-in-Chief, González, second in command and other officials appointed down the line. The Gómez tribe came in for colonelcies mostly. Juan Vicente was given his old job of Chief Commissary. That was all he asked. He was studying these fellows, now, and learning from them. There was a lot he could learn from them about this war business. Besides, he would handle the funds and the supplies. And the funds were all his, anyway.

A name was decided upon for the movement. They would call it La Restauración, The Restoration. Ever since it has been known by that name and Castro attributed to himself the title, The Restorer. The restoration of what and the restorer of what, no one has ever known.

Castro, at this time, was undoubtedly the ablest general in Venezuela. He was cunning, resourceful, shifty, fast. A small, light man, physically, his war tactics resembled his bodily movements. He was never still. He planned his course of action in the instant that he perceived a situation and he seldom had to alter it. Now, he lost no time. There was a small force of Andrade's troops guarding the frontier. He fell upon them at once, split them in half, and then destroyed each half, one at a time, before they knew that a war was on.

The Andinos came from everywhere to join La Restauración. Everyone, all the little generals in the Cordillera and the llanos, were up in arms against Andrade and Castro seemed a good man to go in with. His prestige as a fighting man had always been great. Besides, he had been out of the country for seven years and whatever his misdeeds had been or his lack of qualifications was, was all forgotten now. The second day after the crossing of the Táchira his forces numbered six hundred men and in a few weeks, two thousand. The way was clear to San Cristóbal, the capital of the state of

Táchira. It was defended by General Peñaloza with a strong force well-placed among the mountains above the town.

Castro moved rapidly to a position before the de- fenses. He made all the preparations that would indi- cate an attack, this to deceive Peñaloza, and then he made a move which was typical of him in this era of his fighting career. He knew that a force under General Sarria was approaching along the Cordillera, coming to aid Peñaloza in the defense of San Cristóbal. He de- ployed quickly to the northeast, leaving Peñaloza to scratch his head and wonder what it was all about, fell upon Sarria's column in a rocky pass and destroyed it. He captured supplies and Sarria, wounded, was made prisoner. Then, without wasting a minute, he wheeled back against Peñaloza at San Cristóbal, surprised him and drove him out of his position.

The capital of the state became their headquarters. They were quite a horde now, all the supplies, herds, pack-animals, personal belongings, their women and children. They took over the town, sprawled all over it, the men setting up their little open-air establish- ments of hammock and open fire and woman and maybe a child or two, with the easy adaptability of people who always carry their homes with them. They bathed and washed their clothes and watered their animals in the Torbes River that swept past the town. Gómez estab- lished a park for munitions and requisitioned supplies from the haciendas in the valley.

Castro always had his little channels of information. He learned now that an Andrade force under Pacheco was moving down from the state of Mérida to dislodge him from San Cristóbal. Instead of digging in there and awaiting him, he left a small force to defend his park and hurried out with his main force to meet him. He selected the exact spot beforehand. The state of

Mérida is the most mountainous of all the Andean states. There are seventy-six peaks of over thirteen thousand feet, ten of them perpetually snow-capped, and toward the south, near the Táchira border, there is a rough, high table-land, the Páramo Zumbador. Over this exhausting country the government troops were laboring along the old Spanish trail southward. Castro chose to meet them at the spot where they would be most fatigued, the foot of Zumbador, where the páramo dropped down to the valley of La Grita.

As the Andrade men filed down the steep trail and spread out, dog-weary, on the plain below, the Restorers swooped upon them, a mad, shouting horde, swinging machete and güinche, smothering them as you smother a fly with wet wings. Castro returned to his position at San Cristóbal.

Gómez kept his pack-animals moving over the trails, bringing up the supplies as they were needed, watching all this and learning. Not once in this whole campaign of the Restauración was there a moment's delay in action for need of supplies. They were always there.

There was a brief rest in San Cristóbal and then came word of another movement against them, this time a large force, five thousand men, coming from Maracaibo, over the lowlands south of the great lake. Castro was ready with a new plan. He gave the order to break camp. Everything was going out this time, the whole force, park, women and all.

Great excitement in San Cristóbal. Women bundling their hammocks, packing their cooking things, men driving the animals in from the pastures. The pack-mules reared and plunged with the feel of the loads roped upon them, the burros brayed, the goats bleated, chickens dashed underfoot, squawking. Dust rose in clouds from the sunny plaza. At daybreak the column filed out of town. It moved rapidly northeastward, the men urging the animals with shouts and prods, the women swishing their long skirts, the children trotting to keep up, shivering with the mountain morning chill.

That was a hard, fast march, driving hard the whole way. They crossed the high range above San Cristóbal at the headwaters of the Torbes, following the Spanish trail, dropped down into the valley of La Grita, where they spent the night. The women and children dropped, exhausted, not bothering to swing their hammocks. They had marched thirty miles. The men hobbled the animals, chewed on cold arepas and lay down to sleep as the sun went down. The leaders squatted over the flickering fires, talking over their plans, their dark faces reflecting the yellow light.

The next day they crossed the wide valley of La Grita. At noon they reached the ascent of the Páramo Zumbador, the spot where Castro had fallen upon the troops from Mérida. They entered the pass and began the long, laboring climb, twisting toward the summit. As the shadows of the peaks grew long and dark and the night chill settled, they came out upon the level of the páramo. They slept huddled to the fires, wrapped close in their woolen ruanas.

On the third day, Castro divided his army. The supplies and herds and women and children with a small fighting force were to proceed northeast along the trail for a half-day's march and wait while he with the main fighting body would cross the range to the northwest to meet the troops coming from the Maracaibo basin.

Castro led his men over the high Cordillera de Tovar by way of the pass of Yegüines, dropped down to the valley on the other side and awaited the enemy. When the advance guard appeared, he sallied out to meet them. He drove the advance guard back to within sight of the main column, then he gave an order, his men wheeled, back-tracking up the trail, apparently in retreat. They climbed the Cordillera once more, passed over the ridge and came back again to the main trail on the páramo, the enemy well behind in slow pursuit. Here Castro headed northeast, not southwest toward San Cristóbal. No, he was going to Caracas, not San Cristóbal. He turned northeast, to join the other section of his army, leaving the enemy behind to continue on to San Cristóbal in pursuit of an army that was going the other way. No, El Restaurador was headed for Caracas.

The army joined once more and they could take it easy now for a while. They proceeded along the old trail leisurely, in good order. There was an advance guard, then the main fighting force, then Gómez with his supply train, then the women and children and finally a small rear guard. They were in the highest section of the Cordillera now. All around, the peaks rose in gray columns, white at the top with mists and glistening snow and the icy winds poured down into the valleys at night. To the east the Pico Bolívar reared sixteen thousand, four hundred feet. There were haciendas here and there along the trail where they stopped to rest the animals and feed them up in the rich potreros. The army enjoyed these little stops as all Venezuelans do when they travel. There was always an excuse for a fiesta. It was Bolívar's birthday, or the anniversary of the battle of Boyacá or Carabobo, or Independence Day, or somebody's saint's day or a child had been born in camp. Anyway, the guitars and tiples rippled and the marracas swished. The Indians danced the joropo on the bare earth around the fires. Much aguardiente was drunk and sometimes there were fights among the men. The blue moonlight washed over the white peaks and high valleys and the little huddle of flickering fires made a brave, warm sally into the vast expanse of cold.

Gómez dickered with the haciendados over the pur-

chase of food and of course he made good bargains,
under the circumstances. All his life his bargains were
made under circumstances.

On toward Caracas. An enemy force of seven hundred men was met and defeated and the way was clear
to Mérida. This, the capital city of the state of the
same name, was entered without the firing of a shot.
Castro lost no time here. Slowly, by the nature of the
rough country they were traveling, but without pause,
they crossed the state, along the trail of the old Spanish
conquerors that followed the high valley of the Chama,
always northeastward toward Caracas. Nearing the border of the state of Trujillo they had to climb again,
this time to the Páramo de Muchuchíes, ten thousand
feet above the sea. They crossed the plain, again the
snowy peaks rising on all sides, and moved down into
the valley of the Trujillo beyond. Here General Leopoldo Baptista awaited them with two thousand, five
hundred men hidden among the lofty crags. Castro
spied him out, skirted him and hurried on ahead, leaving his enemy behind for the second time.

He had to move fast now for Baptista came on in his
rear. He crossed the state rapidly, meeting little resistance. It was hard going here. The state is criss-crossed
with rivers. Into them the column went, one river after
another, splashing in the cold, swift water, driving the
animals, shouting at them, beating them, packing and
unpacking the loads time and time again. Through the
capital city, Trujillo, without stopping, always to the
northeast. At the border of the state of Lara where the
trail dropped down into the valley of the Tocuyo another large enemy force was waiting.

Castro knew this country from childhood. He knew
a side-trail down the mountain, a little-used and pre-
cipitous path called La Viciosa, the Vicious One. Off
the main trail the column went, into the gloomy,

wooded, narrow path. It was rightly named. In places
the mules could scarcely squeeze between the rocky
sides. They fell and pitched down the smooth, hard surface. They were unpacked, helped to their feet, re-
packed and urged on again, their knees bruised and
bleeding. There were fallen trees and underbrush that
had to be cleared by machete. At last they were down
to the valley. They came out upon the plain and fell
upon a small force guarding the enemy's park at a place
called Parapara. They dispersed the guard and took the
whole supply train, leaving the enemy back in the
mountains, waiting for them by the main trail. On
toward Caracas. For the third time the enemy was left
behind.

Easier going now, across the state of Lara. A few
rivers here, too, but mostly dry plains, the mountain
peaks lowering a little as though tired of their long-
sustained loftiness. Herds of cattle grazed on the sparse
grass over the great arid stretches. The tropic sun beat
down upon the aching shoulders of the Indian horde
straggling along. In their nostrils was the smell of
Venezuela; the smell of goats on a bare hillside, of
drifting, wood-smoke and burro dung. It isn't a bad
smell, really; it is acrid and virile and somehow satis-
fying. You'll remember it, once you've smelled it, and
you'll sniff it with pleasure when you come to smell it
again.

At Barquisimeto, the capital of the state, a large force
of government troops had united to defend the city
against the Restauradores. Castro skirted the city and
continued on into the valley of the Yaracuy, once again
leaving the enemy behind. Here a large force of old
Mochistas joined him, bringing his strength to three
thousand men. On he went, across the state of Yaracuy,
still moving fast with the enemy behind.

At the town of Nirgua near the border of the state

of Carabobo, he defeated a force of eight hundred men under General Rosenda Medina, taking nearly all of them prisoner. He crossed into the state of Carabobo and worked along the Cordillera and took up a position among the mountains near the city of Valencia. Behind him came Leopoldo Baptista and Antonio Fernández with two thousand men. These were joined by government reinforcements and in all five thousand men were closing in on him. The phantom was going to have to fight now.

Gómez had learned a lot. He had seen many miles of new country and memorized it all. He had handled the most difficult and important job of the campaign, next to the job of commander, and he had done it well. He had watched a master guerrilla in action. And next he was to see the guerrilla's masterpiece.

Chapter VII

TOCUYITO AND A NEW WORLD

❖

J UAN VICENTE GÓMEZ had already taken a few cautious steps along the road that he had decided upon. He knew his man, Castro, thoroughly by now, he knew just what use he could make of him.

Castro was arrogant, high-handed, intolerant with his men. He was a stickler for discipline and not concerned with the welfare of his soldiers. They were there to win battles for him and nothing more, to obey him blindly; and they were free, mountain Indians, mostly, to whom these methods were distasteful. They had always been accustomed to the easy, familiar relationships that existed between the caciques and their tribesmen.

Furthermore, by this time there had been attracted to the movement many young military men of the aristocracy, of Castro's own class, some of whom had been educated abroad and had served in the armies of foreign countries; capable officers in their own right. Among them were such men as Eleázar López Contreras, now president of Venezuela (1936), Régulo Olivares, now president of the state of Zulia, Félix Galaviz, Pérez Soto and many others. And these, too, suffered from the despotic methods of Castro, the little man with delusions of grandeur. Resentment was stirring in both the rank and file.

Gómez, as Commissary, was in a nice position to take advantage of this; little favors in the way of extra equipment, good riding animals, extra rations of food passed out surreptitiously. Besides, his personality invited confidences. His silence, solidity and general capability, as well as his humble origin, drew the men to him with their grievances. Nothing tangible, not at all, not an indiscreet word. Just a word here and there, a sympathetic gesture, a fleeting facial expression. It was much too soon for any more than that. This was a long way ahead of time, years ahead of time. But it was just as well to begin now. Gómez had an Indian's patience.

The bitter ones formed a group and called themselves, secretly, La Liga de los Descontentos, The League of the Discontented. Gómez was its leading spirit in his subtle way.

Castro is now before the city of Valencia, the capital of the state of Carabobo and the largest city on the Cordillera next to Caracas itself. Before him are the defenders of the city and behind come Baptista and Fernández. There is no opportunity for retreat in case of disaster. The terrain is not to his liking. Again he is ready with a plan, a perfect beauty of a plan this time.

He gives the order to break camp, to abandon the position. It is done rapidly, efficiently. The lines are formed, the cavalry drawn up, the park mobilized, the infantry ranks filled. Then the command to march, *to the southeast*. For the first time during the campaign the northeast route is abandoned. The advance guard moves out, the whole column draws out like an accordion stretching, the army heads away from its main goal. Along the trail toward the town of Tocuyito. Flatter country now, wide valleys and rolling hills, room to maneuver. They march nine miles along the road to the outskirts of the town. Here is the place Castro was looking for and he gives the order to halt.

He wheels his men so that they are facing northwest along the road whence they came. The road is wide here, stretching straight as a plumb-line across the plain of El Palito valley which they had just traversed, and on either side are high barbed wire fences. Castro places his men among the low hills in a V-shape, a wing of infantry on each side of the road, the cavalry concentrated at the apex. Now he is ready.

No enemy behind, now. The llanos sloping down to the Apure, all clear, an escape to Colombia in case of disaster.

They wait among the hills. The men, sprawled on their bellies on the knolls, sight their guinches down the straight road below, across the sleepy, sun-drenched plain with the heat-waves dancing. The animals of the mounted men stamp and sniff. One whinnies and strong, brown fingers clamp its nostrils.

There is a faint movement away off across the valley, just a flicker like the movement of a wren in deep foliage; and little spots of color appear against the dark green of the mountains beyond.

A hoarse whisper from one of the men on the knoll, "*Ahí vienen!*" "Here they come!" The whisper goes back along the V, little waves of hoarse sound rippling back to the mounted men at the rear, "*Ahí vienen!*" A short order returns along the line of sprawling men, "Esperan el mando!" "Await the order!"

The enemy column is plainly visible now. It creeps slowly along the road, a compact mass, its swinging motion of march accentuated by the shimmering heat. It grows as it comes nearer, changing from a dark, gliding snake to the little, colored sections of a caterpillar; and then the sections, too, break up into smaller segments that are men. They move between the lines of barbed wire. The advance guard rides right into the clump of knolls. The sprawling men can look down upon them now and their fingers twitch on the triggers.

"*Fuego!*" The command is drowned in the roar. The

güinches blaze down into the mass of human and animal flesh that churns like a boiling vat of tortured insects between the lines of barbed wire. The hills utter a din of triumph, the drumming of muskets and the wild yells of the Indians, and the plain, the din of horror—the shrieks of animals and men. The horses rear and plunge among the foot-soldiers. The wounded ones fall, struggling, trampling and crushing. The officers push about in the mad confusion, waving their machetes, their faces livid with screaming. "Deploy!" "In the name of Mary, deploy!" But they can't deploy. They are torn against the barbed wire by the press of bodies. Here and there one gets out. He breaks across the plain and the men on the knolls pot him calmly and gleefully as a boy knocks over clay ducks at a street fair. There is no room for the animals to run for a leap. Then, some of them break the wire with the weight of their surge and there is a feeble sally into the open plain.

Now Castro with his horsemen come out from the apex. They flank the wings of the V and charge over the rough plain, cutting down the fleeing ones, echando plomo—throwing lead—into the imprisoned column along its whole line. Castro's horse stumbles on taking a ditch. Horse and man go down together and Castro lies there with his leg broken.

Diego Ferrer, the Andrade Minister of War, is far in the rear with a few pieces of artillery. He gets out upon the plain, trains his pieces and fires them. Now, worse carnage still. The shells fall among his own men in the advance column. Right into the bloody mess between the wires. Pieces of men and pieces of animals scatter over the earth when the shells blow, one after another.

Gradually the rear falls back, making room, and the trapped ones drag themselves away in slow retreat. Castro's cavalry keeps at them, hurrying them back along the trail to Valencia. What is left of the army melts away into the hills and Castro's men are called off. They wheel back to the hills of Tocuyito.

They gather up the dead and the wounded. Among the latter is Aníbal Gómez, one of Juan Vicente's brothers.

The next day the Restorers follow the remnants of the government army into Valencia. The column moves slowly. Castro lies in a hammock suspended between two mules, his leg propped up before him. He laughs and jokes with the officers riding beside him. He is a very genial man on these occasions.

Tocuyito. The master guerrilla's masterpiece.

Valencia was the headquarters while Castro recovered and the army rested. It was a great occasion for the hillmen from remote Táchira. Here was a city of twenty-five thousand people, there were cotton mills, paved streets and a narrow-gauge railroad that came from Caracas, eighty-five miles away.

What was left of Ferrer's army had fallen back to Maracay and then to La Victoria where they joined a force led by the president, Andrade himself. When Andrade learned of the defeat at Tocuyito he went back to Caracas, leaving a force of four thousand, five hundred men under the command of General Luciano Mendoza. This was the same Mendoza who had fought against Páez years before, who had defeated Páez's man Torres, causing him to commit suicide, who had cut off the genitals of the mantuanos.

Castro now remained with only one thousand, three hundred men and it was a good opportunity for Mendoza to attack him. But he held off. Things were going on in Valencia. Things among the business men. Also, among the other government generals. The banker of Valencia, Manuel Antonio Matos, the merchant, Manuel Corao, the newspaper man, Manuel Pimentel Coronel and the opportunist, Ramón Tello Mendoza, were conferring with Castro. Something was afoot. He'd better look into it. He sent out feelers, learned what was going on and declared himself in.

There was a whole month spent in negotiations in Valencia. The result was that everyone went over to Castro, including Leopoldo Baptista with his three thousand men who had been hurrying after Castro from somewhere away back along the Cordillera, Luciano Mendoza with his four thousand, five hundred men and many other caudillos. Manuel Matos was the banker of the movement. There were all sorts of contracts let and bargains made. The Restauración had now become a great political movement. Gómez and his mountain tribe were somewhat lost in all the fuss and probably considerably confused. Gómez stayed in the background, calmly waiting.

The way was clear to Caracas. Andrade had fled the country. The Restorers, now marching side by side with many who had been firing upon them shortly before, headed northeast once more toward the capital city. They had come seven hundred and fifty miles in six months over the roughest kind of country, fighting all the way. They had grown from a group of sixty men to an army of upwards of ten thousand.

Hermenegilda Chacón sat in her hammock at Buenos Aires, back in the Andes.

Gómez rode his white mule in the rear of the column, studying this new land. It was warmer now in the Valley of Aragua and the mounted men carried their ruanas across the saddle, the men on foot carried them folded on their shoulders. Hills rose around the basin of Lake Valencia, shutting it in, so that no breeze entered, and the sun-warmed air lay there like water in a stagnant pool. Every mile brought new wonders to the men from Táchira—the fine haciendas, the broad, cultivated valley, rich with dark green of sugar cane and maiz, the narrow railroad, twisting its way by the river bank, darting in and out of tunnels where the rocky mountain sides dropped steeply.

This was Bolívar's land and Gómez knew all about it from the stories he had heard. He rode it now, absorbed in it as a religious man is absorbed when he trods for the first time the ground where his god has walked. He spoke to a companion now and then but he was really speaking to himself. They rode through the little, flat village of Maracay.

"Páez lived here," he said, speaking to himself. "And Bolívar came to see him here many times. Think of it, Bolívar rode these very streets."

They came to San Mateo and a little beyond the town, were the ruins of Bolívar's own hacienda, up on the hillside, looking out over the wide valley of the Aragua.

"There is where he lived," Gómez said. "He lived right there on that hillside, compadre."

A little further along, a large, wide-spreading tree rose from the center of the road and the column had to go around it to pass.

"This is it," Gómez said. "This is the Samán de Güere. He rested here, compadre, many times, and he conferred here with Miranda. Think of it. Under the shade of this tree."

At La Victoria the column rested and Castro brought General Luciano Mendoza to meet Gómez. Under way again, Gómez said to his companion, speaking to himself, "I have met Mendoza, compadre. Think of it. He defeated Páez! When I was a boy in my mountains, there were three things I always wanted. I wanted to see San Mateo where he lived and the Samán de Güere where he camped, to meet Mendoza who defeated Páez and to see La Puerta. I have done two of those things in two hours. Now it remains to see La Puerta."

They crossed a mountain range and dropped down
into the valley of the Guaire and approached Caracas.

It was six o'clock in the evening of October 26, 1899,
when the Restorers entered the city. The sun had already dropped down below the hill of El Calvario. The
mountains rising over the city to the east were dark
green in deep shadow, tinted golden at the crests by
the long, slanting rays, the mists about them, rose-
colored, with the reflected fire from the western sky.
The colors of the city, the red roofs, the pink spires,
the patchwork of blues and lavenders and yellows and
browns that were thousands of houses, were sharp and
clear, intensified by the neutral gray of rapid dusk. The
yellow flare of gas street lights blinked into life, one by
one, washing out the colors, bringing on darkness suddenly.

The mountain horde poured into the city over the
cobblestone streets. The narrow sidewalks were lined
with staring people. Castro rode at the head of the column in a coach, with flaring torches and a military
band, and women tossed flowers from balconies and the
crowds cheered him. But they laughed at the array that
followed after him. The bewildered, straggling column
of Andes hillpeople.

Venezuela was and is a country of one city. All the
material wealth of the country is concentrated there.
There the landowners live and enjoy the riches that
come to them from the labor of their peons in the interior or from the bounty of the public treasury. There
are the theaters and public buildings and parks and
colleges and the gay, cosmopolitan life of a capital city
fashioned after the European plan. It is said that a
Frenchman believes he goes to heaven when he dies; an
Argentine, that he goes to Paris and a Venezuelan, that
he goes to Caracas. Maracaibo was little or nothing at
that time. Valencia had a population of twenty-five

thousand, Barquisimeto twenty thousand, and Ciudad Bolívar ten thousand; and aside from those there was nothing in the country larger than a village. Caracas had one hundred thousand people.

They came through the streets, staring at the buildings, the thousands of glaring gas lights, the amazing horse-trams, the gorgeous, glittering carriages with brass lamps, the odd and richly dressed people who stared back at them, laughing. The Indian women with their wide hats and straight black hair plaited down the back, carrying their children wrapped in blankets on their hips, driving their burros and goats. The pack-animals clopping over the strange cobblestones, loaded with woven-palm crates of chickens and cooking things, earthen jugs and totumos. Even pets—dogs and parrots and trupials. The dark men with their ruanas and rifles and machetes and their little mules with hand-made saddles.

They over-flowed the city. There wasn't room for all of them. They made their camps in the city parks. The Plaza Bolívar, in the center of the city, became the temporary home of some five hundred of them. They hung their hammocks between the trees, built their charcoal fires and cooked their plantains on the paved plaza walks and answered the calls of nature among the flower gardens.

Castro came out on the balcony of the Casa Amarilla, the Yellow House, overlooking the Plaza Bolívar, and made a speech promising "new ideals, new men, new methods." The people cheered him wildly but they were more interested in the strange beings camped there in the Plaza.

The high, bronze grill fence was lined four deep with Caraqueños, like children watching the monkeys at the zoo. A constant stream of carriages, bearing beautifully-dressed women and men who stared down into the scene in the sunken plaza, rolled along the streets on the four sides. The mountain men mixed with the crowds, pushing into the theater lobbies and cafés, fascinated. They wore nondescript garments they had picked up along the long march but their hat-bands indicated their partisanship with Castro. Some of them wore bands bearing the names of Mendoza and Castro and some of them wore three bands with the names of Mendoza and Baptista and Castro. The Caraqueños snickered.

An oddly cynical city, Caracas. Oddly susceptible, too, with a Latin sentimentality. She recognizes her own weaknesses and makes a joke of them. Much too complicated and perverse for a mountain man ever to win.

Gómez stood by the statue of Bolívar in the center of the Plaza. He watched the milling crowds, the moving necklace of carriage lights, with his sleepy, heavy-lidded eyes.

He was forty-two years old. He still wore the wide hat, ruana and alpargatas of his country. After this he would wear different clothes and he would wear the ruana again, on occasions, but up to his forty-second year the man who was to become one of the world's richest men had worn the costume of the mountains.

Chapter VIII

CASTRO

❖

HE had no plan of government at all. The Restoration was an empty catch-phrase as were all of Castro's high-sounding political utterances. "New ideals, new men, new methods." There were new men but that was all. There were no ideals whatever and as for the methods, they were the oldest methods in the world.

From his first act, the naming of his cabinet and the presidents of states, he demonstrated the incompetence, favoritism and disregard for the public good that was to mark his whole administration. He gathered about him a group of robbing, aristocratic ruffians whom the people referred to as Los Bastoneros, literally, the men with canes. Of these, Tello Mendoza became known as El Gran Bastonero.

Revolutions broke out immediately he came into power and continued for four years, until 1903, when Gómez ended them. The only reason that he was able to maintain his power for so long a time was because of his despotic methods, his military cunning, and toward the end, when women had weakened him, because he had Gómez.

Castro had always recognized the strength that was hidden in Juan Vicente Gómez. He had watched him closely during the Andean campaign. He was always faintly baffled by him. He knew that he was a man to keep on one's side. On December 8, only six weeks after coming into power, he named him Governor of the Federal District. This has always been an important position, requiring special qualities of strength and intelligence, for the Caraqueños are difficult people to deal with.

Gómez took a house in Caracas and sent for his mother, Hermenegilda, his mistress, Dionisia Bello, his children and all the other women of the Gómez clan. His brother, Aníbal, had been brought to a hospital in the city but his wound became infected from lack of proper early treatment and he died.

Castro embarked at once upon a mad career of arrogant confiscation and moral debauchery. Tello Mendoza, the Valencian opportunist and libertine, was his particular companion. He was made Minister of Hacienda, an important cabinet post, so that he would have easy access to the funds necessary for their little pastimes together.

El Mocho Hernández, out of prison, was named Minister of Fomento, a post of no value whatever at that time for there was nothing in the country to foment. Always the old irreconcilable, he left the city for his beloved llanos and gathered up his scattered partisans, declaring revolution against Castro.

The national treasury and the Bank of Venezuela were completely without funds. Castro called upon Manuel Matos, the banker of the Restoration movement, to provide money for the campaign against Hernández. But he had none available either. Castro then turned to the Bank of Caracas. This bank, too, was in bad straits and refused him aid. He ordered the directors to be arrested and sent to the prison at Puerto Cabello with Manuel Matos as well.

Soldiers went to the houses of the bankers, dragged them out and marched them on foot through the city streets to the railroad station and their wives followed by their sides, weeping. However, at the station they came to an agreement of some sort and were turned loose. Those were the methods of the little tyrant, Castro, with his delusions of grandeur.

Guzmán and Crespo had left the country saddled with obligations to foreign countries. For instance, there was a contract with a Russian engineer for the construction of a new market in Caracas. The market had never been built but the debt of eleven million bolívars to the foreign banks which had lent the money still stood. The money had simply been divided among the politicians and the Russian engineer.

A Belgian company had been given a contract for an aqueduct and sewers for the city which had never been constructed, either, and this debt, too, of some millions of bolívars, was outstanding, because of similar negocios.

Germany had a claim of fifty million bolívars, the sum that Crespo had borrowed for the railroad.

England and France had large sums coming to them either as interest or principal on loans made for various purposes.

All of these countries, now that Castro was in, seeing the reckless extravagance of his administration, got together and demanded payment. The total sum demanded amounted to some one hundred million bolívars or twenty million dollars at the normal exchange rate of five bolívars to the American dollar.

Guzmán and Crespo had contracted the debts and the incompetents who had followed them, including Castro himself, had completely ruined the country's resources. Castro couldn't pay, of course.

His actions now were typical of him. He insulted the foreign ministers, refused to see them when they came to talk. Taigny, the French Minister, was accustomed to go down to La Guayra whenever a French liner was in port for a visit aboard. On one of these trips he was refused permission to return ashore, by order of Castro.

He had to stay on board and return to France without baggage. Castro then proceeded to arrest the ministers of the other European countries. Germany sent cruisers to block the Venezuelan coast. They fired upon Puerto Cabello and Maracaibo. Castro rose up in his might and declared war on practically the whole world.

Theodore Roosevelt was president of the United States at that time. He ordered battleships to the scene of the blockade and informed Kaiser Wilhelm that if the German vessels did not withdraw within forty-eight hours they would be fired upon; adding that he would not permit an American country to be "made another Egypt." Roosevelt's defenders in this affair say that there was evidence that the move of Germany was the first step in a plan to establish a permanent base on the northern coast of South America; but whether that was true or no, the results were that Germany withdrew, the demanding nations quoted the Monroe Doctrine back at Roosevelt, and the problem of collection was thrown into the lap of Uncle Sam, who became the holder of the bag, as usual.

The American Minister, Mr. Bowen, negotiated with Castro and the disputing nations. He brought about an agreement whereby Venezuela freed the foreign ministers, recognized a total debt of seventy millions of bolívars and agreed to retire it over a period of years on a pro-rata basis, the United States guaranteeing the payments.

So, eventually, the American taxpayers had to pay for some of the good times of Cipriano Castro and it would be interesting to have a look at what they paid for.

Castro had all the moral vices except those of sexual inversion and he practiced them with glee and enthusiasm. His debaucheries during his time as president were so continuous and so spectacular that they became the most notable part of his whole career and are about the only things that the old-timers remember about the man. They have forgotten, mostly, the able general, the master guerrilla. They love to repeat the stories of his wild doings—how he would drink a quart of Napoleon brandy during the course of a game of billiards; of how he bathed, naked, in the fountain of the Casa Amarilla; of the time he jumped from a balcony into the street, thinking there was an earthquake, and lay there in the light of early morning with his leg broken.

He gave banquets for the men of the aristocracy, hiring French prostitutes to give lewd performances, and he would go down into the barrios and join the fiestas of the common people, distributing champagne and dancing with the girls, delighting in the vivas that greeted him.

He established twenty-two girls as mistresses in various parts of the city, giving them good houses to live in and generous money allowances, maintaining them thus up to the time that he left the country. They were girls of the peon or middle class, mostly, daughters of laborers and tradesmen. His pimp and court jester, Tello Mendoza, arranged all the details of these affairs. He negotiated with the parents, rented the houses and bought the furniture. He was constantly on the lookout for girls whom he thought would please his chief. Castro's principal requirements were that the girls be young and virgin, particularly, virgin. He delighted in rupturing the hymen with his fingers. On one occasion Mendoza had a girl brought from Cuba because he had heard that she was beautiful and of the type that pleased Castro most.

Castro treated his women well. He kept them in comparative luxury, gave parties for his cronies at their houses and was generous and indulgent with the many children that they bore him, even sending some of them

abroad to be educated. Of these, two grew up to become well-known actresses of the stage and motion-
pictures in the United States. Altogether, his women
and their families seemed to have been a happy, contented lot, even though they lived in the social ostra-
cism that Castro imposed upon them in adherence to
the traditions of his class.

Fernándo González, in his book, "Mi Compadre,"
lists the names of eight of Castro's mistresses together
with the monthly sums expended upon each and from
the sizeable amounts it is clear that they were well cared
for.

His wife, a woman of good family of Táchira, lived
quietly in her house, Villa Zoila, in El Paraiso, the
fashionable section of Caracas. Juan Vicente Gómez had
known her from his early days and he visited her often
at Villa Zoila.

Castro named officials, removed them, sent them to
prison and freed them again, with no apparent reason
other than his own caprice. The Ministry of Hacienda
was the easiest post by which he could enrich his
friends so he appointed them to it one after another,
leaving them in office until he judged they had gotten
as much as they should have. They all took full advantage of their opportunities. They followed the advice
of a former president, Linares Alcántara, who said,
"Hurry up, while you have the chance. The treasury is
like the Guaire; we all have the right to drink and the
only argument among us is the size of the dipper."

For four years there were revolutions all over the
country. Practically all of Castro's old caudillos rose
against him at one time or another and he had a hard
time holding on to his job. Gómez proved to be his
anchor. He came to rely upon him more and more, till
in the end, Gómez was really the power. So, as well as

HIS CHILDREN BY DIONISIA BELLO

Standing, left to right: GRACIELA, VICENTICO, ALÍ, SERVILIA
Seated: FLOR DE MARÍA, JOSEFA. ONLY GONZALO IS MISSING

his own twenty-seven years of dictatorship, Gómez can be credited with at least four of the reign of Castro.

Gómez was waiting. Always taking the jobs that were given him, doing them well. He was made Military Chief of Táchira, First Vice-President of Venezuela, Commander of the Center Army, Commander of the Western Army, Commander of the Pacification and finally, Commander-in-Chief. But this all came slowly, very slowly. He was working and fighting and learning. Waiting. Very quietly.

One of the most important things that he learned from watching Castro was the power of the great nations, the power of the musiús, as the Venezuelans call all foreigners. Castro had a genius for getting into trouble with the large nations. Besides the time we have already related, there were two other occasions on which Venezuela faced the possibility of military conflict with them. Gómez watched this and profited by it in a way that Castro never could. He conceived a holy respect for the power of the musiús. He wanted no part of it. "Hombre! They had lain outside of the San Carlos bar and shelled Maracaibo! Think of it, compadre, Maracaibo! Fifty kilometers!"

This attitude had a great deal to do with his policies in later years.

He did his fighting and watched his numbers and was silent. There was a banquet one night in Caracas given by Castro. Gómez was there and all the bastoneros were there. He sat by himself against the wall, watching with his sleepy eyes. An old caudillo from the Andes pointed to him and said to the bastoneros:

"There sits Gómez. He's going to —— on all of you and —— himself with Baptista."

Chapter IX

THE PACIFICATION

❖

THE first revolution that was raised against Castro, that of Mocho Hernández, required a full year to subdue. The old guerrilla roamed from place to place over the llanos and it was impossible to trap him. There were several skirmishes and finally a battle at Mañacal against Castro's troops under General Nicolas Rolando which pretty well destroyed him. He had to flee and he was captured eventually and sent to Caracas.

Castro prepared a reception for Mocho that was something after the order of a Roman holiday. He had him paraded through the streets in a cart between files of soldiers while Castro and his bastoneros and his women looked down from the balcony of the Casa Amarilla. Then Mocho was shipped off to the prison at Maracaibo, where he had been imprisoned before so he knew what to expect.

In the meantime trouble had broken out in Táchira. The mountain states were declaring themselves seceded from the Venezuelan union and there was talk of their joining the republic of Colombia. Gómez, only recently made Governor of the Federal District, was now named Civil and Military Chief of Táchira. So, on February 22, 1900, four mouths after he came into Caracas and only nine months after he left Táchira, an obscure officer in a horde of rebels, he went back there with the supreme power of the representative of the national government. He stayed a year and in that time he persuaded his old neighbors out of their contrary notions, by peaceful means, mostly.

On the 20th of February, 1901, the Congress met at Caracas to carry out the wishes of Castro and to give to his eccentric governmental antics a semblance of legality. Gómez was named First Vice-President. He returned from Táchira and assumed his new duties,

Manuel Antonio Matos, the Valencia banker who had arranged the negotiations among the opponents of Castro after Tocuyito that had resulted in their selling out to the cause of Restoration, had been in difficulties with Castro from the beginning as we have commented upon. He was imprisoned when he failed to provide funds that Castro expected him to produce from thin air. Upon his release he went to the British island of Trinidad and began to make plans for a revolution against Castro.

Matos was an honest man of good family and he had been educated in Europe. He was primarily a business man and was a good organizer but he was lacking in tact and he was ambitious for power.

This was the time of the blockading of the Venezuelan coast and the dispute with the foreign nations over debt payments. These nations now lent their support to Matos. Then, too, there had been a dispute between two American companies, the Felicidad and the Bermúdez, over the concession of the asphalt lake, Guanoco, in the eastern part of Venezuela and the State Department of the United States had been involved, causing the ire of Castro to fall upon the Bermúdez company to which he had been forced to concede the asphalt rights. Now this company, feeling that the Castro government couldn't last, supported the plans of Matos, giving him funds. The result was, with this outside help, the Matos revolution took on most formidable appearance. Following established tradition a name

was given to the movement. It was called La Liberta-
dora.

Matos established communication with all the dis-
satisfied little generals throughout the length and
breadth of the country. He won them over and sent
arms and ammunition to points all along the coast.
Soon the whole country was up in arms against Castro.
Our old friend, Luciano Mendoza, now president of the
state of Aragua by appointment of Castro, again dis-
played the changeable nature for which he was famous
and declared in revolt. General Antonio Fernández rose
in Carabobo, Luís Loreto Lima in Cojedes, Riera,
Solagnie, Peñaloza, and Montilla in Falcón and Lara
and in the east, Nicolas Rolando, Domingo Monagas,
Zoilo Vidal and the Ducharnes. Matos bought an old
British vessel, the *Banright,* rechristened it the *Libertador,* armed it, loaded it with men and supplies and
sailed to the coast of Falcón, landing at La Vela del
Coro. Castro called a council of war.

There was no money and very few men. The
Mochistas who had comprised the largest element in
the Castro following were now quite sullen and unde-
pendable, for their hero lay in prison by Castro's orders;
though they had not actually gone over to Matos, for
he, too, had been guilty of certain acts of desecration
against the deity, Mocho Hernández. The chief threat
was Mendoza, for he was operating within striking distance of the capital. Castro had no intention of going
out himself. He was too occupied with his women. He
turned to Gómez. Gómez was named Commander of the
Center and ordered out against Mendoza.

Mendoza, the man who had "defeated Páez," the man
whom Gómez had dreamed of meeting when he was a
boy in the mountains. Now, he was going out to fight
him and with only a handful of soldiers, "with three
cats" as the expression was. "Hombre!" Gómez said.

"How am I going to fight Mendoza with these tres gatos? Well, I'd go out for him even alone. If he beats me, I'll be beaten by the best man in the country. If he kills me, I'll be killed by the best man in the country. The bad thing would be to send me out against a little fellow."

He was appointed the 20th of December, 1901, and he left the city the next day, just two and a half years after he left Colombia with La Sesenta. He transported his men by railroad to San Mateo and struck the enemy at Cagua the same day, taking them completely by surprise. They dropped back to Villa de Cura and he was right after them and struck again. They fell back to La Puerta.

La Puerta is the gateway to the llanos. It is a narrow place in the trail, a gateway, literally; great, odd pinnacles of rock rising sheer from the valley on both sides, a bottle-neck pass that has always been one of the most strategic points in Venezuela from the military viewpoint. Bolívar fought there several times against Boves, the Spanish butcher. It was the other place that Gómez had dreamed of seeing when he was a boy. Now, he saw it for the first time and he was fighting there against Mendoza, the man whom he had dreamed of seeing. Furthermore he defeated Mendoza there, Mendoza, "the man who defeated Páez."

The battle at La Puerta lasted one hour. Gómez moved so quickly upon Mendoza that he had not time to take advantage of the terrain and it was Gómez who distributed his men about the rocky peaks of the pass. He stood on a high rock himself and fired a rifle. He watched the troops of Mendoza break and flee for the llanos. "It was then," he said, "that I knew I was going to be the president of Venezuela." The goal was a long way off, still, but not too far for him to see.

Mendoza fled with all haste southward and Gómez

was right after him. It was a chase of seventy-five miles into the rolling upper llanos of Guárico before Gómez cornered him at San José de Tiznados and struck him again. He tried to cross the river at Paso de Esteves but Gómez was upon him and completely demolished him this time. Mendoza barely got away himself.

Gómez dropped back to La Puerta again to await General Antonio Fernández who was coming to join Mendoza. This was the same Fernández whom Castro had sidestepped coming in along the Cordillera, who had followed the Restorers for weeks and who had finally caught up with them at Valencia. Gómez placed his men about the crags at La Puerta and waited for him. Fernández thought Gómez was still down in the llanos.

Gómez had quite a large force now. Many men had joined him along the way, some of the enemy forces coming over to him. He attracted men. He didn't arouse their affections as El Mocho did, he was too cold for that, but he drew them to him by his victories, by his solidity of character, by the reputation he had for uncanny discernment. His men feared him and followed him. He was brujo, they said.

Fernández came to La Puerta on the 30th of December. The rocky crags belched fire at him, demoralized his men. He was defeated decisively in a few hours. Gómez went back to Villa de Cura.

Mendoza had gone into the Sierra of Carabobo and raised another force. Gómez went after him at once, caught him at El Barro on the 5th of January and defeated him, taking some of his officers prisoner. He visited all the haciendas along the Sierra and told the owners that they had their choice of joining him or laying down their arms and going to work.

General Luís Loreto Lima was operating in Cojedes with a force of llanero lancers. Gómez dropped down from the Sierra into the plains below Tocuyito where Castro had trapped Ferrer in the final battle of the Restoration, caught Lima at Tinaco, defeated him and took him prisoner, wounded. Then he hurried north again into eastern Carabobo and defeated General Guillermo Barraez.

His present job was finished. The insurrections in the center had been put down, the first step in the Pacification accomplished. He returned to Caracas on February 26, 1902. He had been out sixty-five days. Even Castro had not moved faster nor fought more nor covered more country in that space of time. The Commissary had become a fighting man.

Things had been going badly for Castro over the rest of the country. The states of Falcón and Lara in the west were completely in the hands of the revolutionists and Matos was bringing in men by sea. In the east, the government forces under Calixto Escalante and Ramón García had been defeated at Guanaguana, almost all the troops falling prisoner.

Years after this, when Castro was in exile, he said, "I was always suspicious of the sly smile of Juan Vicente."

Nevertheless, he was the only man he had now who could win battles. Gómez was named National Delegate and Military Commander of the states of Falcón, Lara, Yaracuy, Zulia, Trujillo, Mérida and Táchira, the whole west. On the 17th of March, the day after the appointment, Gómez went to La Guayra and took a boat for Puerto Cabello.

This was the Andean's first voyage upon the sea. The Caraqueños tell that, on seeing the Caribbean before him he said, "Hombre! What an expanse of waste! If it were grass, think of the cattle that could feed upon it!"

He reached Puerto Cabello the next day. He put his

men aboard a gunboat, *Restaurado,* and two schooners
and sailed west for the coast of Falcón where he landed
on the 19th. He established himself at Coro, sending
out two forces, one under Luís Varela to engage General Montilla, the other under Régulo Olivares to meet
Riera and Peñaloza. Gómez's plan was good but it failed
because he wasn't there himself to carry it out. Varela
defeated Montilla at Jacura but Riera flanked him and
fell upon him before he had recovered and drove him
back to Churuguara. He was wounded and Gómez sent
Tobias Uribe to replace him. Olivares had been de-
layed, failed to engage Riera and join Valera as the
plan had been, so that Valera had been confronted
alone with the superior forces of Riera.

Gómez went out himself, then. He ordered Olivares
with three battalions to defend Coro, left a force of
two hundred men at La Negrita to prevent the enemy
getting away to the coast and attacked Riera and
Peñaloza, now joined, at Urucure. He defeated them
and they retreated, leaving their dead and wounded.
He followed them to Sabaneta where he dispersed
them. On April 15 he was called back to Caracas. He
left Ramón Ayala in command at Coro. No sooner had
Gómez embarked for La Guayra than Riera and Peñaloza struck at Coro, captured it and took Ayala and the
president of the state, Tellería, prisoners. Gómez, alone,
of Castro's generals, could win battles.

He was now given command of the eastern army and
ordered against Rolando and Vidal.

He arrived in La Guayra from Coro on the 29th of
April. He got his orders there and left the next day
for the east without going to Caracas. He landed his
men at the Gulf of Santa Fé, some fifteen kilometers
west of the town of Cumaná which was occupied by
Zoilo Vidal. On May 3 he moved his troops to the hills
above the town and conferred with General José

Antonio Velutini. They attacked the same day at four o'clock in the afternoon and Vidal evacuated the city. Leaving Olivares and Araujo to defend Cumaná and Puerto Sucre, he sailed eastward with eight hundred and fifty men and landed near Carúpano which was held by Rolando with two thousand men. At six o'clock in the morning of May 6 he attacked. The fighting lasted till five-thirty in the afternoon, when Gómez received a rifle ball in the thigh. He was carried away, his troops became confused and abandoned the attack. Gómez was taken in a sailboat to Margarita. Later, he was taken to La Guayra in a Dutch steamer. He arrived in Caracas on May 16.

The physician who attended him was Dr. Rafael Requena. It is interesting to note that this was the beginning of a long association. Requena later came to replace Dr. García as the General's private secretary and to exert some influence upon him for moderation in the extreme measures which Gómez used against his enemies when he became dictator.

Castro realized now, at last, that he must do something himself. Gómez's wound had healed but Castro determined to leave his women and take the field. On July 5 he issued a proclamation to the effect that: "I shall take to the field myself and, with the efficiency of my own personal direction and the steel of my oft-proven sword, tear Victory from the ardent breast of Battle!" He was pompous enough still, the little upstart whom Theodore Roosevelt had referred to as a monkey, but women had done him in. He sailed for Barcelona in the east, leaving Juan Vicente Gómez to occupy the presidency for the first time.

He had three thousand men. He drove the enemy, numbering five thousand, from the town of Barcelona to Aragua on the edge of the llanos where they turned and defeated him and then retired into the plains.

That was all Castro could take. The old drive was gone. The master guerrilla had gone down the rocky road. He couldn't stay away from his women in Caracas any longer and he returned, leaving the forces in the east under Rolando free to move west and join forces with the Libertadoras in Guárico. In Caracas he made a few pompous speeches and rested with his friends.

Nevertheless, something had to be done, for the revolutionists had joined forces at Altagracia de Orituco and were threatening the center, driving a wedge toward Caracas itself. Castro went out again, going south to the valley of the Tuy. He took the defensive, permitted the enemy to further unite. This, from Castro, the elusive, the phantom of the Cordillera. Fortunately Gómez, back in Caracas, kept the railroad clear.

Eventually Castro found himself bottled up in La Victoria, a difficult place to defend, lying spread out in the valley. Around him were twelve thousand men, all the forces of the Matos movement united; Generals Riera, Mendoza, Rolando, Matos, Montilla and Solagnie, all of the best caudillos. Of this united force, Mendoza was made commander, although his bad showing in this movement did not warrant it. His plan now did not justify it. He occupied the hills roundabout, fortified them as though he himself were on the defensive and contented himself with a timid sort of maneuvering with wing attacks that dragged on long enough to permit Castro to get word to Gómez in Caracas. Gómez was waiting for that word. He had kept the railroad open on his own volition against the receiving of it.

His reply to Castro's telegram was as follows: "Oct. 12, 1902. Yours received. I do not believe that I should merely send you a battalion as you request. I shall go out myself with the one thousand men that I have held in readiness, leaving two battalions, 'Mariño' and 'Cojedes' to guard this city. I shall proceed there at once by rail, leaving General Pacheco in Los Teques and General Adolfo Méndez in El Guayabo. I shall destroy whatever force opposes me en route and upon my arrival there, fall upon the enemy by the rear guard. Your friend, Juan Vicente Gómez."

The Andean peon has become assertive. He doesn't make suggestions nor ask for orders, he simply tells Castro what he intends to do. He is Provisional President at this moment and he can get away with it.

His plan is good, too. It is worthy of the Castro of the old days. He will use the railroad and leave forces behind to hold it.

Gómez arrived in La Victoria the next day by train. Mendoza, in his hills, hadn't the wit to intercept him and prevent the union.

For fifteen days the two enemy forces lay there looking at each other, Castro and Gómez in the town and Mendoza in the hills. Gómez indulged in a little trickery. Each night he sent small groups out to similate an attack. Each time the enemy, believing it a general attack, sounded the alarm and opened fire along the whole line, wasting their ammunition, until morning revealed the truth. This was done until the enemy tired of it and relaxed. Then Gómez opened the real attack, in the middle of the night, caught the enemy unprepared, drove them from their position and forced Mendoza to retreat southward. The victory was complete.

Castro had the grace to give Gómez full credit. He wrote him, "I salute General Juan Vicente Gómez and congratulate him upon the triumph of La Victoria, for the glories are legitimately his."

On November 9 Gómez returned to Caracas. Castro had him occupy the presidency until March 20, 1903, while he himself rested and engaged in his favorite pastimes.

The Battle of La Victoria had broken up the revolutionists once more and scattered them, but it had not destroyed them. Matos had fled to Curaçao but now he returned to the coast of Falcón. Nicolas Rolando gathered together three thousand men and moved against Caracas, arriving at Petare, within twenty kilometers of the city. There, however, he wasted time and was forced to fall back into the hills of Miranda. Furthermore, the government cause was daily losing adherents, two large bodies of troops under Pérez Crespo and Palacios having gone over to the enemy in one lot during the Castro fiasco at Tuy, while the revolutionists were increasing in numbers, principally by recruits from the Mochista element.

This last situation was met by Gómez during his time as provisional president by an astute move. Knowing that Hernández and his followers had no great affection for Matos, he had intercepted a letter from Matos to a caudillo in Zulia in which he was offering a trade involving Hernández's continued incarceration after the revolution succeeded in return for the caudillo's services to his cause, and had the letter published. Then, he set Hernández free. A wise move. El Mocho immediately wrote all his partisans among the Matos ranks, asking them to lay down their arms. So once more a situation was met by the shuttling back and forth between prison and liberty, of the ever-popular Mocho Hernández.

Gómez was ordered out against Rolando on April 3. Rolando had taken up a position at El Guapo about one hundred and fifty kilometers east of Caracas. He had a force of three thousand, a good park, and was entrenched in the hills in an almost impregnable position, prepared to wait it out. Gómez had a much smaller force and a meager park. His only hope was a quick, violent assault.

He attacked Rolando on April 11. The battle lasted three days and it was the bloodiest of Gómez's career up to this time. On the third day, when assault after assault had failed, one of Gómez's old veterans came to him and said that it was hopeless.

Gómez replied, "Hopeless? Que va, compadre! We have reinforcements."

"Reinforcements, General?"

"Claro! Of course! I shall explain. Now you, you are worth a thousand men. That battalion, the 'Gómez,' is worth another thousand. And I myself am worth many thousands more."

Then he ordered another assault, led the charge himself and drove Rolando from the position. Rolando fled to the llanos and holed in at Ciudad Bolívar on the Orinoco, four hundred miles away.

The threat on the capital was removed and Gómez returned to Caracas.

On May 1 he was made Chief of the Western Expeditionary Force and ordered back to Falcón to fight the revolutionists who had taken everything over when he had left after driving them out the first time.

Matos, the revolutionary leader, had returned from Curaçao with reinforcements. The railroad from the port of Tucucas inland to Barquisimeto, the capital city of the state of Lara, was in the hands of the revolutionists along its whole length.

Gómez sailed from La Guayra and landed at Tucucas before the enemy had any inkling that he was in the vicinity. They thought that he was still busy with Rolando in the east. He attacked the advance guard immediately, drove it before him, and then worked out the railroad toward Barquisimeto, striking the enemy time and again, zigzagging back and forth across the line "like a streak of lightning," González says. He gave the enemy no rest and took none himself. The railroad was fortified everywhere, guarded by Matos forces, well-entrenched. Gómez avoided the narrow defile of the cut along the valley of the Arao, keeping to the hills, following mountain trails, falling upon the enemy from the rear, zigzagging, mopping up, moving fast. Matos gave way before him, yielding the railroad all the way to its terminal, Barquisimeto.

Gómez had learned well from Castro, the Castro of the Restoration. Speed. Always speed and more speed. One night the old general, Filipe Franco, commanding the advance guard, had lain down to rest in his hammock at ten o'clock after several days of forced marches and fighting. Shortly, Gómez came up with the main column. The old general jumped to his feet.

"Never mind," Gómez said. "I'll follow the enemy, for that is the way to finish with these fellows."

He rode off into the dark and Franco, ashamed, wakened his men and started after him. He didn't catch up until nine the next morning.

Gómez took Barquisimeto the 23rd of May and he followed after the retreating enemy the same afternoon and caught them at Mata Palo on June 2. He attacked at eight o'clock in the evening. The battle lasted until six o'clock the next afternoon. The enemy broke then and fled. The Matos revolution was done for in the west. Matos and Riera, the leaders, went to Curaçao.

On the 6th of June, 1903, Gómez sent a cable from Coro to Castro in Caracas. "I have the satisfaction of communicating to you that on the third day of having put foot in the state of Falcón I gave the lance to and defeated the generals, Matos, Riera and Lara in Matapalo. On the second day at eight in the evening I assaulted the enemy camp with two battalions and from that hour until six of the afternoon of yesterday, at

which time the enemy, from the formidable drive of
the Battalion 'Gómez,' declared themselves in complete
defeat, fought fiercely. We have to lament the loss of
many officers and troops but greater have been the
losses of the enemy, whose persecution I continue
actively in order to seal the peace of the State of Falcón
and of the Republic. Your friend, Juan Vicente
Gómez."

Castro answered this with a telegram couched in
glowing terms, heaping praise upon Gómez, calling him
"Salvador del Salvador," "Savior of the Savior," declaring his eternal gratitude. Castro had one general who
could win battles and he knew it.

The whole Matos movement was crushed, the country pacified, with the exception of the extreme east.
There, Rolando held out with a force of three thousand
men and ample park. Peñaloza had joined him there,
Peñaloza, another whom Castro had side-stepped coming in along the Cordillera.

Chapter X

CIUDAD BOLÍVAR

❖

GÓMEZ had become a man of affairs by now, affairs involving considerable clerical work, dispatches, accounts, proclamations and so on. And he was still practically illiterate. He had acquired a private secretary and it is interesting to note who it was he had selected. It was Dr. José Rosario García, of Cúcuta, Colombia, his own blood-uncle, the brother of his real father. García remained with Gómez for many years as his personal adviser. Gómez never intimated that he was his uncle, nor indicated in any way that he knew that Pedro Cornelio Gómez was not his real father. Nevertheless, the close association between Juan Vicente and Dr. García for so many years suggests that Gómez knew the real facts of his birth. It is likely that the general use of the name Gómez by all the tribe was a deliberate effort toward maintaining the clan solidarity with which Juan Vicente was always greatly concerned.

Gómez was given command of the eastern forces and ordered out to subdue Rolando. He left La Guayra on June 27 with three gunboats and two thousand men. Two days later he arrived off Carúpano where he waited while one of the vessels proceeded to Trinidad to pick up pilots for the navigation of the Orinoco. Then he proceeded along the coast of the Paria Peninsula, entered the Gulf of Paria by the Dragon's Mouth and sailed westward along the southern coast of the rugged, mountainous promontory. On the 1st of July he landed his men on the rocky beach at Soro under enemy fire from the hills above. He moved quickly into a position among the hills himself, placing his men to dominate the enemy camp.

At daybreak of July 2 Gómez attacked Generals Antonio Paredes and Manuel Morales at Campo Claro and destroyed their force of five hundred men in two hours of fighting among the crags of Güiria. This cleared the way to Ciudad Bolívar. There was no other enemy left in the east but Rolando and Peñaloza.

Gómez boarded his gunboats once more and entered the Orinoco River on July 5. For six days the boats twisted their way slowly among the maze of deep caños of the delta, the still heat bearing down up the brown, smooth water, upon the shining tangle of mangrove. This was new country for Gómez, and the naked Indians who paddled their dugouts quietly along the banks were new to him, too.

On the 10th they passed the village of Barrancas and on the 11th they disembarked at Santa Ana, below Ciudad Bolívar. Dr. García was sent on to the city to confer with Rolando over the possibility of arranging terms of surrender. Gómez sent word by García that he would attack within twenty-four hours. He moved his men closer to the city and the gunboats moved up in support. The American warship, *Bancroft,* and the French warship, *Jouffrey,* came up the river and stood by to protect the property of the foreign citizens.

On the 13th García returned to Gómez's headquarters, bringing with him General José Manuel Peñaloza, the French and German consuls and the Bishop of Guayana. A conference was held and Gómez offered his terms—not very liberal ones for this was his day, the thirteenth, and he was very sure of himself. Peñaloza pointed out the difficulty of attacking the city, the strength of their position and the great quantity of stores they had which would permit them to sustain a long period of siege. He refused outright the terms Gómez offered.

Gómez said, "Very well, General. But I tell you one thing. As there is a God, I shall take Bolívar." He turned to the Bishop of Guayana and said, "And you, little father, will drink my health there."

Ciudad Bolívar comes down to the river bank, the .main street skirting the shore, a sea-wall forming the river-side edge of it. Hills rise behind the city to the southward, the city streets coming part way up the northern slope, facing the river. Four of these hills dominate the Orinoco valley in both directions; the hills of La Esperanza, El Zamuro, Cerro Colorado, El Convento and El Cementerio. These were all fortified, some of them having small artillery pieces, and the flats below the city, known as Punta Mateo, were occupied by entrenched infantry.

At three o'clock in the morning of July 19 the gunboats opened fire on the city. They raked the trenches at Punta Mateo, clearing the way for three battalions that attacked simultaneously the hills of La Esperanza, El Zamuro, Cerro Colorado and El Convento. By six o'clock the trenches were reduced and La Esperanza fell to the Gómez forces. At eight, Cerro Zamuro was taken. The Rolando forces launched counter-attacks, sallying out from the city streets with support from the artillery, but they were driven back. Now, Gómez moved his artillery up within range and by evening the Rolando artillery on the hills was silenced.

The fighting continued all the next day. The three hills remaining to the defenders resisted stubbornly but their task was hopeless without the artillery pieces. They fell to Gómez, one by one, and late in the day the government troops entered the city streets. Every block was defended stubbornly, Rolando's men falling back inch by inch, utilizing every cover. They fired from the roofs of houses and from the cathedral. They fought all night, the guns blazing from the aqueduct, the customs house, the capitol building, the jail, the theater; the fire from the gunboats flashing in the darkness on the river. The Gómez men poured in, dragging up the small artillery pieces, setting them up in the city streets, raking the barricades. By early morning all the buildings had been taken and Rolando surrendered.

This was Gómez's greatest victory and the final battle of the Pacification. His loss was two hundred and fifty dead and four hundred wounded and the enemy, eight hundred dead and wounded.

The officers of the *Bancroft* and the *Jouffrey* sent their congratulations to Gómez.

Castro was overjoyed. The whole country was subdued, his power unchallenged. Probably a little drunk, he sent a telegram:

". . . the man who, from 1901, comes fighting, with victory, for the republic . . . . . . this glory no one can dispute to the gigantic Venezuelan . . . when in the infinite secrets of Providence it pleased God to save Venezuela from the disorder and chaos into which she had fallen, you had been destined to be the head and the arm of that most important work—the salvation of a people." The little monkey was slightly delirious.

Gómez returned to Caracas. His fighting days were over.

This was July, 1903. Gómez was forty-six years old. Four years before, at forty-two, he had been an obscure mountain peon. He had never seen a city, never seen the sea, never been more than a few miles away from the place where he was born. In four years' time he had come to be the most powerful man in his country, to have occupied the presidency, to have directed large armies over the whole area of his country, to have commanded steam-driven war vessels, to have utilized such modern and, to him, ununderstandable, machines as telegraph, telephone and railroad.

Yet, essentially, he was the same man. Completely un-awed, perfectly self-assured. Silent, soft-spoken, calmly studying his men, watching with his heavy-lidded eyes. Speaking the ungrammatic vernacular of his mountain people.

How could he have learned so much in so short a time? He couldn't have learned it. It was impossible. It was more than learning, it was instinctive knowledge, it was something he had been born with.

He had handled armies with the judgment that is supposed to come only through study. López Contreras, a soldier by profession, a graduate of military colleges, says of him that he possessed by instinct the knowledge that he himself had learned in school.

As Commissary he had learned the value of mainte-nance of supplies and from Castro he had learned some-thing of tactics, but that doesn't account for it. The cam-paign of the Cordillera was not enough to make of him the military leader that he had become.

He possessed the traditional qualities of the success-ful generals of all times, qualities which have been axiomized by centuries of repetition. He thought slowly and acted quickly. Rapidity. Persecution of the enemy, relentless follow-up of victory. Mobility, maintenance of communication and supply bases, room for orderly re-treat, utilization of the fastest means of troop transpor-tation, of topographic features, of the errors of the enemy. Besides, he had an uncanny knowledge of his men. He knew how to get the best from them. Often he would say, "You, compadre, you undertake this mis-sion for you do things well and you are not afraid of anything."

He knew the importance of reserves but he knew

when they should be used. At El Guapo, when he was outnumbered by Rolando and had assaulted him time after time for three days, he had one battalion in reserve guarding his stores. Rolando came out in a counter-attack after one of the assaults. Gómez threw in the reserve battalion. The situation was desperate. He drove Rolando back and, with the impulse of his fresh troops, carried the position.

On the other hand, in the final campaign against Matos along the railroad to Barquisimeto, he stationed reserves all over the country, being careful to maintain contact with them all. He drove on, himself, with a small, fast-moving force of only two hundred, striking here and there, dividing the enemy into segments, destroying them one by one.

Four years of constant fighting. In July, 1903, it is all over. The Castro régime is secure for five more years of despotic exploitation of the people. All the work of Juan Vicente Gómez.

The defenders of this man, those who quote the economic good which he accomplished for the country later, during his own dictatorship, must consider this problem. Where were this man's patriotic motives at this time? Where were the evidences of his benevolence and his desires for the well-being of his people that later were attributed to him and that he attributed to himself? No one could possibly argue for the merits of this economic fiasco, this bedlam of abuses and strangulation of political liberty that was the Castro administration. Yet it was Gómez who sustained it, who supported it, single-handed, for eight years. At any time during those eight years he could have destroyed it with a word.

Chapter XI

BRUJO

❖

GÓMEZ returned to Caracas after Ciudad Bolívar, not a national hero exactly, for the cause he defended had come to have a distinctly bad odor for the people at large, but certainly, the darling of Castro. Among the Castro bastoneros, under the superficial cordiality with which they treated him, lurked a certain resentment, for they sensed in this man a threat to their easy access to the public purse.

Castro suspected nothing. He had complete confidence in Gómez. He said, "I was always suspicious of the sly smile of Juan Vicente." But now for the time those suspicions were allayed by the proofs of loyalty which Gómez had given. On May 3, 1904, Castro had the Congress elect Gómez First Vice-President of Venezuela for another time.

The fighting days were over, but Gómez now entered into another sort of campaign, a campaign that he had begun years before, among the Restorers with the League of the Discontented, that he had conducted ever since, during the fighting years, very subtly, very cautiously, among the men and officers who fought with him. It was the campaign to win to himself a personal following; to create within the Castro organization an element that would be ready to repudiate that organization when the time came; to accomplish this in such a manner as to arouse no suspicion in the mind of Castro that such a thing were going on, nor, indeed, in the minds of the men themselves, that they were being so deliberately won. It was a campaign even more suited to the talents of Gómez than were his military campaigns. It utilized his Indian cunning and patience, his instinctive knowledge of men and their weaknesses, his brujeria, witchcraft.

The nucleus of his party was there, of course, in his clan, in his old neighbors from the mountains of Táchira. From his earliest rise to influence with Castro, he had looked after these. He had obtained government posts for them of one kind or another, or got them parcels of land or taken them with him in his campaigns. Now, as First Vice-President, he was in a position to do more. He placed his men where they would do the most good. All of them, Juancho, Eustóquio, Evaristo, Santos Matute, Dr. García and the rest, were placed in positions of influence and they worked constantly for the prestige of Juan Vicente. Dr. García was particularly successful at this sort of sotto voce propaganda.

Some of them, Eustóquio in particular and many of the younger proselytes as well, were wild by nature and inclined to be impatient for more immediate action. Gómez counseled them to bide their time. He warned them that the time for action had not arrived. He had to reprimand Eustóquio and threaten him with punishment should their plan be spoiled through his rashness. Curbing this element, keeping them in hand always, became the most difficult part of his task. But by accomplishing it, he won over many new partisans; for these actions of his took on the color of self-abnegation, causing many sincerely righteous men to mistake for nobility of purpose what was nothing more than expediency. Thus, an element of honest citizens became incorporated in the organization which Gómez was developing.

Gómez went quietly about his tasks. At his office

every day, handling the affairs of the government, carrying out the orders of Castro like an office-boy, from early morning till late at night. Never a word spoken unless he was spoken to, bowing to every wish and whim of Castro. Never taking a drop to drink, never mixing in the social gossiping of the other government officials that was always an annoyance to Castro. Castro, delighted to have this staff to lean upon, to have someone upon whom he could foist the details of government that were always irksome to him, spoke of him ". . . this great, fighting general, the most humble of my soldiers." Humble, efficient, trustworthy. Above everything, trustworthy.

In the last months of 1904 Castro fell ill. His excesses began to have their effect upon him at last. He had been drinking prodigious quantities of liquor ever since coming into power and then, there were the twenty-two women. Twenty-two of them, all young and anxious to please. He had been making great efforts with them all. He had been taking aphrodisiacs. He had tried every sort of pill and powder and herb that any quack doctor or Indian medicine-man prescribed for him, or that his pimp, Tello Mendoza, whispered to him.

He began to have intermittent fevers, pains in the bladder and in the glands of the groin. His doctors failed to diagnose the trouble but they all agreed that he should temper his sexual indulgence. He decided to get away from temptation for a while and go on a trip to the interior for rest and recreation. On April 11, 1905, he left Caracas for a tour of the eastern states, leaving Juan Vicente Gómez in his place as Provisional President. This was the second time that Gómez had held this office.

Gómez performed his duties faithfully, redoubled his efforts to keep his followers in check and he kept Castro informed constantly of the course of affairs.

Castro returned on May 15, somewhat recovered in health and delighted with the way in which his trusted friend had handled things. On June 7, he had the Congress elect Gómez for the office of First Vice-President for a term of six years.

At this Castro's old bastoneros became panicky. Here was Gómez, the legal successor to the presidency for a period of six years, and Castro was ill. In Caracas again, he had gone back to his old habits and his condition had become aggravated. The bastoneros got their heads together. Gómez was no friend of theirs, he had done nothing for any of them, ever, his influence had always been exerted in favor of his tribe from the Andes. He was not the man to succeed Castro if they could help it.

During the whole year of 1905 the old group of Castro followers cast about for a means of discrediting Gómez in the eyes of his chief. They knew of the large party that was forming among the army and various other government branches in favor of Gómez and they hit upon this for their weapon. "Ambition," they whispered to Castro. "Be careful of the ambition of Gómez." They organized a spy system among the Gómez partisans and relayed to Castro everything that came to their ears.

Among this group were the Valencianos who had gone over to Castro after the battle of Tocuyito: Torres Cárdenas, Manuel Corao, Ramón Tello Mendoza, Dr. Celis, Rafael Revenga, Francisco Alcántara, Angel Carnevali, Monreal and so on. They conferred upon who would be their man to succeed Castro in the event of his death. First, they considered General José Antonio Velutini but eventually resolved upon Francisco Alcántara.

Meanwhile Castro was growing steadily worse. His fever was almost constant, now, and he was irritable and slightly delirious with it, always. He was in a good state to be worked upon with propaganda such as this.

The financial affairs of the country were in the usual sorry state. He fretted over this and over the extravagances of his friends and over his women. Little by little the whisperings of the bastoneros had their effect upon him. He began to believe them. He began to be suspicious of Gómez. He never did become fully convinced of Gómez's disloyalty until it was too late but the germ was planted and it flourished. He was in a frightful mental state. He knew that he couldn't trust the bastoneros, he was too good a judge of men not to know that. He had always known that they were his men just so long as he kept them well-paid; and now, when he thought he had hit upon a man whom he could trust implicitly—it was too much to bear. His reaction, in his feverish state, worked rather to Gómez's advantage than otherwise. He determined to prove him. He conferred more and more powers upon him to tempt him to outward acts of treason. He arrived at the place where he almost wished that Gómez would tip his hand and prove his guilt, just to get it over with. This reaction didn't please the bastoneros at all.

Gómez, meanwhile, saw through it all. He redoubled his efforts to appear humble, to keep his men in line, to allay Castro's fears.

Castro determined to prove him to the limit. On April 9, 1906, he announced that he was taking a rest and that Gómez was to occupy the presidency. This was in the nature of a temptation, nothing more.

Nothing happened. Gómez continued to perform his duties and to report daily to Castro. On July 5, Castro returned to office, almost angry that his trick had failed, such was the mental state into which he had fallen. He issued a public proclamation accusing Gómez and he accused him to his face. But he didn't remove him. He wasn't really convinced. Such was the hold that Gómez had upon him through his years of planning and his brujeria.

Gómez took these accusations in his calm way. He denied everything. He mentioned his services to the Restoration, to the Pacification, his loyalty in the exercising of the presidency. Castro was more confused than ever. He became sullen. He refused to see Gómez, but he didn't remove him.

In the early days of 1907 something happened that almost ruined Gómez's plans, but in the end he utilized this event, too, to his advantage and to build up confidence in his honesty of purpose among his partisans and even, indeed, to win new ones.

His brother, Eustóquio (he was not really a brother, nor even a Gómez, we remember, but an adopted son of Pedro Gómez who had grown up to use the family name) was a wild, bloodthirsty ruffian whom Gómez had always had difficulty in curbing. He had been useful to Gómez in the mountains and was to be useful to him again, in his own machine, but now, for these delicate times, he was a danger. Eustóquio spent most of his time carousing in the botaquínes in the barrios with some of his old friends from the Andes.

One night he was with two of them, Isaías Nieto and Rafael de la Cova, in a saloon in the Puente de Hierro. They drank heavily and became very loud, creating a scandal in the neighborhood. Eustóquio shouted some indiscreet remarks about politics. The people of the neighborhood informed the police of the disturbance. The Governor of the Federal District at that time was Dr. Luís Mata Illas, a gentleman of good family and good record of public service. He heard of the affair in the Puente de Hierro and decided to go there himself to look into it, since the persons involved were closely connected in government circles.

He went to the botaquín, spoke to Eustóquio and

asked that he make less noise. Eustóquio received him most politely. He offered him a drink and then he drew his revolver and shot him dead.

Eustóquio fled to the mountains of Miranda. General Domingo Antonio Carvajal was named by the authorities to follow and arrest him. After some days of trailing Eustóquio among the rocky crags and jungle valleys, he caught him.

It is an interesting light upon the character of this man Eustóquio, whom we shall learn more about later, to observe what happened when he was arrested.

Carvajal came upon him suddenly, stepping out from behind a rock, his revolver drawn. Eustóquio drew his own gun but it trembled in his hand. He cried out, "Don't kill me, for God sake, don't kill me! I'm all in. I'll go with you." Carvajal took his gun away from him and said, "Never mind, I won't kill you. I don't assassinate in cold blood as you do."

Eustóquio was taken back to Caracas and stood trial for murder. He was convicted and sentenced to fifteen years in prison, the maximum penalty by law at that time.

The significance of this from the political angle is that Gómez did nothing. He did absolutely nothing to save Eustóquio from prison. He was First Vice-President and that position under the Castro government was good for a pardon any day. But Gómez did nothing; said not a word to Castro in favor of Eustóquio. Eustóquio was known to be an ardent partisan of Juan Vicente, had been shouting for him publicly at the time of the crime.

Gómez was very sure of himself, very sure that he could do something for his tribesman at a later, more convenient time. Meanwhile, he used this little incident to convince people of his good faith, to reassure Castro.

When he finally did assume the supreme power, one of his first acts was to release Eustóquio.

Things went along in this way through the year 1907 and into 1908. Castro became more ill every day and was finally confined to bed at Villa Zoila. The bastoneros were now running the country and it became their chief concern to eliminate Gómez. They laid many plans to assassinate him but Gómez was brujo, he discovered the plots, eluded the traps set for him with uncanny ease.

Years later, Gómez himself spoke of these plots to Fernándo González. He told of them in his own words, in the short phrases of mountain vernacular that characterized his speech all his life. He said:

"Pues, sí. It was thus. Sometimes, sleeping, and again, when I am walking about, these things occur to me, suddenly. That they are going to kill me, in such and such a part. Good. I say to myself, uh-*huh*, those vagabonds, they are not going to kill *me*.

"One day, during those times of Castro, when they were trying to trap me every moment, General Galaviz told me that they were going to assassinate me in La Vaquera. (An hacienda belonging to Torres Cárdenas.) Something told me that I ought to go there and I called a coach.

"Those who were there were Dr. Carnevali, Governor of Caracas, Dr. Eduardo Celis, Minister of Hacienda, and others.

"I arrived at La Vaquera and I saw there a peon, plowing. Something said to me, 'It is he who is to kill me.' I went up to him and I said, 'Tell me something, compadre. Is it possible to plow with two oxen?' Imagine, can you plow with two oxen? I, who know nothing if not oxen. Diverting, eh? And I watched him, talking to him, my hand in my pocket, saying to myself, 'If you move, you bastard, you die in your tracks!'

"All of this, I asked him to get him into conversation.

I told him that I needed peons for my hacienda, that I was going to take him there.

"I asked him what was going on in the house. I said I bet that there were going to be cock-fights, for Dr. Cárdenas was as fond of cocks as I was of oxen, that I was so fond of oxen *that I came to see them even when I knew that they were going to assassinate me!* Diverting, eh? The man's knees were knocking together.

"I went up to the house and told them all about it. Dr. Celis said, 'Gentlemen, I retire from this conspiracy. We can do nothing with Gómez.' "

Gómez made a trip about this time to the state of Trujillo, well out into the mountains, and the bastoneros thought that they had him for sure. It would be very easy to kill a man in those lonely places. There were four states to cross on the way back to Caracas and the state presidents were instructed to see that Gómez did not pass the borders alive. Nevertheless he appeared back in the city, perfectly calm, as though nothing had happened, and no one ever knew how he had eluded the assassins.

He took a house in Paraiso near to Villa Zoila where Castro lay ill. Castro refused to see him, but Gómez spent every day at his house, all day, sitting in the corridor with Mísia Zoila, Castro's wife, who had always been his friend.

The doctors examined Castro's urine and discovered the eggs of ascarides. The diagnosis was that the walls of the bladder had been eaten away, making an opening to the intestines, and fecal matter was entering the urine. Excessive drinking and the use of violent aphrodisiacs had inflamed the delicate tissues, causing, finally, an open fistula. The only cure was surgery and it had best be done in France or Germany.

Whatever can be said of Castro, it cannot be said that he was infatuated with Europe and foreign culture as had been Guzmán Blanco and other presidents. Quite the contrary. He despised foreign countries, mistrusted them, and now, in his feverish state, he became enraged at the idea of going abroad. He dismissed his physicians and engaged others. One after another doctors examined him, made the same recommendations, were paid and politely dismissed.

Gómez sat outside the bedroom door, quiet, faithful, humble. Castro knew he was there but refused to see him. One of the doctors, Juan Iturbe, was dismissed because someone committed the imprudence of asking him in Castro's hearing, "How is General Gómez?"

Eventually, Dr. Revenga operated upon Castro, there in his house. The operation was not entirely successful. It became more urgent for him to go to Europe.

Gómez worked upon Castro through Mísia Zoila. Day after day he sat there, talking to her, winning her confidence; dwelling upon old times, talking of things back in Táchira, speaking of family affairs, relatives and neighbors; speaking, very tactfully, of the misdeeds of the bastoneros, of their ambitions, of their attempts to put him out of the way. Very tactfully, very innocently, sitting there, the tips of his gloved fingers together, playing, with little movements, a way that he had, his sleepy eyes very innocent because you couldn't see them well.

Simple, faithful Mísia Zoila was completely won over. She came to believe that Gómez was their only loyal friend; that everyone else was in conspiracy against them, that they were waiting like vultures for Castro to die.

Then Gómez began to speak of Castro's health. He quoted the opinions of the doctors, dwelled upon the grave state the man was in, emphasized the necessity of getting him to Europe while he still had strength to withstand the operation, spoke of the terrific blow to the country should Castro die. He convinced the woman that the trip to Europe was the only means of saving her husband's life, that if he died it would mean the utter ruination of their country.

Mísia Zoila used her influence upon Castro. Always sincere, faithful, in the face of the suffering that he had caused her, her influence was great. He had always relied upon her and respected her judgment. That is the way in which Castro was finally brought to consent to the European trip.

He went, unwilling, muttering objections, muttering his distrust of Gómez and everyone else. But he went.

Gómez arranged everything for the journey. He was the true family friend. He arranged a letter of credit for Castro of one million bolívars, guaranteed by the government, and helped Mísia Zoila to gather together three hundred thousand bolívars in gold. He went to La Guayra and saw them off, repeating his assurances of loyalty to Castro, pledging to guard well his power and to put down any revolt against it while he was away.

Castro sailed on the French liner, *Guadalupe,* on November 24, 1908.

This was the man whom Castro had called "son." After the battle of Ciudad Bolívar, the little man, in his ridiculous, grandiose vanity, had written:

"I, always enamored of everything good, of everything grand, of everything sublime and of everything related to the spiritual and moral life of humanity, especially in that which shines with the spirit of justice and equity . . . . . . it is as if, in this instance, the honor of the father (meaning himself) were incarnated in the glory of the son (meaning Gómez)."

PART FOUR

THE YEARS OF POWER

1908-1936

Chapter XII

THE REHABILITATION

❖

H E waited for twenty-seven days. He had waited for eight years and twenty-seven days more were nothing. There were things to be done which couldn't have been done while Castro was there, things which would make his plan more perfect. There was the outside, for instance. He had to get the leaders who were in exile, all the caudillos who had fled the country during Castro's reign, lined up. He had to make sure of his following among the rank and file of the army.

Then, too, there was trouble with a foreign nation again and it was just as well to let this work itself out to the discredit of the Castro government rather than to his own, should the results be for the worst. Meantime, it could serve as an excuse to brighten up the army a bit and to assume for himself extraordinary, emergency powers against the day.

Castro, before he left, had managed to get himself into trouble with a foreign country for the third time of his career. It was Holland this time. On December 1 Dutch warships blocked the Venezuelan ports and the cruiser, *Gelderland,* captured the Venezuelan gunboat, *Alexis,* at Puerto Cabello. Gómez had learned from Castro's mistakes, had formulated his own doctrine of fair-dealing with the musiús, and he got this affair settled with little trouble.

When the news of Castro's sailing for Europe reached New York, the exiles there, among them General

Arístides Tellería, Nicolas Rolando and Oscar Lar-
razábal, this last acting as agent for our old friend,
Mocho Hernández, formed a pact and stipulated the
terms upon which they would support a new government with Gómez at the head. They sent Tellería to
Curaçao so that he could negotiate with Gómez at close
quarters. The result of this was that Gómez found the
terms acceptable and many exiles came back into the
country, supporting him, many of them men whom he
had fought and defeated in the battles of the Pacification. Among them were Generals Zoila Vidal, Gregorio
Riera, Juan Peñaloza, Ramón Ayala and Ortega Martínez and Doctors Pedro Rojas and Carlos Garbiras.

There are those who claim that Gómez invited all the
political exiles to return. That is not true. He permitted
the old enemies of Castro to return under definite,
stipulated terms, because he needed their support.
There were many who were not permitted to return,
now nor ever.

By December 20, everything was ready. In the morning Gómez left his house in El Paraiso with a group of
some of his more violent Andean friends, all well-armed,
and went to the army barracks known as Maméy. This
was the only one of the various barracks in the city of
which he wasn't sure.

He entered the building and demanded to see the
commandant. The officer appeared and glanced around
at the group of Andinos.

"Do you recognize General Juan Vicente Gómez as
President of the United States of Venezuela?" Gómez
asked him.

"Yes, General," the officer answered.

"Good!" Gómez said. He turned and walked out, his
men following him.

They took coaches and rode across the city to the Casa
Amarilla. They entered the government building and

Gómez asked to see the Governor of Caracas. This one appeared and he refused to recognize Gómez. He called Gómez a traitor and Gómez knocked him down with his fist. That was all there was to it.

Gómez was president. He had only knocked a man down.

He issued a proclamation to the people and cabled Castro that he was not expected to return. Following the custom established by tradition, he gave a name to the new political set-up. He called it La Rehabilitación, a high-sounding name, probably suggested by Dr. García.

He named a new cabinet immediately. He cleaned out the bastoneros completely, only three ministers of the Castro cabinet remaining in office, and put his Andeans in all the government posts.

The public accepted the situation calmly, rather pleased for the most part, for Castro's abuses had been flagrant, but there was no great demonstration of joy. There were a few minor disturbances in the streets and the office of the newspaper, El Constitucional, was sacked and burned.

Gómez set about putting the nation's affairs in order, as he had done with his haciendas in the Andes. He was about to appropriate a new hacienda now, a much larger one, and he intended that it should be operated on a paying basis. He faced quite a task. Castro had left the finances in a terrible state; there was the huge foreign debt, the income from taxes, duties on imports and so on had long been appropriated almost in toto by the politicians charged with the collecting of them; the banks were insolvent. He attacked these problems with the same direct methods and the same instinctive understanding that had characterized his actions in battle.

For example, the French Minister, a former army officer, was treating with the Minister of the Treasury over the collection of a debt of forty million bolívars which was owed to France.

Gómez said, "Send the Minister to me. He and I will understand each other as military men."

The result of the conference was that Gómez offered to pay three million bolívars, ended up by paying four million. And the French Minister went away, his friend.

He recognized ability in men and used it, regardless of their political views, so long as the men behaved themselves and kept their views to themselves. He had complete confidence in his ability to handle any political situation and he could use these talents, keeping constant watch over them. He had Vicente Lecuna reorganize the Bank of Venezuela and he had Ramón Cárdenas as Minister of Hacienda for nine years. But he watched them constantly. He utilized many of the returned exiles, put them into positions that their talents merited; but he was very, very careful that the power for mischief-making did not come to their hands. The moment one of them expressed a free opinion or made an independent move, he was banished from the country or jailed. In the really strong spots, in the army and in the strategic posts from the military angle, he placed the men of his clan or of his Andean henchman. Still looking far ahead, he built his structure to last, planned the economic growth of the nation from the very beginning so that when it matured the fruits would fall in the right direction.

The Caraqueños, even more than other Venezuelans, if possible, possess a remarkable sense of humor. It is a peculiarly keen, perceptive kind of humor, almost communal, it is so generally uniform, gallant, cynical, bitter. It has an undertone of seriousness, always. It respects nothing. It creates jokes about the crucifixion of its own people. It has developed among the pueblo, the common people, out of the many years of oppression, as their only defense against despair.

Now, watching the new methods of Juan Vicente, finding them good, too good, suspicious, out of long experience, they called this period of the Rehabilitation, the "honey-moon." They said, like a honey-moon, it would last a year.

They were right, of course. It was just about a year when the trend of things began to be apparent. It began to be seen then how Gómez had solidified his power, how he had started the process of appropriation of all the revenue-yielding properties of the country, how he intended to convert the country into another hacienda for himself and his clan.

Many of the old irreconcilables who had returned from exile and many of the old régime who had been incorporated into the Gómez government now began to see these things, too. Old caudillos, nearly all of them, in another day they would have risen in revolt. Now, it would be useless to try. Gómez had planned too well. Disgusted, one after another, they left the country. Some of them were sincerely patriotic, others merely angry because they saw no share for themselves in the distribution that was taking place. They were not of the Gómez clan. Among them were Generals Juan Pablo Peñaloza, Régulo Olivares, Francisco Alcántara, Arístides Tellería and Doctors J. M. Ortega Martínez, Leopoldo Baptista and Martín Requena.

The first act of Gómez to reveal the methods that he would use in his administration was the release from prison of his foster-brother, Eustóquio, the murderer of Dr. Mata Illas. As in all his subsequent, self-interested maneuverings, he attempted to disguise this process with a semblance of legality. Usually, almost invariably, he succeeded, but this time he failed. He appointed a judge, Dr. Juan José Abreu and a secretary,

Rafael Bruzual López, to review the case. The findings of these men upheld the decision of the court which had convicted and sentenced Eustóquio.

Now, the lightning strikes. The calm, heavy-lidded, almost genial composure is gone for an instant, there is a flare of action, and then he is back in his chair again, playing with his fingers, slowly, almost as though he were asleep. Abreu and López are in prison and Eustóquio, the murderer, is free.

The Caraqueños look at one another and smile. The honey-moon is over.

And now comes the "most genial," as the Caraqueños say. Gómez recommends to Régulo Olivares, the Minister of War, the appointment of Eustóquio Gómez as commandant of the prison of San Carlos to replace General Jorge Bello. From prison to commander of the prison. "Que divertido, eh?" How diverting. A typical Gómez jest.

Olivares flatly refuses to make the appointment and waits for the lightning to strike. Nothing happens this time. Shortly, another name is given him for appointment to the post, the name of one Evaristo Prato. Olivares accedes and signs the papers. When the new man appears at San Carlos to take over the post, he proves to be the cut-throat, Eustóquio. Furthermore, he brings as his assistant, Isaías Nieto, another of the Gómez clan, the man who was an accomplice in the murder of Dr. Illas.

It is interesting to consider the false name which Gómez gave to Eustóquio for this little deception. Evaristo Prato. Prato was Eustóquio's real family name for he was a bastard son of a brother of Pedro Cornelio Gómez by a woman named Prato. And Evaristo was the name of Juan Vicente's real father, Evaristo García, of Cúcuta, Colombia. Again, there is evidence that Gómez knew all the facts of his own birth and of the others who

THE GENERAL REVIEWS THE CAVALRY

used the name of Gómez and always claimed to be brothers and sisters.

Eustóquio remained in charge of San Carlos prison for a number of years and, afterward, was given many different positions in Gómez's government. While he was not of much importance, actually, in the dictator's machine, he was too stupid for that, he was one of the most fiendishly cruel of the clan and was used by Gómez in the perpetration of atrocities by which he maintained his power and so is of interest to us. We shall deal with him at greater length later.

Gómez lived now in the president's palace, known as Miraflores. His family was established in houses in various parts of the city and his mother, Hermenegilda, lived in a large quinta [1] at Macuto, a small beach resort near the port of La Guayra. His younger sisters and his own recognized children by Dionisia were growing up and marrying. In their present elevated position as kin of the dictator, they were marrying into wealthy Venezuelan families. Juan Vicente watched these unions, directed them to some extent, carefully measured the capabilities and resources of the men and incorporated them into his governmental machine. In the end, the illiterate Gómez clan from the mountains came to embrace within its fold doctors, lawyers, engineers and modern military men, all active in some phase of government, their loyalty assured by ties of family and mutual interest.

Meanwhile, Dionisia Bello had grown too old for him. There was a girl of sixteen, a dark-eyed, plump and attractive person whom he had seen about the city at the homes of some of the educated men with whom he now associated. Her name was Dolores Amelia and her father was Dr. Nuñez de Cáceres, a distinguished

[1] A modern suburban house in the later real estate developments of the cities. Villa was the old word.

writer, philosophist and linguist. Gómez decided to have her. He used more or less the same methods that he had used when he took Dionisia away from her Italian husband in San Cristóbal. The sixteen-year-old girl was established as the dictator's mistress and Dionisia was given a fine house in El Paraiso. Some years later she went to Spain to live.

Dr. Nuñez de Cáceres, an elderly, rather timid man, was helpless to deal with the situation. He died soon after, grieving over the disgrace.

The Congress, made up of Gómez appointees, met in April, 1910, and named him Commander-in-Chief of the Army and Constitutional President of the Republic for the next four-year term.

Chapter XIII

THE HACIENDA GROWS

❖

THE first concern of Gómez, before he assumed the power and afterward as well, was the army; and the second was the treasury. And these two concerns were closely related, the one depending upon the other. He had organized the army in such a way as to render any successful armed uprising against the government impossible; a thing that had never been accomplished in the country before by any dictator, not even by Páez nor Guzmán Blanco, and he intended to maintain it that way. So, he must get money into the treasury. He bent all his efforts in that direction.

In spite of these efforts and in spite of his natural aptitude for economics, it is very doubtful if his structure could have stood against the constantly increasing tide of resentment for very many years, had not the European war come along to aid him. With the great increase in the prices of the raw materials that Venezuela produced—coffee, hides, cattle, cotton, principally hides and coffee—and the vastly increased foreign market, the revenues began to pour in.

Nevertheless, by 1914, before the war began, he had accomplished considerable. He had raised the balance of income over expenditures to the amount of five million bolívars, from the balance of five million bolívars under expenditures that had existed in 1908 when he assumed the power. And this, in the face of the extraordinary outlays made in the establishing of a money-maintained dictatorship with all the new palms to fill, as well as in the development of the army which he was pursuing on a large scale. It is interesting to note that from 1909 the total annual national income had been increased from fifty million bolívars to sixty-two million, an increase of twenty-four per cent, and the annual expenditures for the army had increased from eight million bolívars to twenty-two million, an increase of one hundred and eighty per cent. Public works, on the other hand, had only increased from three million bolívars to five million. For education there had been no increase made at all. The yearly expenditure of six million bolívars of the Castro reign was continued with practically no increase, not only throughout these early years of the Gómez administration, but well on into the big revenue years of the war and oil development. In 1927 these expenditures had only reached ten million bolívars. These facts may surprise many who were under the impression that Gómez did great things in the way of public education.

The army was the first consideration. He was looking a long way ahead and he was providing for the security of his property as he had provided for the protection of his herds in La Mulera. Improvements could come later. He was using the same men, too, in the organization for the protection of this property—Andinos. He placed Andinos everywhere, over the whole country. In charge of all the garrisons and prisons, presidents of all the states, jefe civiles of all the little villages from the Colombian border to the Orinoco delta, from the Caribbean Sea to Brazil, in every post that required the strong arm and the clean machete—Andinos. In the llanos of the east where the resentment against his government was always particularly strong, he doubled his force of Andinos.

In Venezuela there is a species of large ant known as

bachaco that burrows into the ground in cultivated places in huge colonies and constructs wide-spread labyrinths of tunnels from which it sallies to strip clean every bit of greenery in the vicinity. It is the major pest to agriculture in most parts of the country. The universal, primitive means of combating it is to tie goats with a short tether upon the mounds over the nests and these, annoyed by the swarming and biting of the ants, stomp wildly until the mound is destroyed.

Gómez said once, "For the bachacos, goats, for the people of the east, Andinos."

Gómez had learned from Castro the value of the "little channels" of information. Now, as a further protective measure for his rule, he set about the organizing of an elaborate spy system throughout the country. His uncle and secretary, Dr. José Rosario García, was the secret chief of the system and was largely responsible for its development into the vast system that it came to be over the years. At first only a national system, as more and more disgusted Venezuelans left the country and took refuge abroad and the threat of revolutionary invasion became constant, it became international and spread its branches into every country in Europe and the Americas. Now, at the beginning, it was small but efficient. Nothing could take place anywhere in the country that Gómez wasn't informed of it immediately. To this system can be attributed many of the "voices" that always spoke to him and told him of danger, many of the uncanny feats of divination and mind-reading that built up for him a reputation for brujeria among the peons. Nevertheless, the man did possess extraordinary powers of character-reading and a flair for applied psychology, though he wouldn't have understood you had you told him so. The nearest he could come to expressing his own power was, "Conozco a los hombres." "I know men."

He was a cattle-man. The cattle business was the business he knew. Even as an old man, many years later, he talked of cattle and the cattle-business as though they were the things that interested him most. His first steps toward the appropriation of the nation's wealth were, naturally, made in that direction. He knew the whole country, he had the map in his head, and on that map was marked every grassy plain, every fertile valley where cattle would thrive. He knew exactly the number of head that they could be made to support.

Gradually, he went about the acquiring of lands. Hacienda after hacienda fell into his hands. He used whatever means he could, legal ones preferred. He had his lawyers look into old titles to find flaws, look into the tax records to discover delinquencies that would justify forced sales, look into the financial and family affairs of the owners to find out if their circumstances were such that a low offer would be acceptable. Not all of these properties came to be held as his own. They were distributed discreetly among kinsmen, held in the names of dummy agents and of corporations thinly disguised with patriotic-sounding titles. Thus, many acres of llanos cattle-lands in Guárico, covering nearly the whole state, came to be held by Félix Galaviz and his brothers, old Andean companions and officials in the Gómez government. Tracts were held in Táchira and Lara and the valley of the Aragua by Eustóquio, Juancho, Gonzalo and the others, and elsewhere by the sons and daughters and in-laws of Hermenegilda and Dionisia.

During Castro's period an English company, the Lancashire Cattle Company, Ltd., had purchased a large tract of grazing land in the llanos state of Apure and had acquired the rights to establish an abattoir and refrigeration plant at Puerto Cabello on the coast. This company was operating successfully, exporting its hides and frozen meats to Europe. For Gómez, this was a constant source of irritation, this invasion of his chosen enterprise, this one obstacle to the monopoly that he wished to create. It rankled his avaricious soul. He set about the suppression of the company's operations.

The plan which he evolved was simple, effective and perfectly legal. He was very careful that it should be perfectly legal, for he was dealing with a company of musiús.

If we look at the map of Venezuela we shall see that the state of Apure lies well to the south, south of the Apure River which flows into the Orinoco a great distance from its mouth. Here were the grazing lands of the Lancashire Cattle Company. In order to get their cattle to a seaport where they could be slaughtered, the meat frozen and shipped, there were two routes to be considered: one, by water, down the Apure and Orinoco to some point on the coast of the Gulf of Paria, the other, overland, due north, to the coast of the Caribbean. The first route was found to be unfeasible. It involved a journey by boat of a thousand miles, the enormous outlay necessary to purchase and maintain a fleet of vessels—for there was no established line capable of handling great numbers of cattle—as well as to pay freight royalties to Manuel Corao, who had been given a monopoly of the navigation of the Orinoco by Castro, and the tedious and expensive process of loading and unloading. The obvious route was overland.

So, the English company built its abattoir at Puerto Cabello and drove the great herds of cattle northward across the llanos states of Zamora and Cojedes and over the mountain and jungle trails of Carabobo to the coast. This route proved practical, the cattle finding good forage along it, plenty of water, arriving at the abattoir sleek and ready for butchering.

It will be noticed that this route northward involved

the crossing of three state borders. This was the feature that Gómez utilized for the strangulation of the Lancashire Company. He simply passed a law creating high *state tariffs* on cattle entering one state from another. Very simple and quite legal. It did not interfere with the movements of his own herds for with him it was only a question of taking money from one pocket and putting it into another. The Lancashire Cattle Company was forced to abandon the abattoir and refrigeration plant at Puerto Cabello and go out of business. It still holds its lands in Apure and maintains a nucleus of its organization there.

So the whole cattle business, the principal industry of Venezuela until the development of the oil fields, became the private monopoly of Juan Vicente and his clan.

Antonio Pimentel, a wealthy land-owner and friend of Gómez, had a large hacienda in the state of Aragua that he wished to dispose of and that Gómez wished to acquire. It was a valuable piece of land and Gómez had a natural aversion to paying real money for anything. The two of them got together.

In 1912 Gómez purchased a huge tract of unexplored land lost in the jungles of the state of Bolívar, known as Hatos del Caura.[1] He paid one hundred and sixty thousand bolívars for it. Then, with Pimentel's assistance—Pimentel being Minister of Hacienda—he sold this land to the nation for seventeen million bolívars! One hundred and six times the amount he paid for it! The cash went to Pimentel and the hacienda in Aragua went to Gómez.

In all his negotiations and in the handling of every

[1] Grazing lands or a small ranch with grazing lands. A Venezuelan word, it differs in meaning from hacienda, which means a large country estate and usually implies wealth. Hatos del Caura means simply the grazing lands in the vicinity of the Caura River.

sort of problem that arose during his whole career, legal, technical, diplomatic, economic, Gómez utilized the hombres de talento, men of talent, as he called them. He consulted them, listened to their advice, and then made his own decisions. He paid them well, honored them, but he was never awed by them. Quite the contrary. His attitude was rather one of genial tolerance, of the master to the capable hireling. His self-assurance was such that no amount of education, nor technical knowledge, nor familiarity with the modern things of the outside world on the part of another man could affect it. He was accustomed at times to refer to these men as hombrecitos, using the affectionate, faintly condescending diminutive. He appreciated their capabilities, could use them for his purposes, but he, himself, was gifted with powers beyond these petty talents.

Once he said, "Look at Dr. García there. He has read so many books that his eyebrows are burned. Yet he isn't capable of interpreting my thoughts."

His admiration for other human beings was given, reservedly, to men of strength such as Theodore Roosevelt and the German Kaiser; unreservedly, to only one, Simón Bolívar. Bolívar was his idol. He spoke of him constantly. He mused of him, aloud, whenever anything reminded him of him, whenever he was in the vicinity of any of the places hallowed by him. "He sat there. In that house he spent the night. He hung his hammock between those two trees the night before San Mateo."

His first efforts in the direction of public works were the construction of monuments to the Liberator, statues and plazas in towns throughout the country, the restoration of the old tree, the Samán de Güere, creation of a museum of Bolívariana in Caracas, construction of a memorial arch at La Puerta, a monument at the battlefield of Carabobo, and so on.

He always thought of himself in connection with the

Liberator. He falsified the date of his birth so that it would coincide with that of Bolívar, so that, on the holiday honoring that date, his own picture would appear side by side with his. He saw nothing humorous in that at all. He even saw to it that all public buildings display his picture beside that of Bolívar and that the newspapers feature the Rehabilitation always in connection with the Liberation, and treat of them with equal respect and as of equal importance.

It is difficult for us to realize the egotism of such behavior, being so far removed from the scene and so unfamiliar with the psychology of the race. Perhaps by making some sort of comparison we can get some realization of it. We may be able to get something of the effect such behavior ought to have upon us if we transport it to familiar scenes and familiar people.

For example, it is as if President Franklin Roosevelt owned outright all the newspapers in the United States, and that he should cause to be published on every occasion his own picture beside a picture of George Washington, with captions, over one, "The Father of His Country" and over the other, "The Savior of His Country." Or that Abraham Lincoln had done such a thing, or Theodore Roosevelt or, much more accurately, some swash-buckling capitalist such as Harry Sinclair or William Randolph Hearst or Al Capone.

Well, that is how most of the Venezuelans felt, even though they were more accustomed to egotism in their rulers. And they had to feel that way for twenty-seven years and they didn't dare say a thing about it.

Chapter XIV

THE GENERAL

❖

FROM the days of the Pacification Gómez was "the
General," a military man in his dress and all his
habits. His fighting years, comparatively few, actually
only four out of his whole life, left a lasting mark upon
him, obliterating the outward traces of all the other
years of his early life. He fitted so naturally into the
military life. His orderly habits of thought and actions,
his simple tastes, his natural self-discipline and most of
all, his insistence upon blind obedience always, which
had been characteristic from the days when he ruled
the tribe at La Mulera, made the military life perfectly
suited to him.

So, from now on, a uniform was his regular dress. He
had uniforms of many types, some of them quite ornate,
as nearly like the grand ones of Bolívar, with the high,
gold-braided collars, huge epaulettes, skin-tight trousers and jack-boots and cocked hat, as he could come
without being too ridiculous; but mostly they were
very simple. In the years before the war he admired
Teddy Roosevelt and his uniforms were designed to
make him look as much like Teddy as possible—the
Teddy of the African game-hunts; khaki breeches, field-
boots, wide hat turned up at the side, his foot on a
dead lion. In some of the photographs of Gómez taken
during this period, especially those in which he wears
glasses, the resemblance to Roosevelt is striking. Later,
when the war in Europe broke out, he conceived a great

admiration for the Kaiser and his uniforms became very German. There are pictures of him wearing a spiked helmet, carrying a sword, his mustaches trained upward, and in these he looks almost exactly like the Kaiser.

The soldiers, too, were uniformed according to these changing tastes of the General. While his mounted soldiers always wore the wide hats turned up at the side, these being rather a natural part of their regular Andean dress, his foot-soldiers, from the time of the European war, wore uniforms resembling the field uniforms of the German army, but made of light khaki and having visored caps instead of helmets. Their drill, too, was based upon the German system. Gómez hired German officers and some of his regiments were even trained to a modified goose-step for parade occasions.

His way of life was always that of the soldier. His room was as bare and simple and orderly as a barracks-room. He rose at daybreak and retired early. He never drank nor smoked. From the Andes he had brought a short, bow-legged, dark-skinned Indian named Tarazona, who was his body-guard, valet and orderly till he died. Tarazona cleaned his room, laid out his uniforms, took off his boots and stood guard at his door. He was given the rank of colonel. Later, when attempts were being made constantly upon the dictator's life, Tarazona tasted all the food, water and medicine that was given him.

Even in the matter of his women, he was like a general in campaign. He never had what you might call home-life. His established mistress lived in another part of the house or in a different house, where she ran her home and looked after his children, coming to his bare room when she was sent for. He would visit her and her children when it pleased him, arriving like an honored guest, throwing the establishment into hushed turmoil.

He visited other women, too, in other houses. Many

of them. And many attractive young girls were brought to his bare room and taken away again, after a short stay.

No one woman, of all the women he had, ever exerted any influence upon him. He had no weakness in his character, not even for women, though he indulged in them. He did raise two women above the status of the others, making them his official mistresses in their respective times, maintaining them and their families in wealth; but that was because he needed a large blood-clan in the carrying-out of his plans and because his egotism demanded an extension of his life-stream through sons begotten on the bodies of especially worthy women. That he was indulgent with these sons, even affectionate, is not incompatible with an essentially cruel nature, for parental love is a form of egotism.

If any women had any influence upon him, they were his mother, Hermenegilda, and one of the older of his sisters, Regina, who never married and who was always close to him. These were the only women with whom he did condescend to talk of serious subjects and affairs of policy and government. But even with these, there is no known case of his being influenced by their counsel. But he did listen to them.

His chief companion was Antonio Pimentel. Castro had had his Tello Mendoza, pimp and court jester, and Gómez had his Pimentel. But there was a vast difference. Mendoza was a sly, undistinguished opportunist. Pimentel was wealthy, educated, aristocratic, capable. Gómez could have had nothing but contempt for Mendoza, while he respected Pimentel probably more than any other man among his associates. He always had negocios with him, to their mutual benefit.

Pimentel was a small, keen man, very witty, a great dancer, a linguist and a favorite among the foreign dip-

lomats and their wives. He was corrupt, gleefully cynical. He was a pimp because the rôle delighted him. A
little, dancing satyr, whispering filthy jests into the ears
of the lovely ladies from Paris and London. He believed
in the essential baseness of human beings and his chief
pastime was bringing it out. Gómez enthralled him.

He was the only man who ever made Gómez roar
with laughter. He was the only man ever permitted to
embrace Gómez with the casual shoulder-pat that is the
common form of greeting in Venezuela between friends.

Pimentel owned estates in the country and buildings
in the cities. These he used for staging parties. In the
buildings in the cities, in Caracas and Valencia and
later, in Maracay, they were evening affairs, somewhat
after the nature of Roman or czarist-Russian orgies, and
at the haciendas, particularly Trumpillo, southeast of
Lake Valencia, they were all-day, sometimes week-end,
picnics. The men invited were always a certain few, the
women, many and ever-changing. Pimentel had a vast
list of attractive young girls lined up for these affairs,
most of them from the lower strata but some of them
discontented ladies of good family. They were given
fine clothes and gifts of money. Pimentel had a staff of
maricos and city loafers employed in seeking out likely
girls.

The girls would be taken to the scenes of the parties
in coaches, later in automobiles, and sent home afterward in the same way.

The General was always invited. Frequently he attended. Pimentel delighted in watching the effect, on
this austere, self-disciplined mountain man, of his refined orgies. He delighted, too, in sending to his room,
unannounced, some particularly charming morsel he
had discovered.

At the evening parties the General would sit quietly,
listening to the orchestra, watching the dancers, playing

with his gloved fingers. Occasionally he would respond to the urging of one of the girls and dance a bit, perhaps take her to one of the bedrooms. At ten o'clock he would rise from his chair, wave his hand, bidding everyone to go on having a good time, and leave for his barracks-room.

At the haciendas there would be cock-fights, in which the General always took a great interest, sometimes fighting his own birds. Here, the atmosphere would be less refined, the girls of a rougher, louder type, sometimes mountain girls from the vicinity. There would be a barbecued steer, rum, brandy and champagne, served out-doors. A peon orchestra would play joropos. The General would sit under a tree in the shade, Tarazona at his side.

Pimentel had no fear whatever of Gómez. That is why he could take the liberties that would have been disastrous for anyone else. He chided Gómez about his ignorance and dared to relate to him the latest jokes that the Caraqueños were making about him.

From his first arrival in Caracas, that night when he stood in the plaza by the statue of Bolívar, in his ruana and alpargatas, watching the lights of the coaches circling the square, Gómez had been vaguely baffled by this city. There was something about it that evaded him, annoyed him. He couldn't grasp it, make it his, as he could with everything else that he encountered. This was too subtle for him. These Caraqueños with their assurance, their complicated jokes that he couldn't understand, they evaded him. The men, yes, he could handle them. In dealing with them directly, in business matters and matters of government, he could understand them and dominate them. Individually, yes, he could conquer them; but collectively, these men, with their clothes and manners and their fine, educated women, seemed to be mocking him. They seemed, collectively, to shut him out, as he shut them out, individually. Even the pueblo, the boot-blacks and the street-vendors, even they were too wise, their jokes were too subtle and keen.

The Caraqueños always regarded Juan Vicente as a barbarian. At first they tolerated him, were amused by him, hoped that he would prove to be a mountain messiah who would lead them out of their troubles. Then, when they saw the truth, they despised him. Helpless, they resorted to ridicule, to making very discreet, cynical jokes about him. The time came when they feared to mention him by name. They invented names for him in self-protection. They spoke of him as Don Gregorio or Tio Gregorio or El Bagre, the Catfish. Then, when he took Dolores Amelia Nuñez de Cáceres, he horrified them; and when he established her as his official lady, he insulted them.

Caracas is an old city, was an old city when Gómez entered it. It was conservative, loath to change. It clung to its old-world traditions and social and moral codes, those being one, for here there were no sins but social sins. Mistresses? Of course. Everyone had mistresses, it was the universal custom; but they should not be flaunted, they should not be established in the palace of Miraflores. They should be visited in the back-streets, late at night; they should not be greeted in passing. A man's family, his wife and children and his home, they were his social badge, they were to be shielded against the corruption of the world, so that they could stand, in their innocence and ignorance and purity, as the ideals for which he really stood, in spite of his behavior. They were a sort of proof that a man's sins were only in fun.

Castro, as well as many others of past presidents, had scandalized them, but he had not insulted them. They could understand his behavior. It fitted into their code.

They knew of all his affairs, of course, everyone did, their wives whispered about them, but he had not violated the tradition by flaunting them. He had had his Mísia Zoila, his respectable, married wife, to provide his proper back-ground and conduct his social affairs.

Now, this man Gómez, not married, flaunts his mistress. It is out of ignorance, of course, for his codes are of the mountain Indians; but it is shocking, none the less. He has her in his box at the theater, she is his hostess at all government social affairs. And he is the dictator. He and his mistress and his bastard children cannot be ignored. One's wife must greet the dictator's mistress, one's children must associate with his children at the exclusive schools. One's private, shielded family must be exposed to contact with sin, something which they are not supposed to know anything about. A man must present his wife and daughters to the dictator's mistress, for his position and even his life depends upon it. Some of them try to evade the situation by leaving their families at home. Gómez asks them, bluntly, where they are.

Pimentel, of course, is delighted with the situation. He does everything he can to encourage Gómez to further social efforts. He, himself, gives balls in Dolores Amelia's honor, invites all the diplomats and all of Caracas society, dances with Dolores and makes a big fuss over her. His own sons become the intimate companions of the growing Gómez boys.

Of course, that is not the attitude of everyone in Caracas, by any means, but it is, of the great majority.

Gómez did not like Caracas. He couldn't conquer it. He satisfied himself by ruling it and, on occasions, punishing it.

He owned an hacienda in the valley of Lake Valencia near the village of Maracay, about one hundred kilometers over the mountains from Caracas. He began to develop this hacienda into an ideal ranch. He spent more and more time there.

From a military stand-point its situation was perfect. It dominated the whole country. It was high and surrounded by mountains. By La Puerta, close by, it dominated the llanos, to the east, by the pass over the ridge, it dominated Caracas and to the west, it commanded the trail in from the Cordillera states. North, was quick access to the sea, thirty kilometers away.

Chapter XV

THE REIGN OF TERROR BEGINS

❖

FROM the time of the Spaniards there have existed three major prisons in Venezuela—El Libertador, built upon a rocky promontory in the harbor of Puerto Cabello; San Carlos, on a small island near the entrance to Lake Maracaibo; and La Rotunda, The Round House, in the city of Caracas. All of these are places of unspeakable horror, constructed in the best Spanish manner, the Spanish manner of the colonial times which has never been improved upon for things of this nature. Nothing has ever been done to modernize them, consequently, the accumulation of filth through the centuries, the breeding of vermin of every sort and the growth of mold and slime has served to enhance the works of the sadistic imaginations of their builders. At high tide, sea-water seeps into the lower cells at San Carlos and El Libertador.

Gómez had his prisons to hand. It only remained for him to man them with the lowest and most fiendish of his henchmen. There were plenty low and fiendish ones to choose from.

As we have mentioned before, Eustóquio was made governor of the prison of San Carlos and his kinsman, Isaías Nieto, his assistant.

The arrival of guests to these prisons began almost immediately Gómez came into power and was to continue throughout his whole period of rule. It would be impossible to calculate the total number of those sent there but it was certainly well into the thousands, and the number of those among them who died from torture and starvation and poison, would be still harder to estimate. Then there are the other thousands who escaped by fleeing the country. These totaled many times more, some sources placing the number as high as three hundred thousand; but that is an exaggeration. We shall have to content ourselves with mentioning a case now and again as time goes on.

In 1909, when the eyes of the Venezuelan people were opened to the sort of rule they were in for, by the illegal liberating of Eustóquio and the imprisonment of the judges, Abreu and López, the first public protests were raised by the newspapers, *El Pregonero, Sancho Panza,* and *El Nacional.* The papers were suppressed at once and their owners, Arévalo González, Flores Cabrera and Rafael Martínez, arrested. With sixteen others, whose crimes were of a similar nature, they were locked into the hold of the gunboat, *Zumbador,* and taken to the prison of San Carlos. There was no trial of any sort, no stipulated sentence, not even a pronouncement of the offense of which they were considered guilty. They didn't know where they were going nor how long they were going to stay.

The experiences of these men after their arrest were not at all extraordinary—as a matter of fact they were probably less horrible than in the average of the hundreds of cases of the sort that occurred—but we might recount them for this case was among the first under Gómez and we happen to have specific information about it.

The *Zumbador* took thirty-six hours for the passage to San Carlos, a storm causing her to anchor for some hours in the lee of a headland, and the prisoners were thrown about in the darkness of the hold and the loose casks and boxes and other junk that you always find in the holds of ill-found vessels were tossed about on top of them till they were all bruised and bleeding. They had been given no water nor food since their arrest.

At San Carlos, Eustóquio was there to meet them with another Gómez, Evaristo, who turned out to be something of a chief turn-key. Sick, starved and thirsty, the prisoners staggered between two files of soldiers to the prison doors, urged by curses and blows from Eustóquio's verga. The verga is a sort of quirt or swagger-stick made of the penis of a bull, covered with leather. It is carried by nearly every male in Venezuela who considers himself at least slightly above the peon class.

Inside the gates, they passed into a small, open square where the tropic sun beat in upon some bundles of bones and rags that had been men once, chained to the walls. The place was literally boggy with excrement. The stench made the new prisoners retch blood for there was nothing in their stomachs to vomit. They were lined up and everything was taken from them but the clothes they wore. Some of them carried extra clothing and González and Cabrera had six hundred dollars in cash between them which they never saw again. They asked for water and were threatened with vergas. They were divided into groups of six and taken to cells that faced upon the square.

In the group with González, Cabrera and Martínez were Dr. S. Leopoldo Maldonado, Temístocles Poleo and Manuel Angulo. These six were pushed into the same cell.

When the door was closed behind them they were in almost total darkness. The cell was bare of everything but filth. There was no place to sit or lie down except on the slimy floor. They spent the night fighting off rats and centipedes and cockroaches, wondering what was to happen to them, convinced that they were to be left to die of thirst and starvation.

In the morning Evaristo showed up with a small can of water, enough for about a cupful for each of them, and a gasoline can filled with a thin onion broth on the surface of which floated six plantains. This was their ration after forty-eight hours without any food or water.

After eating, the men were fitted with grillos. These are the leg-irons that were invented in the Venezuelan prisons, being unlike any other known form of shackles and much more painful, for their whole weight rests constantly on the bare ankles. They impede any kind of bodily movement and make it impossible to assume a comfortable position even lying down. Two solid iron U-shaped shackles with eyes at either end of the prongs are placed about the ankles. Then an iron bar is passed through the eyes, behind, and a pin is driven into a small hole in the ends to prevent the bar from coming out. The total weight of the grillos varies from twenty to eighty pounds and the eighty pound ones were nearly always reserved for "enemies of the Rehabilitation." So that the prisoner can walk, two ropes are tied to the bars at either end and these are passed over the shoulders and the weight lifted from the ankles by pulling on the ropes held in the hands. Even then, the best movement that can be achieved is a slow, forward shuffling. In time, the ankles become chafed and swollen and distorted. In many cases gangrene set in. Some of the prisoners died, lying in the shackles, the iron rings imbedded in their swollen, rotten flesh. Others had their feet amputated and so saved their lives, whatever they were worth.

The months went on. Day after day the six men lay in the semi-darkness in their own filth and the filth of others who had been there before them, the vermin crawling over them, nothing to do, scarcely able to move, no word from the outside. Every day they were brought the cupful of water and the can of broth with the plantains. Never anything else and never any more. It was just enough to keep them alive. Cabrera tells that even this ration was sometimes denied them. On several occasions Evaristo and the others went on drunken benders and the prisoners were neglected entirely. They could hear the sounds of the drinking and cock-fighting outside the prison and their shouts for attention were met with curses. On one occasion they were left without food from Sunday till the following Saturday.

Sometimes the size of the plantains varied. In order that each of them should get an equal amount, they had gotten a penknife from Evaristo which they used to cut up the plantains so that they might be divided more evenly.

One morning, Dr. Maldonado, who usually did the cutting-up, moved a little away from the others and sharpened the penknife on the bar of his grillo. Then, without a word to anyone, he plunged the knife into his throat and hacked back and forth with it, in one quick spasm of motion. He died before the others could drag their way over to him.

Cabrera and González were released, eventually, through the influence of friends.

Cabrera went to New York but González stayed in Caracas and went on with his propaganda. He was back in prison again before long and then out again. He spent the rest of his life in prison, with a few days of freedom now and then, which he devoted to making speeches and printing pamphlets against the Gómez government. In all, he served fourteen terms in prison, one of them of nine years' duration, some of them, only a few months. He wrote constantly. He managed to smuggle bits of pencils into his cell and he wrote on anything he could find in the way of paper. If there was nothing else, he wrote upon the walls of his cell. He was a scholar and a brilliant man. Some of his writing is as fine as propaganda literature can become. He died in 1935 of a disease contracted in prison. In the new Venezuela he will become possibly the greatest national hero.

Why Arévalo González was not put to death by poison or torture as were many other less-prominent enemies of the Gómez régime is only explainable by the tremendous esteem in which he was held by the whole nation. News of his murder would have meant a general up-rising, which, though vain against the armed machine, would have involved the slaughter of more Venezuelans than even Gómez cared to undertake.

The further adventures of Eustóquio at San Carlos prison may be worth the telling.

He ruled the prison colony, the guards, the storekeepers, the blacksmiths, the shoemakers, the barbers (all these of course for the officers and guards, not the prisoners) like a demon ruling in hell. He made a negocio out of everything, handling the funds that were sent him by the government for the maintenance of the prison in a way that would leave a good balance for himself. He appropriated all the belongings of the prisoners as they arrived and he pocketed the sometimes large sums that were sent by their families in the belief that they were purchasing decent food for them.

Further, in keeping with the general practice among officials of the Gómez government charged with the disbursement of public funds, he had on his list of employees large numbers of "imaginaries"—people who did not exist at all and who drew salaries and sustenance. The result was that the prison was sadly undermanned. The guards and other attendants had to do much more work than they were supposed to or even physically able to. So, in May, 1910, there was an uprising of the prison employees against Eustóquio. Isaías Nieto and a Colonel Uzcanga were killed and Eustóquio and Eva-

GÓMEZ IN 1916, WHEN HE ADMIRED THE GERMAN KAISER

risto hid themselves till things calmed down. Then they
made their way along the shore to where a fisherman
was with a small sailboat. They induced the man to
carry them to Maracaibo, promising him a good sum
of money. He carried them there all right but, instead
of the money, he received Eustóquio's gun in his ribs
and the advice to get back where he came from.
Eustóquio telegraphed his situation to Juan Vicente.

The reply to his telegram was a money-order and an
appointment as President of the State of Táchira. Que
divertido!

There was in Caracas a well-known priest, Presbyter
Dr. Antonio Luís Mendoza, universally admired for his
fearless oratory. In May, 1912, he delivered a sermon
against the practice of concubinage in which he made
some rather indiscreet allusions to the country's outstanding example. That was his only offense. He was
immediately put into prison in the Rotunda in Caracas.

Here, perhaps, the prisoners were a little better off
than at San Carlos for they had cells to themselves and
a board to lie upon, though the cells were only six feet
long by four feet wide. Padre Mendoza remained in
La Rotunda until the end of 1921. He was freed then,
an old, sick man, and died in 1924.

During his years in prison he spoke from his cell in
a loud voice so that the other prisoners could hear him,
delivering sermons and hearing the confessions of those
who were dying. He aroused the particular hatred of
the "executioner" as the prisoners called him, one
Nereo Pacheco, a man even worse if possible than the
Gómez boys at San Carlos, who subjected him to every
cruelty in his power. He placed on Padre Mendoza's
ankles an extra pair of grillos as punishment for calling
out, demanding aid, when another prisoner, General
Pablo Monagas, was dying from a heart attack.

So it went. There was no public criticism of Gómez or his government if you valued your freedom. In 1909 the writer, Rufino Blanco Fombona, had to flee the country. Dr. Abreu got out of prison and was back in again in no time, much the same as González. In 1918 the poet, Elseo López, died in the Rotunda of arsenic poisoning. The list, if it were possible to make a complete one, would be a volume in itself.

The Caraqueños had a joke about a peon who went about the streets selling pets. On one occasion he went along, leading a burro, holding a monkey in his arms. He called out continually, "The monkey looks like Castro! Look, señores, the monkey looks like Castro!"

A street-loafer called out, "Compadre! Who does the burro look like?"

A policeman grabbed him by the arm and said, "Listen, you. Any more disrespectful remarks about General Gómez and I'll lock you up."

Chapter XVI

EXILES

❖

THE Congress was scheduled to meet on April 19, 1914, to elect the president for the next term. The Congress was strictly Gómez as everyone knew and there was no possibility of any other candidate being considered. Most of the members had never seen the states they were supposed to represent and a rather comic feature of it was, they received traveling expenses for themselves and their families and servants from these places to Caracas and return every time Congress met, when actually they lived in the city all the time.

On July 11, 1913, the newspaper *El Pregonero,* owned by our friend Arévalo González who happened to be out of jail for a few days, announced as its candidate for the presidency in the elections of the coming year, Dr. Félix Montes, an educated man of liberal views and general popularity. González and two employees of his paper, Carlos Brandt and Angel María Garrida, were arrested the same evening that the paper appeared. Montes, on leaving his house next morning, was told by people on the street that González had been arrested and that the police were coming for him. He hurried to the home of a friend, Adolfo Frágenas, who lived in an outlying residential section called La Pastora, where he remained in hiding for two months. Meanwhile his home was searched and a guard posted to watch it day and night and all the members of his family were trailed constantly.

Montes managed to establish communication with his two sons who laid plans for his escape. They secured the help of a priest, Padre Monteverde, who knew the mountain paths over the ridge to the coast and who had friends among the fishermen. This same priest was the one who had gotten Flores Cabrera, publisher of *Sancho Panza,* released from San Carlos and out of the country to New York.

Montes, disguised as a peon, was taken by an abandoned trail to Maiquetía where a sailboat waited to carry him to the Dutch island of Bonaire. From there he went to Curaçao. His life, up to the time of Gómez's death, was spent in exile, in various places in the West Indies.

Padre Monteverde was arrested on November 16, 1913, and stayed in prison until 1921. He was returned to prison in 1924 and released when it was seen that he was about to die. He died a few weeks later. He was a man of good family, a son of General Manuel Monteverde.

As we mentioned before, there was quite a large element of sincerely patriotic and honest people who had been won over to Gómez while he was preparing his coup against Castro. Many of these now deserted him, but there was nothing much they could do except go into exile. Many, on the other hand, still remained loyal and did remain loyal throughout his whole reign. It must be remembered that these arbitrary acts of Gómez were carried on with great secrecy. There was nothing ever appeared in print about them in Venezuela and what was written in the exterior was never permitted to enter the country. They were whispered about, of course, but to many they were just idle gossip, not to be taken seriously. The country was beginning to show the outward signs of economic betterment and Gómez himself always gave the appearance of such a sober, sincere, almost benevolent person that it was difficult to believe such things of him. It was not until after Gómez died that the truth became known to everyone. Further, some of them were convinced that these methods were necessary for the good of the country, that economic good was paramount to political liberty, that the "good man and strong" was the only type fitted to rule their country.

Many, on the other hand, knew the truth, but forgot their patriotic scruples in the prosperity that came to them by continuing to support him.

There were others, too, not so many of these, but a few, who knew the truth, deplored it, but felt that their influence, working upon Gómez from within in the interest of moderation of his methods, would be of more benefit than the hopeless business of attempting to overthrow him. Meanwhile, of course, they might as well enjoy the wealth that came their way. These are not wholly to be condemned but they did contribute to the tyranny by partaking of its benefits and are not to be mentioned in the same breath with such uncompromising patriots as Arévalo González, Dr. Abreu, Bruzual López, Félix Montes, Jorge Luciani, Néstor Luís Pérez, Blanco Fombona, Pio Gil, Flores Cabrera and all the hundreds of younger ones who came later. Nevertheless, some of them did manage to temper the methods of the dictator in a few cases and win a bit of mercy from him for a few of his victims, as we shall see later.

In the exterior, the exiles got together and plotted constantly. Some of them had considerable means. One of these was Dr. Leopoldo Baptista, the old warrior of the Cordillera whom Castro had side-stepped in his famous march. He had carried out of the country with him some one hundred thousand dollars that he had made in a deal with Gómez before he broke with him.

Others of the indefatigable early plotters were the old caudillos, Mocho Hernández, Peñaloza, Régulo Olivares and Arístides Tellería, Doctors Roberto Vargas, Carlos Leon, José Heriberto López, Bruzual López, Abreu, Blanco Fombona, Carlos López Bustamente and Generals Ortega Martínez, Francisco Linares Alcántara, José Antonio Dávila, Rafael María Carabaño and Arévalo Cedeño. López Bustamente had been editor of the Maracaibo newspaper, *Fonógrafo de Maracaibo,* which had been suppressed for articles against Gómez. Bustamente had been imprisoned in the Rotunda and fled to New York on his release. Alcántara was a graduate of the United States Military Academy at West Point and was the same Alcántara who had been a Castro follower, having been the bastoneros candidate to replace Castro in the presidency. Arévalo Cedeño was a newcomer. He had been a telegraph operator in an isolated post in the llanos and had risen against Gómez and taken refuge across the Colombian border from where he made innumerable raids into Venezulean territory. He never accomplished anything considerable by these exploits but, on the other hand, he was never defeated. He made some twenty such raids in all and plotted in New York between times. Arístides Tellería sold out to Gómez later and returned to Venezuela to enjoy the dictator's patronage for the rest of his reign but at this time he was among the exiles, plotting revolution.

These men kept in communication with each other, met to discuss plans, wrote articles, published books at their own expense. There were groups in Brooklyn, París, Germany, Havana, Trinidad—nearly everywhere. Gómez learned of their activities, of course, and it was then that his spy system became really a huge organization.

The nucleus of the foreign system was the Venezuelan diplomatic corps. Every consul and minister was responsible for the activities of the Venezuelan exiles in his area and he maintained his own staff of informers to keep them under surveillance. He used his influence with the state departments of foreign countries (Gómez himself did a bit of this, too, through the foreign ministers in Caracas with whom he always cultivated cordial relations) to impede their movements, discredit them and even, in some cases, imprison them. (Alcántara in Holland, for instance.)

Dr. José Rosario García was in full charge of the system in the islands of the Caribbean and in North and South America, giving all of his time to this work, Dr. Rafael Requena now being private secretary to Gómez. In Venezuela, the system was under the supervision of Rafael María Velasco, one of the original Restorers and a typically brutal Gómez henchman. In Europe, the head man was Dr. José Ignacio Cárdenas, Minister of Venezuela in Holland and the Low Countries. The system became so vast that the monthly expenditures to maintain it reached the sum of three million bolívars.

In Venezuela it became impossible to speak a word in either direct or implied criticism of the government or of the personal conduct of Gómez or any of his clan without the near-certainty of having it overheard and suffering the consequences. Spies were everywhere—behind barber chairs, in the botaquínes, among the shopkeepers, chauffeurs, prostitutes, tradesmen, and the passengers of steamers. There was a beautiful, cultured señorita who traveled constantly on the vessels of the American steamship line that runs between New York and La Guayra and Maracaibo, ostensibly as the representative of a dress manufacturer, who was responsible for many Venezuelans being met at La Guayra by police and imprisoned.

Small wonder then that revolutionary movements failed.

The first of these that actually took the form of action, was instigated by Cipriano Castro. Castro had been operated upon in Germany and his trouble was eliminated. Dr. Iturbe said that "they opened him up like a trunk." He was an older man now, repentant, and content to live a decent life. Consequently, he got well. He spent the rest of his life in bitterness against Gómez, scheming to overthrow him. All the money that he had taken with him and the money that Mísia Zoila had, as well as two houses that she had owned in New York City, had gone to pay the doctors and in promoting his revolutionary schemes. Nevertheless, he managed to finance an expedition.

From Germany he had gone to the French island of Martinique. Through the activities of Gómez the French government ordered him out. Castro refused to go. They rolled him up in a blanket and carried him aboard a French steamer and took him to the Canary Islands where he would be farther away from the Venezuelan coast. Later he went to Mexico and then to Puerto Rico where he remained until he died in 1928. His last words were: "How pleased Juan Vicente will be." It must be said in justice to Gómez that afterwards he sent money to Mísia Zoila regularly and she came to Venezuela to visit him frequently.

Besides Castro two other Venezuelan exiles died on the island of Puerto Rico. They were Doctors Francisco de Paula Reyes and Martín J. Requena. Requena died in the insane asylum there.

In 1913, an expedition organized by Castro landed on the Venezuelan coast at La Vela del Coro, the traditional spot for such disembarkations. On August 3, Gómez declared himself in campaign and left with a force to meet the invaders, naming the Vice-President, V. Márques Bustillos, to exercise the presidential powers.

Gómez moved westward, leaving a garrison of troops in reserve at Maracay. Upon leaving that place he received word that the president of the state of Falcón, General León Jurado, had fallen upon the invaders as they landed and destroyed them. That was the end of the affair and of the dreams of Castro. The spy system had functioned and Gómez's men had been prepared.

Gómez returned to Caracas but he permitted Bustillos to occupy the presidency till the Congress met for the elections on April 19, 1914. Then he was elected President again and Commander-in-Chief of the Army as well, a job which he had always held anyway, but this made it official.

In 1914, the Ducharnes attempted an armed rebellion in the state of Monagas but it was discovered and smothered before it got fairly under way. Horacio Ducharne was killed in Maturín.

The outbreak of the war in Europe put an end to the activities of the exiled revolutionists. Gómez's strong hand at home and his spy-system maintained the peace there during the war's duration. He was free to take advantage of the benefits of Venezuela's position as a neutral nation and a producer of raw materials to build up the nation's revenues.

Gómez admired the Kaiser because, he said, "He defied the whole world. I like men like that." He felt that Germany was in the right. Great pressure was brought to bear upon him to enter the war on the side of the Allies both by the foreign ministers and by his Venezuelan advisers. He resisted the efforts, scarcely listening. His only answer was, "I am responsible. It is I who says what we shall do."

His old respect for the great nations was still strong. He was determined to remain at peace with all of them. "For," he said, "that is how a small nation prospers."

He argued, very sensibly, that what little Venezuela

could do would be of no benefit to anyone. "Money?" he said. "Perhaps we could send them nine millions. That would not last a minute. Men? Twenty thousand at most. They would not serve for one cannon meal." Those were his arguments to all discussions of international law, human rights, imperialism, treaties and so on that the diplomats bombarded him with.

He could remain neutral and sell his hides and coffee and cacao to whomever would buy them. And that is what he did. He attended to the business of developing his haciendas and lived his life, watching his cock-fights, directing his machine, watching the war closely as a man watches a game of chess.

By 1917 he had increased the balance of income over expenditures from a deficit of five million bolívars in 1909, to thirty-three million, besides having reduced the foreign debt by twenty-three million and the internal debt by twenty million. And this was still prior to the era of oil.

Chapter XVII

PETROLEUM

❖

IN dealing with the subject of the petroleum industry in Venezuela we shall have to abandon the system of chronological sequence which we have been following more or less and confine ourselves to that subject alone, without attempting to record the other events that paralleled its development in time. Otherwise we shall find ourselves lost in a maze of rather unrelated happenings.

Petroleum has been by far the most important factor in the modern history of Venezuela and in the life of Juan Vicente as well. Without it, Venezuela would have remained just another small South American republic and Gómez, an obscure, petty tyrant. With it, Venezuela became a nation of commercial importance to the whole world, a nation enjoying the soundest economic standing in the world, and Gómez became one of the world's richest men. And this happened over a period of a few years.

In 1917 there was no oil whatever produced in Venezuela. In 1928 Venezuela had become the second oil-producing country in the world, replacing Mexico, and now, in 1936, she is a close third with the Soviet Union in second place. The United States has always been first by a margin of some five hundred per cent over her nearest rival.

For some years before it was known that there was oil in Venezuela and seeps of both gas and oil had been

163

found in various parts of the country but great quantities were not suspected until the Dutch, English and American companies began to drill in 1918.

Prior to that time there had been some large and rather vague blanket concessions granted to individuals, principally to Julio Méndez, married to Juan Vicente's daughter, Graciela, and Dr. Requena, Gómez's private secretary, but nothing had ever been done with them. They had been granted under the terms of the old Mining Law which was designed to cover gold concessions in Guayana and coal and asphalt in the eastern states, because that was the only law in existence for the mining of minerals.

When the boom began and the oil business assumed immense proportions it became necessary to work out a new law, apart from the old Mining Law, to meet its particular problems. The new law went into effect in 1920 and, while it underwent some minor changes later, it remained basically the same for the rest of the Gómez era. The old concessions, those granted to Venezuelans before the boom, were sold to foreign companies, mostly to the Sun Oil Company, the Maracaibo Oil Exploration Company and the Standard Oil Company, and had to be converted to the new law. So, from the time of its beginning, the oil business in Venezuela has been conducted in an orderly, efficient manner, controlled by the Venezuelan law, with none of the hectic scramble, claim jumping, court fights and general confusion that had marked the oil booms in Mexico and other places.

The first oil wells were brought in along the shores of Lake Maracaibo. That area was the sole producing area of the country for some ten years and it still is the principal area, although new fields have been opened up recently in the eastern states of Monagas and Anzoátegui which show prospects of becoming even greater producers than the fields of the Zulia region.

The development of the Lake Maracaibo region took place with great speed. From 1918 the production of oil practically doubled in quantity each year till 1928 when it reached the amount of one hundred and five million, seven hundred and forty-nine thousand barrels. Then the progress became less rapid and the estimated production for 1936 is around one hundred and forty-five million barrels.

The city of Maracaibo, which became the center of the oil activities and the site of the companies' main terminals, changed, in a few years, from a sprawling village, in almost exactly the same state of advancement as it was in the days of the Spaniards, with about fifteen thousand inhabitants, ninety per cent of them of Indian and Negro blood, to a city of seventy-five thousand people, thirty thousand of whom were white foreigners. There were paved streets, modern docks, electric and ice plants, sewerage and so on.

Naturally, in the process of such rapid growth, with the sudden influx of vast numbers of foreigners into a village ill-equipped to take care of them, there was a period of great disorder. The place took on some of the aspects of a frontier boom town. Prices were ridiculously high, sanitary conditions were terrible and moral conditions worse. The town is a hot, unhealthy place, anyway, lying low on the shores of the almost tepid lake, visited at times by clouds of mosquitos that literally darken the sky, and there was considerable sickness.

At the end of the war, foot-loose citizens from everywhere drifted in. The Mexican fields had gone to saltwater, the American fields had passed the peak of their drilling period and oil-field workers and the riff-raff that follow in their wake came to Maracaibo. Wages were high and it was all clear money for you got your living as well and few questions were asked. Well-known gamblers from Alaska and Mexico opened up large establishments. There was roulette, faro, crap, every sort of gambling game. Prostitutes came in from Panamá and out from Paris and London and New York to compete with the very plentiful local variety. On tropical rainy nights you would see French girls, in evening dresses and high-heeled gold slippers, picking their way along the filthy, muddy streets, going from one saloon to another.

The oil companies began by quartering their men in tents pitched along the shores of the lake and ended up with large modern office buildings, club houses, golf courses, swimming pools and hospitals.

Drilling went on as fast as possible. Most of the wells were drilled along the swampy shores of the lake, out in the water, the rigs standing on piling, long boardwalks on piling connecting them with land. Whole villages were built thus, on stilts in the water or on swampy shore, and in some cases the men lived in two-story houseboats. The fields spread from the edges of the lake inland into the low country of the eastern shore and westward into the foot-hills of the main Andean range along the Colombian border. Later, fields were opened in Falcón and in the far eastern part of the country.

Soon all the American, Dutch and British companies were in, scrambling for concessions, plastering the whole country with them, operating under many different names. The big early producers who managed to maintain their leadership pretty well up to the present time, were the Royal Dutch Shell, operating under the name of the Caribbean Petroleum Company; The Standard of Indiana, operating under the name of the Lago Petroleum Company; the Gulf Oil Company and the Sun Oil Company. They were all in before long, all the big companies, the Standard of California, the Standard of New Jersey, the Texas Oil Company, Atlantic Refining, Sinclair, and a maze of subsidiary companies that would require a puzzle expert to straighten out. Many of the companies were not producers at all, being simply dealers in concessions, buying from the government or from other companies and selling at a profit. Many of the producing companies had less luck than others. The Standard of New Jersey, for instance, drilled a great number of deep wells and is said to have spent some twenty million dollars before getting any oil.

Engineers and geologists swarmed over the whole country. They were young men, mostly, not long out of American and European universities, trained in the most modern methods of petroleum exploration. They traveled with pack-trains over the trails, cutting their way through the jungles, carrying their traverses, setting their monuments, breaking up rocks and studying fossils, covering the vast seas of the llanos, paddling in dugouts among the caños of the Orinoco Delta, dodging the arrows of the Motilone Indians in the Perijá district of the state of Zulia. Here, they worked with detachments of troops lent by the Venezuelan government to protect them; they posted guards at night, kept fires going and built barbed wire fences around their camps.

They took motor trucks and touring cars into the llanos, running over the trackless areas by compass and speedometer as a ship navigates by compass and taff-rail log at sea. They brought in all the newest devices for studying the sub-surface geology—the torsion balance, the seismograph, the magnetometer. They went into places where no white man had ever been and into places that the early Spanish explorers had reached and no one else since. In a few years the whole land area of the country was nearly covered with oil concessions and the water areas as well—the rivers, the whole surface of Lake Maracaibo and the whole seacoast into the water for a distance of a kilometer, against the time when methods for well-drilling in deep water should be discovered.

In the drafting of the Venezuelan Oil Law of 1918 and the later modifications of it, Gómez was guided by the opinions of the technical men of his own departments, many of whom had been educated in American and European universities, and of representatives of various foreign companies. He did not actually draft the law, himself, of course, but it can be certain that he, personally, had to approve all of its clauses. The result was a law that, for fairness to the companies and for the protection of the rights of the nation as well, has never been bettered. From the standpoint of the protection of the rights of the nation, it is miles ahead of our own laws.

Under this law, the land-owners, that is, the owners of the surface rights, native Venezuelans, of course, had the first opportunity to secure the oil rights on their land. A stipulated period of time was set during which they could declare their property as a Private Land Concession after which a tax per year per hectare was to be paid. Those who availed themselves of this opportunity were privileged to sell the oil rights to any purchaser. Most of them did sell them immediately, to the foreign companies, for they themselves were not in a position to finance the development of them nor, in most cases, to pay the taxes on them. Lands which were not so declared within the time limit fell automatically into the areas which were open for oil development under the second type of concession known as Escoger Concessions.

The Escoger Concessions could be purchased on all public lands, those lands belonging to the nation whose surface rights were not owned by individuals, as well as on the privately owned lands which had not been converted into Private Land Concessions. They were granted for lots of ten thousand hectares in area, to be laid out in any form suitable to the purchasers.

These Private Land and Escoger Concessions, bought either from the nation or from the land-owners at whatever prices they could command in open bidding, in the case of the national lands, and in private negotiations, in the case of the privately owned lands, were subject to an initial tax for the conversion and transfer. Then, they entered into a three-year exploration period during which they were subject to a yearly tax per hectare. During this period, should the purchasers wish to hold them for exploitation, the lands must be surveyed. The boundaries must be traversed with chain and transit, permanent corner posts set with suitable reference ties, all rivers, roads and state and district boundaries falling within their limits or within a kilometer outside their limits also to be so traversed. This done, the total area of the concession must be divided into half. This half of the original area became the final area available for oil exploitation by the purchaser. It must be divided into rectangular parcels of five hundred hectares each, these placed within the concession in any manner suitable to the purchaser, the corners to be marked by permanent posts with reference ties. The other half of the concession then reverted to the nation as National Reserves and, in the case of the Private Land Concessions, any area found by final calculations to be in excess of the amount originally declared.

At the end of the three-year exploration period, the concession owners were required to present to the Minister of Fomento for approval, a large scale map of the whole concession made according to strict specifications, showing all details of survey, and individual maps of each five hundred-hectare parcel and copies of all survey notes and calculation sheets. These were checked by the technical staff of the Department of Fomento before approval by the minister and a tax was collected for each map. The maps were retained by the department and copies were sold to the concession owners or anyone else interested in them.

The concession, now consisting of half the original area divided into five hundred-hectare parcels, belonged to the purchaser for a forty-year exploitation period, during which drilling could be done and oil produced. An annual tax per hectare was collected on a graduated scale, beginning at two bolívars and arriving at five.

On all oil produced, a royalty of from ten to fifteen per cent was collected, either as oil, or its value in cash at current world prices, at the nation's discretion, the production figures being checked at the wells by Venezuelan officials of technical training.

A very good law for the nation. It left no loop-holes for shady dealing on the part of the foreign companies. None of that was ever attempted so far as can be proven. Not by the large companies at any rate. There may have been cases of it, certainly there is a lot of propaganda out to that effect, but we have been in a position to observe things from rather a close spot for quite a long time and we never turned anything up, in spite of pretty determined efforts to do so.

This statement is not made in defense of the companies at all, for we know how far big companies will go in that direction if they get a chance. We have lots of examples of that sort of thing on the part of the foreign companies in the so-called banana countries. No, it isn't that, it is to show the perception of this mountain illiterate, Gómez, in grasping the problems of a vast industry, his cleverness in utilizing the talents of educated advisers, his cunning in avoiding the tricks of the foreign legal minds and finally, working out a good, fair law that assured his nation a proper percentage of the profits, that would still not discourage the foreign exploitation which was so much to be desired.

Let us look at some of the benefits to the nation derived from the terms of this law. In the matter of exploration, it assured the accurate mapping of the whole country at no expense whatever. It would be hard to overestimate the amount of money saved by this. And then, we must consider that it would probably never get done at all, otherwise, and certainly not so accurately.

When the oil companies went into Venezuela there were absolutely no accurate maps of the country existing. They were obliged to put down a system of triangulation for control, to traverse all the state and district boundaries, the rivers and trails, in order to insure the legality of their titles. The standard of accuracy demanded by the Department of Fomento engineers was very high; not so high, of course, as those of the United States Coast & Geodetic Survey, by any means, but the methods stipulated and the small error of closure permitted, assured surveys accurate enough for practical purposes. Accurate enough, anyway, to discover errors of as much as ten miles in the old location of certain rivers and of from three to four miles in some state boundaries and to discover that some rivers did not exist at all or were tributaries of an entirely different system than they had always been considered. The common boundaries of many of the concessions with concessions of competing companies worked for the elimination of errors, also.

The limitation of concession areas to ten thousand hectares and the provision for the division of the half-area into parcels of five hundred hectares with the other

half left as National Reserves was the best feature of
the law, probably, for the good of the country. This
assured that at least one-half of the oil-bearing area of
the country would remain to the public benefit. That
is, it should have assured that. It didn't actually, for
Gómez put this little item to his own use.

There were no loop-holes for the oil companies, but
there were for Juan Vicente.

Quite legally, within the law, Gómez managed to
arrange his little negocios.

In the matter of National Reserves. The law did not
stipulate, though the name implied and the spirit certainly intended, that these areas should be held for the
nation. Something in the way of insurance against
future need. Or at least, certainly to be held until the
companies had proven them by drilling on the adjacent
areas, thereby increasing their value enormously. That
was the whole purpose behind that rather complicated
feature of the law.

A company was formed, known as the Compañia
Venezolana de Petroleo. Gómez was the principal stockholder. No sooner were the maps of the oil concessions
approved by the Minister of Fomento and the National
Reserve and Excess Areas determined, than, by some
obscure process, these reserves became the property of
this company. Then, almost immediately, before any
exploitation work was done on the adjacent parcels of
the producing company, they were offered for sale. In
most cases they were bought at once by the company
that held the other half of the concession for that company had made the geological studies of the land and
knew its value.

So that, soon, the foreign companies owned the oil
rights on all the land of the whole country and there
were no National Reserves at all. The best feature of

the oil law from the standpoint of public good was nullified and used for the personal gain of Juan Vicente and his friends.

Another feature of the oil regulations that was a source of much revenue for the country and for Gómez, personally, as well, was the aduana fee, known as "rehabilitation," for some obscure reason. This was a fee charged by the customs authorities on the oil tankers entering Venezuelan ports and was based upon the tonnage and the length of stay. With the great number of tankers that came to load with oil from the producing fields, these fees amounted to enormous sums. There were all sorts of extra charges made for vessels arriving after working hours and on Sundays and days of fiesta. It became one of the most exasperating and costly features of the oil business for the foreign companies and one of the easiest means for the officials of the Gómez government to arrange little negocios.

There were innumerable other ways, some of them small in themselves but reaching sizeable proportions in the aggregate, by which Gómez managed to get his share from the oil income for himself and his friends. The Compañia Venezolana de Petroleo figured in all manner of deals involving trading of concessions and he was a stockholder in many other small companies as well.

The foreign oil companies did not rob Venezuela. Gómez himself did whatever robbing was done in the oil business. There may have been some cases of illegal practice on the part of small land-trading companies and individuals, but the large producing companies obtained their concessions in the manner prescribed by law, paid their full royalties on oil taken out of the ground, paid their taxes and aduana fees; not because they wanted to, if you will, but because they couldn't get out of it. Gómez made hard legal bargains with them and held them to them.

No foreign individual or corporation, nor native one, either, for that matter, ever bested Gómez in a deal. It usually worked the other way.

Gómez was never tempted to sell his country out. The country was his, every inch of it, and he would get out of it whatever there was to be gotten. That was always his attitude. He was not intrigued by foreigners nor foreign countries as Guzmán Blanco had been. He was content to be friendly with them but he never cared to visit them. The oil industry was the only business put into the hands of foreigners during his rule. The railroads and docks and electric plants and gold mines that were operated by foreigners were concessions granted by others before his time, by Castro or Guzmán Blanco or some of the others. He awarded the rights to develop the oil industry because he knew that it was utterly impossible for him or his countrymen to do it themselves.

His usual method of procedure with a foreigner seeking to establish a business of some sort in the country worked something like this. Suppose the business to be ice-cream making by modern methods or the establishment of an American-type soda fountain. The man would be given every encouragement. Of course. By all means. Venezuela needs modern things of that sort. Everything would be done to make matters easy for him. The business would be opened up and begin to pay out a little. Then something happened. The man and his business had been watched very carefully. Somewhere near him, possibly right next door, another establishment opened up, similar to his, this one owned by one of the many relatives of Gómez or his in-laws. But this new establishment had advantages. Everything it used, say ice-cream powders imported from the States, flavoring extracts and so on, came in duty-free under government frank.

And besides, the foreigner found himself swamped with all sorts of ridiculous taxes. He couldn't compete and he had to close up. That sort of thing happened time and again.

Gómez never sold out to foreigners. If their business was of such a nature that he could not conduct it himself or that none of his friends could conduct it, he would permit them to operate on his own terms. He would manage to get his share some way or another, out of the legitimate income for the nation from the transaction. No business was too small for him to apply these methods to. He even worked them on the business of selling the novelty American frozen confection called Popsicle on the streets of Caracas.

There was a considerable amount of paying out to be done in the handling of various details of business, always. It had to be done by individuals traveling in the country and by the oil companies on a larger scale. It was impossible, for instance, to land at or sail from any Venezuelan port without a considerable outlay to petty officials. It was not in the nature of bribery at all, it was just that under the system of the country the officials had to be paid for doing what was their regular duty—what their positions required them to do. It was simply a form of hold-up against which companies and individuals were helpless.

The outstanding example of this type of official was the president of the state of Zulia, Pérez Soto, a cocky, high-handed fellow and a particular pet of Gómez. The oil companies had to handle him with kid gloves, accede to his constant demands for everything from the use of their launches for parties for his women to outright cash.

The wealth poured into the national treasury. More money than Venezuela had ever seen. In 1930 the income to the nation from aduana fees and the exploitation of minerals amounted to one hundred and ninety million bolívars, four times the total amount of the nation's income for 1915, twice the amount of its total expenditures for 1921.

Chapter XVIII

EL BENEMÉRITO—THE WELL-DESERVING

❖

GÓMEZ was fifty-three years old when he usurped the power from Castro. Now, in the days of his great prosperity, he was getting along in years but he still remained vigorous. He grew quite stout. He continued his production of children both with Dolores Amelia and with all the young girls who were brought to him. The children of Dolores Amelia he regarded as his real family and he treated them as such, although he never recognized them legally as he had done with the children of Dionisia Bello. The other children were cared for after a fashion through agents, in some cases, and were simply disregarded in others, their mothers perhaps being given a sum of money. Of the children by Dolores Amelia, there were three sons, Juan Vicente, Jr., Florencio and Juan Crisóstomo, the latter being still quite young when Gómez died, and five daughters, Rosa, Belén, Hermenegilda, Cristina and Berta.

The children of Dionisia had grown up and married. This family lived apart from the second brood and there was always a feeling of jealousy between the two groups. Nevertheless, the fact that Gómez treated them all equally and had them living close to him, either in the palace of Miraflores or in the various haciendas, prevented any outward breaks. The children of the first family resembled Gómez physically, much more than those of the second. The sons, particularly, looked like him.

José Vicente, always called, Vicentico, Gonzalo and Alí were educated and brought up in the military tradition, in the ways of the old Gómez tribe. Neither they nor any of Juan Vicente's children were sent abroad. The three boys were kept at the haciendas, mostly, and taught the ways of the Venezuelan cattlemen. Vicentico was made Inspector General of the Army and Gonzalo, though he carried the rank of colonel, devoted most of his time to managing his haciendas. Alí, the youngest, died in March, 1918, in the epidemic of influenza. He was of a different type than the others, a slender, handsome boy, the only one regarded as simpatico by the people. The Caraqueños said that he died because he was too good to live among the others. They said, too, that Juan Vicente, hiding away at the time at San Juan de Los Morros to escape the epidemic, refused to go to see his son as he lay dying, out of fear of the disease. This is probably not true, for Alí had given signs of being the most intelligent of his sons and his death seems to have affected him considerably. About this time, too, his mother, Hermenegilda, died.

Of his brothers, or rather, those who had been raised with him at La Mulera and regarded as brothers, Juancho, said by the people to be bobo, a booby, was given the position of vice-president of the republic. He may have been a booby, but he was still the steadiest, most reliable of Hermenegilda's brood. Eustóquio, whom we know, was moved about the country as president of various states—Táchira and Lara and Aragua. The half-brother, Santos Matute, was made president of Zulia and held many other governmental offices from time to time. This one was a shifty, cruel individual, given to bloody raping of peon girls and other sadistic practices. In fact, all of the sons of Hermenegilda inherited her strong traits of character, but, unfortunately, they were exerted for evil.

This Santos Matute had begun by using his real name, without the Gómez. Then he began calling himself Santos Matute G. and finally he used as his full name, Santos Matute Gómez. The Caraqueños made a joke out of his use of this name. They called him, "the man of the three lies." He was neither Santos, which means holy, nor Matute, which means petty thief, for he was a thief on a large scale, nor a Gómez. His principal exploit occurred when he was president of Zulia. The oil companies had begun their development in that region and a German air-line, the Scadta, was operating into Maracaibo. Santos Matute took some three million dollars in gold from the state treasury, hired a plane and flew away to the Dutch island of Curaçao. Gómez was so angry that he forbade airplanes to enter his country—a rule which he adhered to obstinately for some years. He did not care to have such an easy means for leaving the country available to anyone. Eventually, with the coming to Venezuela of good-will fliers such as Costes and Lebrix and Lindbergh, he was forced to lift the ban. Eventually, too, he forgave Santos Matute who came back to the country and was made President of Aragua.

Progress, of course, was now beginning to make headway, particularly in the city of Caracas. There were electric street-lighting, motion-picture theaters, automobiles and so on. Gómez began the construction of roads from La Guayra to Caracas and out to his stronghold at Maracay, to Valencia and to Puerto Cabello. He spent more and more time at Maracay as he grew older and his distaste for the city of Caracas increased. Attempts were made upon his life there from time to time. His spies always discovered the plots in time but he became

very distrustful of the Caraqueños. He set about making
Maracay into his idea of a paradise.

His first step was to make it the military center of
the country. He concentrated all the best of his army
equipment there—the artillery, machine-gun units,
tanks and later, airplanes. After the European war he
engaged German officers to train his men and French
and Belgian aviators to fly his planes. He built large
barracks and established an aviation training school. He
had soldiers stationed at short intervals along the roads
approaching the town and along the roads to La Guayra
and Puerto Cabello as well, with heavy chains to stop
all cars and all travelers were required to register. In
addition, he built a concrete road from Maracay along
the short back way to the coast to Ocumare de La Costa,
providing a quick access to the sea without passing
through the capital.

Then he began to make the village an industrial
center, his own industrial center, for everything there
belonged to him. In his cattle business, he employed
foreign experts who developed a type of beef cattle, by
crossing Holsteins with zebu bulls brought from India,
that would thrive better in the climate. He constructed
a modern abattoir and refrigeration plant and monopolized the meat supply for Caracas. He hired Swiss dairy-
men and built a creamery and produced cheese and
butter, the only butter made in the country. He built
a cotton mill, a factory for making candles, for cooking
oils, for leather tanning, for synthetic perfumes and so
on. All of the construction was paid for out of the government treasury, the materials were taken from the
warehouses of the Department of Public Works, the
labor was done by conscripted soldiers, as was all the
labor on his haciendas, but the profits went into his
own pocket.

He watched it all being done, strolling around in the

sun with his Indian, Tarazona, his secretary, Requena, and his friend, Pimentel. Every Saturday the cabinet members drove out from Caracas to get their orders from him and to spend Sunday at his barbecues and cock-fights. He sat in the shade, removed a bit from the others. He asked questions of everyone, short, pertinent questions. To their replies, he remarked, "Uh-*huh*. Good. It is so. Uh-*huh*." Those were his characteristic expressions, always. Sometimes it would be, "Como le parece! Divertido, eh?" "What do you think of that? Diverting, eh?" He carried bits of hard candy in his pockets and he put a piece into his mouth from time to time and sucked on it thoughtfully, as a cow chews her cud.

The Congress began to think up ways of their own to curry favor with him. They conferred upon him the "Order of the Liberator," and ordered that he be invested for life with the title, El Benemérito, the Well-Deserving. From then on, every time his name appeared in public print and every time it was used in public speech, it was preceded by the title, El Benemérito.

The ministers of European countries, because of the courtesy with which he treated them and the willingness which he showed to meet his financial obligations to their countries, recommended him for honors from their governments. He was given orders by Belgium, France and Holland.

At the recommendation of the Papal Nuncio, Monsignor Carlos Pietropaoli, he was made a Cavalier of the Order of Piana by the Pope.

In connection with this last honor, there is an incident that should be told.

There was a priest, Presbyter Doctor Régulo Franquis, who had been something of an anti-Gómez agitator from the beginning of Gómez's rule. He had been a follower of our old friend, Mocho Hernández, having served as chaplain in the field for his troops. In November, 1915, Gómez's spies turned up a plot which had been hatching in Caracas and Padre Franquis was involved. Twenty men were arrested and sent to prison but the priest managed to escape. He remained in hiding for two years. Then, deciding that the coast was clear, he attempted to leave the country, disguised. He started out at night on foot, taking the old abandoned trail over the mountains that went down to the coast at Maiquetía. His intention was to go to Rome and expose Gómez before the Pope.

However, the spies were still on his trail after all this time. They caught him in Maiquetía and took him back to Caracas. He was led through the streets on foot, bound like a criminal. His belongings were searched and a letter was found addressed to the Pope. In the letter, all the misdeeds of the dictator were listed and then a statement in these words:

"Your Holiness: to whom shall pass, on the death of Gómez, the Order which the Church has bestowed upon him? Will it be one of the ninety-seven bastards which he has had upon . . . ?" Here he named, in a long list, many of the women who had borne children to Gómez.

Padre Franquis was imprisoned in the Rotunda. Nereo Pacheco was ordered to give him arsenic in his food. On the first night of his imprisonment, he realized that he had been poisoned. He spoke in a loud voice telling the other prisoners what had occurred. He prayed and asked forgiveness for his executioners. The other prisoners contrived to get some oil of some sort and managed to get it to his cell so that he might take it as a purge.

When Pacheco came in the morning, expecting to remove the body of the priest, he found him still alive. He realized what had been done and all the other prisoners were ordered to be whipped. Then he gave the priest another dose. He succeeded this time. The priest died that night. That was December 17, 1917. His body was carted out, feet first, and dumped upon the dung-heap behind the Rotunda.

The Well-Deserving.

Chapter XIX

REVOLUTIONS

❖

DURING the European War, the revolutionary activities of the exiles in Europe and the United States were confined to arm-chair discussions and Venezuela enjoyed a period of comparative peace, if the helpless submission of a people to the abuses of an all-powerful group of savages can be called peace. If a situation where the least spoken or printed word of protest resulted in imprisonment and torture and secret execution can be called peace; for these things always went on. There was no cessation of these things, ever. They were the common fate of every poet and writer and newspaper-man in the country who dared speak out with conviction. And there were many of them. Doctors Néstor Luís Pérez, Carlos León, Luís Zuloaga, Martín Requena, Generals Aurelio Robles, Norberto Borges, Arturo Uzlar, Zoilo Vidal, Colonels Francisco de Paula Ochoa, Tomás Alcántara, José González and the citizens, Casimiro Vegas, Julio Delgado Chalbaud, Manuel Negrón, were the better-known among them. Some of these went mad or died under torture and the rest rotted into skeletons in San Carlos or the Rotunda or the Libertador.

The exiles who had their refuge across the Colombian border, however, never ceased their revolutionary raids into Venezuela. The remoteness of the territory that was their scene of operations, with the difficulty of the mountainous terrain and the lack of resources, worked against them so that none of their efforts had any success. In most cases the news of them never reached the capital. Arévalo Cedeño was the most active of these border raiders and others were Carmelo París, Alfredo Franco, Roberto Vargas and Pedro Pérez Delgado. Opposing them were well-equipped forces under Eustóquio Gómez, Pérez Soto and León Jurado, some of the choicest of Juan Vicente's "machetes."

Eustóquio, as president of the state of Táchira, held the territory of his childhood in a reign of terror. He took vengeance on his old neighbors, remembering his own low place among them as a boy. He raided their haciendas, drove off their cattle, appropriated their lands and their daughters. The whole state was reduced to misery. The old families abandoned their homes and fled to Colombia. They covered the mountain trails on foot, carrying their belongings, as the Gómez tribe had done years before.

At the end of the war, in 1919, the most ambitious of all the border raids was organized. The leader was General Juan Pablo Peñaloza.

This was our old acquaintance, the same Peñaloza who had followed Castro along the Cordillera, who had been trapped and defeated by Castro at the carnage of Tocuyito, the same old caudillo. He had lent his support to Gómez in the early days of his reign. He became disgusted among the first, went to New York, and he had been plotting there and in Paris ever since. He had met, in exile, another old acquaintance of ours, his old enemy, Mocho Hernández. They had embraced and joined forces in the common cause. They had sat together and schemed and talked over the events of all the years they had fought each other—two caudillos of the old Andean type.

Peñaloza crossed the border with two hundred men and attacked Eustóquio's stronghold at San Cristóbal, determined to rid his old state of the scourge that infested it. He fought six battles among the mountain passes and he won them all. Nevertheless, in the end, lack of ammunition defeated him. He was forced to retreat back into Colombia. Many of his men fell into Eustóquio's hands.

Two of these, Francisco Gómez and Gabriel Chacón, were hung up alive on meat-hooks on a tree beside the road, in a village called Los Pirineos. They hung there for fifteen days, rotting, the buzzards eating them, for the edification of the people.

Peñaloza remained in Colombia and made further raids whenever he could get a few men and a few guns together. Eventually he was taken prisoner and sent to the Libertador. He died there, and those who saw him die have told about it.

He died on June 16, 1932. He was an old man then. He lay there in his cell, a withered, helpless mass of bones, lying in his own filth. He wore two pairs of grillos of seventy pounds.

In Venezuela there is a type of insect called gusana. In its mature stage it is a fly. The fly bites into flesh, human or animal, and deposits its eggs. The eggs hatch, in the flesh, into a worm that lives through the larva stage, there imbedded, until it develops wings and flies away. The nest in the flesh is left as a swollen sore. Those who saw Peñaloza die, say that he died literally eaten alive by gusanas.

His old enemy, the other non-conformist, the other old caudillo, whom he had embraced at last, El Mocho Hernández, died a better death. He spent his last days, dreaming and plotting, in Brooklyn.

Nineteen nineteen was a bad year for plotters. But so were they all, all bad years for plotters.

In January, 1919, Gómez's spies uncovered a plot that had been brewing among some of the younger army officers. It involved officers from the barracks at Maracay and from several of the cuartels of Caracas. Fourteen men were arrested and taken to the old home of Castro, Villa Zoila, in the residential section of Caracas called El Paraiso, which had been turned into an office of the Department of Public Works by Gómez. Among the prisoners were Dr. Pedro Manuel Ruiz and a boy of fourteen years, Manuel Andrade Mora. The boy had done nothing whatever, but his father was suspected and he had gotten away. The officers were Captains Miguel Parra Entrenera, Luís Rafael Pimentel; Lieutenants Julio Hernández, José Ramírez, Jorge Ramírez, Aníbal Molina; Second Lieutenants Ricardo Corredor, Arturo Lara, José Agustín Badaracco, Domingo Mugica, Luís Aranguren, Pedre Betancourt Grillet and Cristóbal Parra. Badaracco, Aranguren and Parra were all under twenty years of age.

Here is what happened to them. We have the story from Captain Luís Rafael Pimentel who is alive, now, in Caracas.

José Vicente Gómez, Vicentico, Juan Vicente's own son, the Inspector General of the Army, was there himself, directing operations. His assistants were General Pedro Alcántara Leal, Colonels Aparicio Gómez, Modesto Torres and León José Zapata and several others.

Captain Entrenera was the first to be hung up. He was heavy and the ropes tore through the flesh and cords of his scrotum and he fell to the floor, leaving his genitals hanging in the knot. He bled to death, lying there.

León Zapata was handling the proceedings. All the prisoners were hung up in order but none of the others fell down. They fainted, but they didn't talk. They were cut down, their testicles squeezed out flat.

It came Pimentel's turn. He was hung up like the

others and fainted almost at once with the pain. He came to, lying on the floor, and they were throwing water on his face.

"We'll try him again," Zapata said. "This is the bastard that knows more than any of them. He'll talk this time."

They hung him up again. Again he fainted. He awoke again on the floor, water being thrown on his face.

"You'll talk, you bastard," Zapata said. "We'll hang you up till you do talk. We'll make you sing."

He was hung up again and again he came to on the floor. Zapata was kicking him.

"We'll make this rooster sing, by Jesus! He's ready to crow all right. One more time and he'll crow!"

"One more time won't make him crow," José Vicente said. "One more time and that rooster will be dead."

"Still better. Come on, hang him up again!"

They fastened the rope and hung him up for the fourth time.

"Sing, you bastard, sing! Tell what you know!"

Pimentel fainted then. They cut him down and didn't hang him up any more. He didn't die and he hadn't sung.

None of the prisoners sang. Most of them didn't know any songs. Most of them were innocent of any part in the plot.

Those who were still alive were taken to Puerto Cabello and imprisoned in the Libertador. Several of them died there, in a few weeks, with the inflammation that resulted from the torturing. Some of them, too, were helped along with arsenic. Those who lived were mutilated for life, of course.

Chapter XX

THE GOOD MAN AND STRONG

❖

THE amazing stealth with which this terrorist dictatorship was conducted! Scarcely anyone in the outside world knew that it was going on. It seems impossible, in these days of modern means of communication when the most remote spots on earth are within a few hours of the great capitals, that it could have been done. Yet it was done. Year after year. Incident after incident of barbarous torturing, wholesale murder; and no word of it ever leaked out.

It was almost ludicrous. The very evening of a day in which something had happened—the arrest of a prominent citizen, say, or the murder, actually by beating to death with clubs, of twenty-four men, as occurred in the town of Guanta on the eastern seacoast—the newspapers appeared and not the slightest word was printed of anything unusual. All was peace and quiet. On the front page of *El Nuevo Diario* and *El Universal* would appear a picture of the Benemérito, with his benign smile and under it, possibly, a statement (written, of course, by Dr. Requena or one of the other "men of talent," but signed by Gómez) commenting upon the happy state of the national treasury or announcing the appropriation of fifteen thousand bolívars for the construction of a new fence around the Plaza Sucre in the village of Aragua. The complete subjugation of the press was, indeed, ludicrous. *El Universal*, on one occasion, printed a statement to the effect that the "Benemérito

General Juan Vicente Gómez had succeeded in changing the climate of the city of Maracay!"

Not a word of the real truth leaked out. And there were thousands of foreigners in the country, traveling over it, working with the natives, month in and month out. Shiploads of tourists were arriving weekly at the port of La Guayra for a day's visit in Caracas. Foreign writers visited the country for a month or two and went home to write glowing articles about the merits of the benevolent old dictator and the progress of the country and the general happiness of the people. Only they didn't use the word dictator, for Gómez didn't like that. He was the "Constitutional President."

Of the foreigners who worked there, probably not more than ten per cent spoke Spanish. The foreigners were there to do their work and they weren't interested in "spig" politics. So long as they were left alone to do what they were there to do, they were satisfied. When rumors of what was really going on came to them, if they had made acquaintances among the natives who came to trust them enough to try to tell them something of it, they laughed and put it down to "Latin exaggeration." It must be remembered, too, that the families of the victims, constantly watched by Gómez's spies, were afraid to open their mouths. Some of the foreigners, of course, saw the real situation, but they didn't dare write home about it.

The average Venezuelan is not, as may be gathered from the rather continuous tales of horror that we have been relating, a cruel person. He is much less so, probably, than the Latin-Indian type of other Spanish-American countries. He is a polite, hospitable, happy person by nature. These atrocities on the part of the few who ruled the country struck him with greater horror, perhaps, than they did those foreigners who knew of them.

Furthermore, the native peons, comprising the vast majority of the Venezuelans who were in contact with the foreigners working or visiting there, felt little of all these things. They were illiterate, mostly, the affairs of politics were not understandable to them, their few bolívars earned daily was enough to keep them content. Those who worked with the foreign companies received higher wages than they had ever known. With their simple needs, under the warm sun, and their homely pastimes, they were content. When one of their fellows fell under the lash of the Rehabilitation, it struck unholy terror into them, and they shook their heads and swore to keep out of "esas cosas."

These were the "smiling, contented faces" that the foreign tourists and authors went home to write about.

The tourists were whisked along the concrete road to Caracas, were shown the wonders that Gómez had worked, the hotels and museums and statues, the country club of the Americans; but they saw nothing of the monstrous cruelties that were being perpetrated upon the bodies of human beings behind the walls of some of the buildings which they passed.

The writers were always given particular attention. They were driven about in cars lent by the government. They were entertained by dinners at the country club and were invited to Maracay. There they were greeted by the genial old man, were shown the wonders of his cattle, his creamery and his factories; but they were not encouraged to go into the interior nor to gad about with the people. They were very courteously attended by the well-dressed, educated, English or French-speaking satellites of the Gómez tribe. More than likely they would be offered gifts of money.

Money. That was the golden key of Juan Vicente. What he couldn't get by other means, he tried to buy. He couldn't imagine anyone who wouldn't do anything

for money. Money was always, to him, the greatest thing
in the world, the only thing worth striving for. He
thought that everyone felt the same way. He was convinced that there was no real honesty of motive in the
behavior of his enemies. They were simply out to overthrow him so that the money he now enjoyed would
become theirs.

He carried packets of bills in his jacket pocket and he
offered them as Rockefeller offers his dimes. He reached
into the breast pocket, drew out the precious bills,
counted them off, very slowly, with his gloved fingers,
and offered them with genial grace. He simply could not
understand anyone's refusing them.

He offered money to nearly everyone who visited
him—artists, acrobats, scientists, bull-fighters, aviators,
anyone who was brought to him as a celebrity. He
offered money to the French fliers, Costes and Lebrix,
and he probably offered money to Lindbergh, unless
someone had been discreet enough to warn him not to
beforehand.

In connection with Lindbergh, the Caraqueños tell a
story which has no relevance here and has the ruinous
disadvantage of having to be explained beforehand, but
perhaps we need it after so much seriousness.

As we have mentioned before, in Venezuela, illegitimate children are called "natural" children and they
become legitimate when they are legally "recognized."

When Lindbergh landed his plane at the field in
Maracay on his good-will tour of South America, Gómez
and a large crowd of his friends were on hand to meet
him. Gómez sat under a canopy.

Lindbergh landed and, instead of going immediately
to the presidential pavilion and greeting Gómez, he left
him waiting there for considerable time while he saw
to the safe stowing of "The Spirit of St. Louis" in a
hangar. Then he went over to where Gómez sat. Every-

THE GENERAL AT SEVENTY-FIVE
SANTOS MATUTE, HATLESS, STANDS BEHIND HIM

one was perturbed about what sort of rebuke this behavior would bring from the mighty one.

What Gómez said was, "Uh-*huh*. That's the kind of
man I like. He looks after his beast first."

However, that is not the joke. Several of Gómez's
younger children, all dressed up for the occasion,
stepped out to present Lindbergh with bunches of
flowers. Lindbergh smiled, took the flowers and said,
"Are they natural?"

Gómez, thinking Lindbergh referred to the children,
replied, "Yes, natural, but recognized."

Nothing ever leaked out. The representatives of foreign news services soon found that it was impossible to
report the truth or to mention any of the abuses to
justice and personal liberty that were taking place. Anything of the sort they sent out, if it did reach print in
their home countries, would be reported back by the
Venezuelan consuls. They would be invited to leave.
On the other hand, if they wrote to glorify the works
of Gómez, they found themselves made wealthy. There
are several outstanding examples of the latter result
among the Americans living in Caracas today.

Anyone who wrote well of Gómez was rewarded.
Foreign or native poets and writers. Any artist who
painted a flattering likeness of him or of the members
of his family. Panderers wrote odes to him, wrote ridiculous biographies of him. Painters made portraits of him
in which he appeared as a noble knight of chivalry.

The Mexican writer, Nemesio García Naranjo, came
to Venezuela, wrote sickening slush about Gómez, such
as his book, "Venezuela y su Gobernante," became a
court favorite and lived in Maracay for some years, partaking of the old man's bounty, receiving the decoration of the "Order of the Liberator."

The Venezuelan Minister to Washington, Pedro

Manuel Arcaya, wrote that "there are no political prisoners in Venezuela. The prisons are empty and no one thinks of revolution." We know all about the political prisoners and there never was a moment when nearly everyone in the country didn't long for revolution and there wasn't a year passed in which an armed uprising didn't occur.

Arcaya said, too, that there was no capital punishment in Venezuela. That is true. There is no crime that calls for execution under the Venezuelan law. The hundreds put to death during Gómez's régime were victims of plain murder.

The foreign ministers probably knew what was going on. They undoubtedly heard stories, even if they had no definite evidence. They probably mentioned conditions in their confidential reports to their state departments. But these things are not for the public. Things were going nicely and what these gentlemen didn't see wouldn't hurt them. Gómez was a nice, kindly old man. He was very considerate of them, always. Some of the diplomats, most of them, probably, felt as did most of the representatives of the big foreign companies who had knowledge of the real situation, that the "good man and strong" was the only one fitted to rule such a country as this and that a few lives more or less were insignificant beside the fact that the foreign obligations were promptly met. Some of the diplomats, too, were under the golden spell of the Catfish. Some of them resigned their posts and joined the little party.

Of the sincere writers and poets who fled the country and, in exile, devoted themselves to their country's cause, few accomplished anything. Few of them wrote in any language except Spanish. Constantly under surveillance, they were discredited by the representatives of their country, and nothing they wrote would be printed. What they did have printed, at their own expense, would only circulate among their own group. Some of them, exiled in Spanish-speaking countries of more liberality in regard to freedom of the press, such as Spain and Colombia and Mexico, under Obregon, and Cuba, before and after Machado, did reach the public ear. But nothing got back into their own country where it would do some good. Everything was watched and reported by Gómez's spies.

The Venezuelan Post Office Department had a formidable system of censorship. Employed in the main office at Caracas were people of every nationality and Venezuelans who spoke foreign tongues. Every newspaper, pamphlet, magazine or book coming into the country was read. Sometimes there was advance information about them from the spies abroad. If there was anything in them dealing adversely with the Gómez government or even relating to subjects which were deemed of inflammatory nature, such as reports of armed uprisings in other countries, they were destroyed. All copies of that number of that magazine or paper were simply confiscated. It was the common experience of all the oil men and other foreigners living in the country to receive only some of the numbers of the periodicals to which they subscribed. The files were never complete. Most of these people suspected nothing and put it down to the inefficiency of the mail system. It was only necessary for a magazine article to refer to Gómez as a dictator instead of as a constitutional president to have all copies of the particular number destroyed. Sometimes even subsequent numbers for a considerable length of time of that periodical would be ruled out. The "American Mercury" was one magazine that fell under the ban.

Private correspondence as a rule was not tampered with, except that of individuals who were suspect by the spies—the friends and relatives of those who were in exile or prison. Nevertheless, on some occasions, after some particularly notorious revolutionary movement, all mail would be opened for a time.

On June 3, 1919, Gómez had Congress pass a law for confiscating and prohibiting the import, manufacture, sale and carrying of arms.

The confiscation took place rapidly. Everything in the nature of arms, except shot-guns and machetes, were taken from their owners. Anyone suspected of possessing a revolver was asked to deliver it. If the possession was denied, the man's premises were searched. The spies reported anyone who was suspected of owning a revolver or rifle and the jefe civiles went after him. The whole country was soon completely disarmed. The reason for this law, obviously a good law, from the social angle, was given as crime-prevention, as a means for making the country safe for the traveler, and so on. That reason was ridiculous, under the circumstances.

There had never been any such thing as a "crime-wave" in Venezuela. The Venezuelan is not addicted to crimes of violence. The country's homicide rate has always been as low, probably, as that of any nation on earth. Crimes of passion and vengeance, there are, yes, but the machete and other weapons, not prohibited by the law, serve just as well for those.

That law was passed for only one purpose—to make any armed uprising against the Gómez government impossible. Yet His Excellency, sitting in Washington, said, "No one thinks of revolution."

On December 31, 1921, something happened that is inexplicable. It is one of those things that make the complex character of Juan Vicente Gómez so baffling. Whether it was a means for testing out the mettle of the "enemies of the Cause," to find out if the prisons had "corrected" them, or whether it was simply that things had been going nicely for a time and Gómez felt that he could afford to be magnanimous, no one can tell. Perhaps he felt that some of his doings were being bruited about too much in the exterior and that he should do something to counteract the bad impression. There is a story, too, that his sister, Regina, had influenced him because of a promise she had made to the Virgin during one of Juan Vicente's sick spells. However it was brought about, on that date, Gómez issued an order freeing all political prisoners.

The Libertador, the Rotunda and San Carlos opened their doors and poured out their miserable victims—those who were still living. Many of the released prisoners left the country. Those who went to their homes were watched constantly by the spies, but they were free, anyway.

Chapter XXI

THE ROYAL FAMILY

❖

FROM January, 1922, until July, 1923, a quiet reigned over Venezuela. It was a quiet too good to be true. It was ominous.

The prisoners were back in their homes. They rested and fed their starved bodies and cured the mangled flesh of their ankles.

Arévalo González was lying in heavenly comfort, scribbling bits for the papers, making great efforts to curb his spirit so that what he wrote would not offend, so that his body might have a brief time, at least, to heal itself.

The newspaper cartoonists, Leo and Job Pim, were back at their work, confining their humor to innocent subjects, relieving their souls in secret, sketching their hate on bits of paper that were immediately destroyed.

The mutilated ones forgot, briefly, the misery that stretched ahead for them all their blighted lives, in the simple blessings of food and drink, at last.

Gentle, gray-haired Porras Bello was back with his family again, writing his theological bits for *La Religión*.

On May 3 the Congress met and elected El Benemérito Juan Vicente Gómez as Constitutional President for the next seven-year term and his brother, Juan Crisóstomo Gómez, First Vice-President.

Revenue from petroleum was swelling the national treasury. The government had initiated a program of public works that was giving work to men and the activities of the foreign companies had raised the wage standard.

It was too good to last. One morning in July, 1923, the dead body of Juancho Gómez, the Vice-President of the republic and the brother of the President, was found in his bed in the presidential palace in Caracas, Miraflores. There were twenty-seven stab wounds in his heart, liver and stomach.

The storm broke then, the calm had been too good to last. The sleepy eyes of the brujo flashed wide, showing for an instant their deadly wrath. The lightning struck everywhere—swiftly, but without thunder. It struck in dead silence. The screams of the tortured victims were muffled behind the thick walls of the prisons.

Into prison everyone, all the old offenders, González, Bello, all the hundreds of them, and new hundreds as well, anyone who looked suspicious or smelled suspicious, anyone who had a brother or a father or a cousin who looked suspicious. The Libertador opened its reeking cells, the Rotunda yawned wide and swallowed.

Confessions. Confessions were wanted. The Well-Deserving wanted confessions. Julio Hidalgo, the Governor of Caracas, Rafael María Velasco, the Prefect of Police, and Pedro García, the chief of La Rotunda, three men well-suited to getting confessions, went about their jobs. Their favorite instruments were put to good use—the tortol, the cepo and the verga. All of the palace guards and the servants of Miraflores were put to the torture. Many of them were never heard of again. Four women servants were hung by their breasts.

They got confessions all right, plenty of them. They got confessions from people who had never heard of Juancho Gómez before.

The Well-Deserving wanted confessions. Confessions

from anybody. He must have confessions to cover up the name of his son, José Vicente.

Gómez knew that Vicentico was guilty of the crime. He didn't know the details of the crime but he knew that Vicente was behind it and he knew his double motive. He knew, too, that others had been involved, and his wrath fell upon these and upon the public at large and upon all his enemies.

When Gómez was told of his brother's murder and went to look at the body, he only said, "Let's bury him." He knew then who had killed him. No outsider ever got into the palace.

The room was covered with bloody finger-prints. When a police officer suggested that the prints be taken, Gómez said, "No." He was afraid what prints might be found. He didn't know then that Vicentico had not done the job himself.

He didn't know then what we know now. He only knew that his son was involved. He had to protect his son. But, after he had gotten his confessions, after he had satisfied his wrath upon the guilty and the innocent, he had the Congress abolish the posts of Vice-President and Inspector General of the Army. Still later, when he thought it wouldn't seem suspicious any more and when he came to feel that José Vicente was plotting against his life as well, he sent him into exile in Europe. He sent him off with his wife and children and servants and much gold and never allowed him to return. That is as far in the way of punishment his peculiar clan and family loyalty would permit him to go; and he was so unmerciful with others.

This is what happened. We know it all, now; not everyone knows it, but a few of us do. It begins back some time and brings us again to Dionisia Bello, Gómez's first mistress, the woman he had brought from the mountains, the mother of José Vicente and Gonzalo.

Juancho Gómez had always enjoyed more of Juan Vicente's confidence than any of the others of the clan. He was steady and sober, more like Juan Vicente himself, though lacking in cunning and imagination. Gómez always felt that Juancho was to be trusted. He had left him in charge of Buenos Aires when he set out with the Sesenta. As President, he made him First Vice-President. This placed him in line to succeed to the presidency upon Juan Vicente's death. Juancho was still a comparatively young man.

Dionisia had been living quietly in Caracas with her family. The boys, Vicentico and Gonzalo, had married but they were still very close to their mother, in the common feeling against the second brood of Juan Vicente. Her other son, Alí, had died.

At one time or another, Juancho Gómez had had a secret love affair with a younger sister of Dionisia who had come in from San Cristóbal to live with her.

This sister must have been quite an attractive girl. Some time after Juancho broke with her (he did break with her for he wasn't the marrying kind. None of the sons of Hermenegilda were) his younger brother, Santos Matute, announced that he was going to marry her.

Juancho sent for Santos Matute and what he said to him was something like this, "You're going to marry that girl? Don't be a God-damned fool. She was my woman. I broke her in."

Virginity, of course, was the first requisite in a woman, with the Gómezs, particularly when marriage was considered. Santos went to the girl, accused her and left her.

Demonstrating the completely unfathomable unreason that many women display in bestowing their affections, this girl had fallen in love with the man. She took poison and died.

Dionisia laid the blame for her sister's death to

Juancho Gómez. She hated him, anyway, for she felt that he stood in the way of her sons, Vicentico and Gonzalo. These two felt somewhat the same about the matter and Dionisia had no trouble in getting their help in a plan to put Juancho out of the way.

Vicentico had married a girl of good family, Josefina Revenga, who was something of a politician. She, too, felt that the way to the presidency should be free for Juan Vicente's eldest son. She probably knew nothing about the plot, but she did goad Vicentico into political ambitions.

Those were the two motives for the murder of Juancho—the revenge of Dionisia for the death of her sister and the ambition to succeed to their father's power on the part of Vicentico and Gonzalo.

The plans were made carefully. Gonzalo arranged to be at one of his haciendas on the night the murder was to be done and Vicentico would spend the night at Los Teques, making sure that he was seen there. They hired seven people to do the murder. They were Captain Isidro Barrientos of the palace guard and two of his soldiers and a cousin who was the Inspector of Gardens in Caracas, a manservant of the palace, Encarnación Mujica, and two women, the cook and her assistant.

On the night decided upon, José Vicente sent for his car in the early evening and drove to Los Teques where he spent the night in company with some officers of the army. Gonzalo had been out of the city for some time.

The manservant, Encarnación Mujica, was accustomed to take a cup of sweet cinnamon-water called canela, a common drink among the countrymen of Venezuela, to Juancho every night when he had retired. This night the canela contained a mild drug that put him to sleep. Mujica then went down to the door and opened it for Barrientos, his cousin and his two soldiers. They all went to Juancho's room, the five men and the

THE ROYAL FAMILY 203

two women cooks as well. The men held Juancho in bed by the arms and legs and it was the assistant cook, a woman, Andara by name, who drove the knife into him twenty-seven times.

Many innocent people confessed to this crime. Those who really committed it were tortured and held in prison but none of them ever confessed. Some of them are alive in Caracas today and that is how we happen to know what actually took place.

Gómez succeeded in terrorizing the country but he didn't fool anyone about the murder of his brother. Everyone knew that Vicentico was involved for everyone knew as well as Gómez knew, what the motives were. The Caraqueños made a joke about it. They said that when Juancho arrived in hell, Alí, already there, sent a message to Vicentico:

"Uncle Juancho, whom you sent yesterday, arrived safely. Send Uncle Eustóquio soon and then the old man and then we all can help you from down here."

After this occurrence the feeling against Gómez became stronger than ever. There were many attempts made on his life. Gómez stayed away from Caracas as much as possible from then on. He practically moved the capital of the country to his stronghold in Maracay. He constructed buildings there to house the governmental departments; the cabinet and the Congress went there for their meetings. All government business except routine clerical work and diplomatic affairs was conducted there. The city of Caracas became the capital simply in name.

Everywhere Gómez went he was surrounded by armed officers. His car, passing over the roads around Maracay or in Caracas, when he did come in for a few days, was preceded by squads of motorcycles with machine-guns mounted on side cars that cleared the road for miles ahead. People said that he wore a steel vest, but that is not true. He did, however, escape death on several occasions when it seemed as though nothing but such a vest could have been the means.

He came to see, at last, that he couldn't conquer Caracas nor break its spirit. He could punish it though. He could leave it at the mercy of Rafael Velasco and Pedro García and Lorenzo Carvallo.

Chapter XXII

THE POTRERO

❖

POTRERO means pasture. In Venezuela it means a particularly fine pasture—a place of deep, soft grass and quiet streams and cool breezes, a place where the pack-animals are turned free after a long journey into the mountains or across the hot plains or into the rank jungles, where they rest and grow sleek with grazing, where the sores on their backs heal and the birds pluck the ticks from their hides. It means a place of fine, easy life with no work.

When the Venezuelans said that someone or other was "in the potrero" they meant that he was within the bounteous fold of the Catfish. He was one of the privileged ones who lived in that magic circle of luxury and splendor that surrounded the Well-Deserving.

There was an American slang equivalent of the expression, potrero, that was used during the war. It was "the gravy train."

The first-string dwellers in Gómez's potrero were the members of the Gómez clan and all their relations by blood and marriage. After that came old friends of the fighting days and newer ones who had won the old man's good will through luck or cunning or even ability, sometimes. Then there was a vast horde of lesser hangers-on, worthless, rascally, mostly—peons from the Andes who hung around and whined, had been hanging around and whining since the days of the Sesenta, probably, and the panderers—the small slickers, perfumed and tailored, the flatterers and cajolers, the truck-ling writers and poets.

To the first two groups fell the best plums. These were the better political jobs—the state presidencies, the cabinet posts, the congressional seats, the army jobs. The others got the minor posts all over the country—jefe civiles of towns, school inspectors, postmasters, sani-tary inspectors, small army officials, tax collectors and so on.

All of these jobs were made remunerative by their incumbents and they were shifted about frequently to give everyone a chance.

The state presidencies were the best spots, probably. These went to Eustóquio and his sons, Santos Matute, Pérez Soto, León Jurado, Arístides Tellería, Félix Galaviz, Gregorio Riera and men of that type—"ma-chetes"—old caudillos, mostly, for these jobs were mili-tary in nature, more than civil, the army forces in the various states being under their command. The possi-bilities here in the way of negocios are obvious. All local public works came under the charge of the state presidents. The feeding and maintenance of troops, management of the prisons, administration of local gov-ernment affairs, all sorts of functions that afforded opportunities to slice off a portion for one's self.

In these posts the system of using "imaginaries" was universal. It was an accepted part of the process of administration, known to everyone, including Gómez himself, though care was usually taken to make it not too obvious. The Caraqueños had a joke about it.

When Marshal Franchet D'Esprey of the French Army visited Venezuela, someone told Gómez that the Marshal commanded an army of one million men.

Gómez said, "A million men! Imagine! Think how many imaginaries he collects for!"

One case, of which we happened to have been an

observer, took place in the town of Barcelona, in the eastern state of Anzoátegui. The commandant of the local army garrison received a rather abrupt notice that he was to be moved to another post and that another officer would arrive in a few days to replace him. It happened that he didn't know the new officer and didn't care to have him discover tangible evidence of the large list of imaginaries that was being carried on the troop's roster. He had to work fast. He set up a table in the town plaza, sent soldiers into the streets and out into the farming country to round up peons and drag them in and he signed them up then and there. This went on till he had gotten enough men to fill out his lists. He didn't bother to change the names on the list. He changed the men's names instead. He checked the list as the men were brought up, reading down it, saying to them, "You are Private Jorge Alvarez. Next. You are Private José Lobos. Next. You are Corporal Juan Sánchez."

The word got around among the peons in no time and they left their work and took to the bush, hiding out until the "recruiting" was over.

The job of Administrador de Aduana or Customs Administrator was another one that gave good results, especially in the ports where the oil tankers loaded and cleared. These jobs, also, were given out in turns, one man succeeding another in rapid order.

The sums of money misused in the Departments of Public Works, Hacienda, Interior and War and Marine would be enormous, if they could be calculated. An estimation, based on the yearly expenditures for roads, for example, compared with the road mileage actually completed, reveals the fact that the cost per mile established an all-time high for roads of their type. There were roads built, yes, but there should have been many times more considering the money spent and the further fact that most of the labor was done by prisoners and drafted soldiers.

The little jobs all had their possibilities, too. The rural postmasters contracted with individuals to carry the mail by pack-train into the remote regions, making bargains that would insure a profit for themselves and as a result, a miserably inefficient delivery system. Sometimes they would buy burros, hire arrieros and run the thing themselves. This allowed still greater opportunity, for the deliveries could be cut down to one a month instead of two, with the consequent saving in number of animals and employees over that carried on the books.

The jefe civiles were one of the greatest curses of the country under Gómez. They were petty tyrants, all of them—ignorant mountain peons, picked as a rule for their "strength." They knew nothing but the rule of the machete. They were the supreme power in all the little, remote villages over the llanos and in the bush and their word was law. They had their little prisons that they used as a threat to attain their own purposes, innocent of any such things as court records, stipulated sentences, jury trial. They were, in this respect, smaller counterparts of the central federal prisons. The little tyrants imposed taxes at will. They preyed upon the business of the community, collecting arbitrary sums from the arrieros who drove their pack-trains into town, upon the number of bushels of corn grown, the number of pounds of fish caught, the number of kilos of goat cheese, the number of tortas of casabe.

These were what might be called the direct rations upon which the dwellers in the potrero fed. There were others, more fattening still, in the way of negocios and monopolies.

It was in these things that the members of the Gómez family profited most, particularly the in-laws, who were educated men, "talented," capable of conducting, to some extent, modern businesses.

The monopolies covered practically everything of any worth in the country. The first and most important fell to the old members of the clan. That was the cattle and meat monopoly. Later, Gómez, personally, monopolized the cotton business, butter, milk, paper, soap, and matches.

To José Vicente went the very profitable monopoly of the lottery and gambling. There were large gambling houses in Caracas and Maracaibo and there was hardly a village anywhere too small to have a roulette wheel in the botaquín. Vicentico collected his share from them all. When he was exiled to Europe, Gómez passed a law prohibiting gambling houses. The lottery went on, though, and someone else got the percentage.

The tax on the sale and making of liquors, also, was a means for large personal benefit and this was handed around a bit. José María García enjoyed it for a long time.

The making of cement was another monopoly. Salt was another. This last was too big an item to give to any one person and it was divided among many in the various states.

The whole country, almost, has access to areas where there is salt for the taking. There are great areas of salina all along the coasts and on the islands where the sea has deposited lakes of white salt. Yet to scoop up a bit of it for your own use was a prison offense. The rights all belonged to individuals. The prices that these individuals charged for the salt worked hardship on all the poor people of the country, for it is a country where there is no refrigeration and the only means of preserving fish and meat is by salting and drying in the sun.

In the city of Caracas there were great fields for negocios. The Gómez family itself stayed out of it mostly, leaving it to the in-laws and the more talented friends. These stuck themselves into every sort of business in the city—the drug business, dry-goods, furniture, importing, machinery, moving-pictures, automobiles. The Santanas, the Andrades, the Pimentels. They enjoyed every sort of favor that the dictator could do them. Their goods came in from abroad duty free, their buildings were constructed with government materials and with government funds. Their taxes were never collected. Naturally, the other merchants and business men couldn't compete against such discrimination and many of them had to give up.

All of these people became wealthy. They lived in luxury, traveled to Europe and the United States, educated their children there, had foreign tutors and governesses. They invested their money abroad, deposited it in foreign banks, bought homes in foreign cities.

When the house of Eustóquio Gómez was sacked after the old man's death, a letter was found and published in *El Universal* which revealed the fact that Eustóquio's current balance in the National City Bank of New York was over two million dollars. That was only one bank, and Eustóquio had never been to New York. No one knows how much he had in European banks.

It must be said in justice to Juan Vicente that he himself, so far as is known, never sent any money out of the country. He never made a foreign investment. He did have a kind of patriotism that forbade that. The chances are that the foreign investments of all the others of the tribe were kept from him, for he wouldn't have approved.

To some extent, Gómez was a victim of all these parasites. Even his remarkable astuteness seemed to have a blank spot when he dealt with his own kin. They fawned and flattered and talked him into all kinds of enterprises. Anything to spend the government's money so that they might get their hands into it.

The greatest example of things of this sort was the ridiculous undertaking which the ministers talked him into of the creation of the port of Turiamo. This was a vast project for building a modern port city at a place on the coast called Turiamo—a rocky, desolate place, miles away from anything. The idea was to build a great harbor with modern docks and loading facilities, modern warehouses, hotels, factories, God knows what. The idea was to make it a free port. This, of course, would be to the benefit only of those in the potrero and they outdid themselves to talk the old man into it. In this effort they were aided somewhat by Gómez's old dislike for Caracas; for the creation of such a port would have been the ruination of the capital city. An American engineer made a survey of the project and pronounced it impractical and fixed the cost at upwards of ninety million dollars. Of course the thing was dropped but not until Gómez had spent millions of bolívars of the nation's money on it. His ignorance was sometimes quite astounding about the most simple, practical things —mostly things, of course, having to do with more or less modern sciences, but which, nevertheless, are familiar to every child these days. This is perfectly understandable considering his absolute lack of schooling, considering the fact that he was forty-three before he stepped upon a city street. The wonder is that he learned so much as he did.

The Caraqueños have made hundreds of jokes about this ignorance of his of simple things.

One of them has to do with the first time he used a telephone. He wanted to call a shoemaker to order a new pair of shoes. When he put the receiver to his ear the operator said, "Number, please?"

Gómez replied, "Number six, but wide, for I've got a wide foot. Carajo! How smart these little machines! They knew I wanted shoes before I said a word about it."

Chapter XXIII

PADRE DE FAMILIA

❖

DOÑA DOLORES AMELIA was a large, heavy woman with a mass of black hair and round, dark eyes, wide-open, under raised eyebrows. The eyes gave her a look of mild wonder, mild frustration, mild stupidity. Her skin had the chalky-whiteness of middle-aged Spanish women who spend their lives indoors in the damp shade of patios—the whiteness that looks so much like a thick coating of face-powder. Her servants and intimate friends called her, Mísia Amelia, and the Caraqueños called her that, too, in derision. She wore too many diamonds on her fingers and over-dressed in a matronly, old-fashioned way.

She sat in the bed-room of her house in Maracay. A maid helped her with the finishing touches of her toilet, patiently doing her best against the woman's nervous fidgetings. She was used to the fidgeting and to the constant complaining chatter.

"What time is it?" Mísia Amelia said. "Has the photographer come yet? Oh, yes, you told me. Did you tell him to have everything ready? You know how the General hates to be kept waiting. Ay, Dios mio. I know the children will do something wrong. I just know it. Are they all ready?"

The maid worked calmly while the woman fretted and sighed, answering the flow of questions mechanically. "Yes, señora." "No, señora." "Of course, señora. It is taken care of." "I told the children. They will be

212

here when they are ready." "Now don't worry, señora, it is only two."

"Ay, Dios mio. Please hurry. It would be a tragedy if we should keep the General waiting. The General is so busy. Just think of all the General has to do. Taking care of all these ungrateful people, giving them money and trying to make them happy and worrying about them. And the terrible things they say about him. The General works so hard for them. He gives his whole life to them. He never has time to be with his own family, that he loves so much. You know how he would love to be with us here all the time. The poor General." She scarcely ever spoke a sentence to anyone that wasn't about "the General." It was as if, by repetition, she hoped to make convincing the fiction she had created about her importance to him.

She went on with her dressing and the children began to come into the room as their own servants finished with them. The girls came in first, starched and ribboned, and the two boys came last. They were dark, rattish-looking adolescents. They stayed together, apart from the others. They muttered to each other in low voices and stood awkwardly like boys at a church reception.

Mísia Amelia looked over all the children and went about, criticizing and rearranging their clothes.

"Rosa, why did you put your hair up? You know the General likes your hair down. He spoke of it the last time. Cristina, stop fiddling with that ribbon. Ay, Dios mio, I know you're all going to disgrace me. Belén, you've got your best dress on. How can I get new dresses for you when you wear your new one? I told you to wear the blue one."

"The blue one was worn out. I gave it to María," Belén said.

"You gave it to María? Ay, Dios mio. Giving such a

dress to a servant. You know it was much too good to give away. Now do you all remember what I told you to say? None of you will say the right thing, I'm sure of it. I know you'll all disgrace me. Florencio, do you remember what I told you to say? Now don't you hang back like a peon. You walk right up to the General and let him kiss you. And if he mentions the car accident, you say, 'I'm sorry, papá, it won't happen again.' Now remember. Ay, Dios mio."

There was a roar of motors out in the street and a manservant came into the room.

"The General is coming, señora," he said. "The motorcycles are here."

Mísia Amelia became as excited as a clucking hen. "Where are the babies? Ay, Dios mio, the babies aren't ready. Run, Carmen, and bring the babies. Come on, children, hurry. The General is here."

She herded the children into the corridor and pushed them along to the patio in the front of the house.

The patio was bare, except for some potted palms and ferns and orchids hanging in wire baskets from the pillars. A group of chairs had been arranged at one end and the photographer stood in a corner with his camera on a tripod and his black cloth over his shoulder. Mísia Amelia fluttered about, arranging the children into her idea of a lovely tableau, giving them last-minute instructions. The servants brought the two babies. Mísia Amelia took the one in long clothes into her arms and stationed herself in the front of the family, facing the street corridor, and a servant stood behind her, holding the older baby. A quiet fell then, over the frozen group. The boys fidgeted a little and muttered in whispers.

There was the sound of motor cars outside—brakes rasping, slamming doors. Then there was the sound of men's voices, laughing and talking, muffled, outside, and then loud, echoing in the corridor, and the sound of many boots on tile.

The dictator came into the patio. A little behind him came the bow-legged Indian, Tarazona, and a group of dark, youngish, voluble men. All were in boots and khaki uniforms. He came in smiling, looked at the group of children for an instant, handed his hat to Tarazona and then went over to Mísia Amelia and kissed her cheek. He smiled at the baby in her arms and tickled it under the chin. Then he turned to the children who came toward him one at a time in order, moving self-consciously. He kissed each child on the cheek, brushing back his long mustaches with his gloved fingers, smiling and saying a few words to each, calling them all by name. The other men moved up behind him and shook hands with Mísia Amelia, flattered her, made a fuss over the child in her arms and filled the patio with genial hubbub. Each child repeated his set phrase.

"How are you, papá?" "It is nice to see you, papá." "I hope you are well, papá." They stressed their "papás" as Mísia Amelia stressed her "Generals."

When Juan Vicente had greeted all the children, patted their heads and given them bits of candy from his pocket, he sat down in the center chair. Mísia Amelia arranged the children in a group around him and the photographer got busy with his plates and camera. Gómez laid aside his cane and took one of the little girls on his knee.

After the pictures were taken, the group broke up and the officers joked with the children while Mísia Amelia and the General talked together. Mísia Amelia talked seriously and rapidly, leaning over the arm of her chair, and the General listened, nodding his head gravely.

After a short while, Gómez's secretary came into the

patio. He went over to the chair, bowed to Mísia Amelia and said something to the General. Gómez rose abruptly. Everyone stopped talking immediately. He moved among the children, kissed them all once more, kissed Mísia Amelia on the cheek and walked out of the patio, the officers following him, voluble once more, laughing and talking.

The sound of motors starting came from outside and again the slamming of car doors.

Mísia Amelia relaxed. The older children gathered around her and asked questions excitedly.

"Ay, Dios mio," she said. "There was so little time. I scarcely had time to say a word. But he did promise that we could have the new house at Macuto."

The two boys had gotten away as soon as possible.

"He said I could have a new car," Florencio muttered to his brother.

He never had any real family life. His nature was against it and the circumstances of his life were against it. He never permitted anyone the intimacy that is the basis of family life. When he grew older and spent most of his time in comparative leisure at Maracay, he became very fond of the younger of his children and grandchildren and spent much time with them, but that is the natural way with old men, however undomesticated their lives have been. The chances are those children had a real affection for him. The other children never knew him. His women never knew him.

In the early days, at La Mulera and at Buenos Aires, he lived apart from his family. The family was under the same roof, but he was apart nevertheless. Later, in Caracas, they lived in separate houses except for the short occasions when they were all together at Miraflores.

When the family of Dionisia was growing up, Gómez

WALKS AHEAD AND THE PRESIDENT OF VENEZUELA, DR. JUAN BAUTISTA FOLLOWS BEHIND. THE INDIAN, TARAZONA, IN UNIFORM, IS BESIDE PÉREZ

was away, fighting, a great deal of the time. Her children, like his own brothers and sisters, admired him, obeyed him and were afraid of him. They all had something of his aquisitive nature and his great respect for money. So he was, for them, the wonder-worker, the source of all the riches that had come to them, something of a god who was to be kept placated. He moved in and out of their lives like a benevolent stranger. The girls married young and when the boys grew up they lost some of their fear and plotted against his life and killed his brother. There could have been no affection there.

The family of Mísia Amelia, the older children at least, were less close to him still. Their hold upon him was even more tenuous for they had never been recognized. He was an elderly man from their earliest memory, the president of the country, the greatest person within the scope of their knowledge. They were raised in luxury, they felt that luxury was their due and they resented having to fawn upon the old man to get it. There was no affection here, either.

The boys, Florencio and Juan Vicente, Junior, grew up to be insufferable bounders. They were sleek, dapper bores, just a little better than half-witted. They acted as though they owned the earth. They went everywhere, insulting people, creating all kinds of scandals, tearing through the streets in expensive cars. They kept up a house in Caracas which they called a club where, with the Pimentels and others of their cronies, they carried on debauches that were worse than the parties of old Pimentel; for these hoodlums lacked the old fellow's refined tastes. They were known all over Caracas as Los Muchachos, The Boys. It was a safe way to speak of them when you wanted to speak your mind.

In the city of Caracas there is a new boulevard that leads out toward the Country Club. At one of the street

intersections there is a sort of traffic circle where two
high concrete columns have been built, presumably for
decorative purposes. They only serve to obstruct traffic.
The Caraqueños always refer to these two columns as
Los Muchachos, for, they say, like Florencio and Juan
Vicente, they are always there and nobody likes them.

Between Gómez and his mother, Hermenegilda, there
had always been a quiet understanding. There was no
demonstrative affection, ever. Gómez went to see her
only occasionally, visiting her house at Macuto, sitting
alone with her for several hours, talking quietly, seriously. There never seemed any need for these two to
see each other often. They were in complete understanding. The old woman from the mountains sat in
her fine house on the seashore. Her eyes were very
bright in her dark, wrinkled face, under the white hair.
Whatever satisfaction ever came out of the career of
Juan Vicente Gómez, it was Hermenegilda who derived
it.

Chapter XXIV

THREE BRUJOS

❖

HE spoke of God frequently. He often said, "God willing" or, "With the help of God." Before the battle of Ciudad Bolívar he said, "As there is a God, I shall take Ciudad Bolívar."

No one knows what God he meant, what God was his. It was not the God of the Christian priests, of his sisters, of his countrymen. He had rejected that God from the beginning; never in words, never by declaration of any sort, but by his actions, all his life, he had rejected him. He had paid no service to that God, ever.

His was his own personal God. He was his own God's chosen son, marked by him for special favors, destined by him to rule over other mortals. Gómez firmly believed in his dreams, in his numbers and his dates. In that sense he was a true mystic. He seldom spoke of these things for they were his alone. He had found his God when he was a boy, among the mountain peaks, in the lonely, high pastures, among his grazing cattle. An illiterate mountain boy, he had found him, secretly, and accepted him against the preaching of the Christian priests that had won his people away from the old gods of the caciques centuries before, against the influence of all the women of his tribe who practiced the religion of the Christian priests. And in this assurance, he was brujo.

He never antagonized the Christian Church in his country except when it dared to interfere with him or criticize him. He tolerated it; even aided it. It was good for other people, this Christian religion. It was good for ordinary mortals. He, himself, with his own God, was superior to it, superior to all its priests and bishops and archbishops and its Pope. He regarded it with rather amused tolerance but he would have none of it for himself. All the pleas of his women and the importunings of the priests to accept its sacraments, to attend its masses, to marry according to its rites, were met with angry silence, with a cold stare from the heavy-lidded, baffling eyes.

He called the priests los curitas, the little priests. He would say, on occasion, "So. The little priests want to build a new shrine in Santa Teresa. Uh-*huh*. Requena, give the little priests three thousand bolívars for their shrine. They keep the people's minds busy and away from things that will get them into trouble."

That was his attitude. He helped the Church so long as it was expedient for his own purposes to do so. He built churches and honored the priests who behaved themselves. The law of the land gave him the power to appoint the bishops and archbishops of the various diocese. So the ambitious ones among the priests curried favor with him, were careful not to antagonize him, permitted him to go his heathen way without a word of criticism, ignored his open flaunting of their moral tenets, pretended to the ridiculous fiction that he was a true son of the Church and a practicing Christian. They sent him blessings and prayed publicly in their churches for his health and well-being. One of them went so far as to obtain for him a decoration from the Pope. Gómez accepted this cynically, as an honor properly due a superior being. He may have seen some humor in it.

This attitude was not toward the Roman Catholic Church alone, but to all religions. The law of Venezuela provides for religious freedom although the Roman Catholic is the established church. Protestant missionaries have always been free to proselyte in the country, even to the extent of passing out tracts to the Catholics leaving the cathedrals, and the Masons have had organizations throughout the country for many years. Nevertheless, little headway has been made against the deeply-rooted teachings of the early Spanish priests and, to the average Venezuelan in the interior, the term Christian is synonymous with Roman Catholic. Gómez continued in this tradition of tolerance, although his support in practical ways went to the established church, simply because the other religions were inconsiderable in point of membership.

It was only when the Church or some official of it dared to assail his power or to criticize his behavior, by inference or direct word, that Gómez threw aside the mask of genial tolerance. It was then that his real contempt for the Church and its God revealed itself. The slightest threat to the only thing that mattered to him, his supreme power, or the slightest word that reflected upon the divine righteousness of his every act, on the part of priest or peon, was met with the same unmerciful wrath. In reality, priest and peon were alike to him in the great perspective of his own eminence.

The priests went to prison with the rest of them. They suffered the tortures of his grillos and of hunger and nakedness. They died from his arsenic and his vergazos. Padre Luís Mendoza, for having delivered a sermon against concubinage. Padre Tomás Monteverde for having aided persons to flee the country, "enemies of the Cause." Padre Evaristo Ramírez, because his brother-in-law was such an "enemy of the Cause." Padre Régulo Fránquis, because he carried a letter addressed to the Pope, denouncing Gómez as unworthy of Papal honor. In October, 1929, the Archbishop of Carabobo, Monseñor Salvador Montes de Oca, published in *El*

Observador of Valencia, an article on the sacrament of matrimony. He was expelled from the country by order of Gómez.

In the prisons, the dying were not permitted the last rites of the Church nor the grace of Christian burial, by order of Gómez—final act of sacrilege for a Cavalier of the Papal Order of Piana. The God of the caciques laughed, surely.

The others, those who flattered and sent prayers and turned their faces from the truth, received the honors and more substantial rewards that were in the dictator's power to bestow, no matter how little their talents merited them. Padre Felipe Rincón González became an Archbishop. Dr. Juan Bautista Castro became an Archbishop. Padre Pérez León, the priest of Maracay, and Padre Aranaga, the Spaniard, received the honors and patronage of the Well-Deserving. Unworthy, all of them. Flatterers who knew the truth and chose to ignore it.

It might help us to understand better the peculiar contradictions of this side of Gómez's character if we tell of his relationship with the priest, Padre Borges, and with the brujo of Maracay, Tomás Meri.

Borges, with Antonio Pimentel and the Indian, Tarazona, were as close to Gómez as any human beings were ever permitted to come. Tarazona was with him constantly and the other two, nearly so. He had made Padre Borges Chaplain of the Army at Maracay so that he might be near him.

He was a Spaniard, a priest who was in the bad graces of the Church officials, who had been removed from office for his unholy conduct. He called himself a "fallen angel" and the phrase was not ill-fitting. Gómez made him his favorite, flaunting him in the face of the Church dignitaries who chose to ignore this truth, too.

He was a brilliant, educated man, a confirmed alcoholic. He staggered about the streets of Caracas, muttering blasphemies and angelic poems. He was the author of a beautiful, lascivious poem about Lucretia Borgia that became famous.

When the dictator established him at Maracay he was an old man—small, emaciated, delicately formed. The habit he wore was half priest, half Venezuelan general. His eyes shone with a brilliance that was half ascetic, half diabolic. Drunk, he feared neither Gómez nor the devil. Sober, he feared them both. Drunk, he insulted Gómez to his face, recited to him his brilliant, satiric poems, expressed his contempt for his ignorance. Sober, he hid from him in terror.

The dictator sent him to prison once "to correct him." It was in prison that he wrote the Borgia poem. When he was released, Gómez sent for him and gave him back his old post.

In the saloons of Maracay he wept and declared that Gómez was God—that Gómez had saved him from hell.

He was a mystic. The memory of his youthful sins tortured him and he drank to forget them. They say that women threw themselves at him when he was young.

The dictator always had him near him. He watched him and listened, fascinated, to his drunken, esoteric brilliance.

Padre Borges was permitted access to Gómez at any time except when he himself told him with a cold glance that he wasn't wanted. Borges always saw, at once, and he would turn and walk away, miserable. Often the General kept important people and affairs waiting while he listened to the demented priest.

Tomás Meri was demented, too. The people called him brujo, primero grado. He followed Gómez about everywhere, had followed him about for years. He was always somewhere close by but he stayed at a distance, sitting by himself, on a curbstone, perhaps, if it were in a city, or on the ground, if it were in the country. Occasionally he would rise, walk rapidly toward the General, push his way through the group that surrounded him, present him with a coin or a relic of some sort, say a few words, and walk rapidly away. He said that Gómez, too, was brujo, primero grado, that he had "seventy-four points." He said that he was a "giant among the ants."

For three years he had been the disciple of an Indian yogi who came to Venezuela. He had learned something of theosophy and numerology from him. His system of divination was based upon dates and numbers. He carried old coins that bore a great variety of dates and these he consulted constantly. He would give one of them to the General occasionally, with a few words of appropriate advice.

He never spoke to him, more than these few occasional words. It is a question whether or not Gómez took Tomás Meri seriously, but, while nearly everyone laughed at him, he never laughed. Frequently he was seen to look about to make sure that Meri was there.

Chapter XXV

UNIÓN, PAZ Y TRABAJO

❖

AFTER the murder of Juancho Gómez in 1923 and the subsequent punishments meted out to all the "enemies of the Cause," there was another long period of quiet that lasted until February of 1928. It was not a peaceful quiet. It was a quiet of terror, of helplessness. There was scarcely a soul in the whole nation, not connected in some way with the Gómez government, who did not desire release from the tyranny in which the country was held. But nothing could be done, absolutely nothing. The people had no arms, no leaders. They could not organize nor even speak to one another of what they felt. The memory of what had happened to their compatriots lingered fresh in their minds. They were frozen into inaction by blind terror of the Andean brujo who seemed completely invulnerable to any human efforts directed against him.

Meanwhile, El Benemérito lived the life he had made for himself in his little Eden at Maracay, surrounded by his friends and satellites and his beloved cattle. The revenue from petroleum rolled into the treasury. He sat in the shade and grunted with satisfaction at the exaggerated reports which his cabinet ministers brought him of the progress of their public works.

Some time before, we spoke of there being some individuals who held positions in the Gómez government or who enjoyed the dictator's patronage, who tried to use their influence in behalf of moderation in

the treatment of the "enemies of the Cause." Among
these was Juan E. París, a brother of the Colombian
border revolutionist, Carmelo París. Juan París was an
educated man and a personal friend of Gómez.

Through his influence, the freedom of some two
hundred political prisoners was obtained. Among them
were Dr. Néstor Luis Pérez, Dr. Pedro José Rojas, Julio
Bustamente and Erasmo Morales. Later, París himself
was imprisoned for some indiscretion.

Another, who succeeded in accomplishing much
more, was Francisco Baptista Galindo. This man held
various posts under Gómez and was his secretary and
personal favorite for a time. He was a poet and something of a humanitarian.

He was something of a diplomat, too. He handled
Gómez properly and obtained the release of many political prisoners, among them the writer, Jorge Luciani,
and helped them to get out of the country. Others, less
fortunate than Galindo, had been imprisoned, themselves, for less than this. He looked after the families
of some of the prisoners who were in need. Finally, in
1927, he accomplished the impossible and secured, for
the second time during the reign of Gómez, the release
of all political prisoners in Venezuela. He had to give
his personal guarantee for the future behavior of the
prisoners and his promise to win them over to the support of the Rehabilitation. An impossible promise, of
course.

Again, the motives that prompted this magnanimity
are obscure. Such acts were so contrary to Gómez's usual
implacability where anything that threatened his power
was concerned. Galindo must have been something of a
brujo himself, as well as a diplomat. It is possible, too,
that Gómez again hoped that the prisoners had learned
their lesson. He always thought of his prisons as sort of
colleges. He seemed to think that sending unruly ones

there would "educate" them. He used to say that he sent so and so to prison to "teach him to be useful."

Anyway, in 1927, all the political prisoners were again set free. There was a great deal of publicity given the occasion and a suggestion was made by Naranjo, the Mexican writer, that the Rotunda be torn down and a park laid out in its place.

Galindo, of course, couldn't live up to his guarantee. He was put into prison himself a little later. He died not long ago, still in prison, if our information is correct.

Again, as had happened after the liberation of 1921, many of the prisoners left the country. Those who remained, our friend, Arévalo González, and the rest of them, tried to keep the peace according to the guarantees they had given.

Nevertheless, the long quiet that had reigned from 1923, was soon broken. This time the trouble was instigated by a new element in the political affairs of Venezuela. It was composed of the young men who had grown up since the beginning of Gómez's reign. They were youths who had never known anything but his tyranny. They had seen their mothers weeping and had been told of their fathers' deaths in prison. They had suffered hunger and want and had seen their brothers and sisters suffer. They were students at the Central University who had studied the laws of the land and had seen those laws abused and ignored by the despotic government that held their country in its grip. They were the sons of once-prosperous merchants and farmers who saw their fathers struggling against the competition of the privileged kinsmen of Gómez. And even here, some echo of modern thought and modern social philosophy was seeping in and finding response in youthful minds.

Their ideals were high and their actions gallant and rash.

In February of 1928, the students of the Central University in Caracas held their annual celebration known as "Student Week." During the festivities there was much speech-making, enthusiasm and gaiety. Some of the student leaders were carried away by their stimulated spirits and became indiscreet in some of the things they said about the political situation. By direct order of Gómez, two hundred and twenty students, members of the Federation of Students, were arrested and put into prison at Libertador, without a hearing of any kind.

This incident marked the beginning of a long series of disturbances and revolutionary movements both inside the country and from without that extended over a period of four years.

Nearly all the youth of the country rose up in protest. There was nothing that could be done other than parade the streets and make speeches. The University was closed by order of Gómez and the College of Lawyers was dissolved. There was a demonstration in the Plaza Bolívar and the police fired on the crowd, killing and wounding women and children. Again, at the bullfight on a Sunday afternoon, some of the young students and clerks of the city got down into the arena and formed a sort of snake dance parade. They shouted such treasonous phrases as "Down with Gómez!" and "Viva la libertad!" and were slaughtered by pistol fire from policemen stationed in the upper tiers of the bowl.

On April 7 there occurred a revolutionary movement in Caracas that really came within an ace of succeeding. It threw a fright into Gómez, away off in his retreat in Maracay, and his actions, after it was all over, were typically swift and unmerciful.

This movement was the result of a plot that involved

four youthful elements. There were the young officers of the army, recent graduates of the Military College in Caracas, students of the Military College, students of the Central University and an element composed of young clerks and sons of merchants of Caracas. They were all of the best families and best blood of the country.

The plot had begun to take shape among the officers and was a result of the discontent that had been spreading because of Gómez's habit of utilizing the army for peon work on his haciendas. The officers were educated men of good family. Some of them, such as the leader of the movement, Captain Rafael Albarado, had studied at military schools in foreign countries. These officers, upon receiving their commissions, were quite often assigned to oversee their men in the cutting of cane, tending of cattle, all sorts of back-breaking, manual labor under the fierce tropical sun on the farms of the dictator. When the protests of the students of the Central University took place, the leaders were cautiously approached by the army plotters and their co-operation was secured. By the same process, all the young clerks and merchants became involved in the movement.

As a result of the unquiet state of the city of Caracas after the imprisonment of the members of the Federation of Students, Gómez recalled the officers and soldiers from his haciendas and ordered them to the city to reinforce the garrisons, taking with them from the headquarters in Maracay, machine guns, extra rifles and ammunition and a light artillery piece. Among the officers assigned to these duties were Captain Albarado and Lieutenant Rafael Barrios, the two leaders of the revolutionary plot.

The artillery and machine guns were placed in the main government barracks and fifteen thousand rifles and twenty million rounds of ammunition were taken

to the barracks known as San Carlos in another part of
the city, not to be confused with the prison of San
Carlos near Maracaibo. Albarado and Barrios remained
with the machine guns at the main barracks in the
center of the city and another of the plotters, Lieutenant Augustín Fernández, was stationed at San Carlos.

The plan of action was this. Albarado and Barrios
were to seize the main barracks, distribute the arms
among the citizens who were to be outside the barracks
at the appointed time and then the main body would
march upon the palace of Miraflores, subdue it and
continue on to San Carlos, where Fernández would give
the signal to attack and open the doors. A small group
was assigned to go to the house of the Commander-in-
Chief of the Army, General López Contreras, and arrest
him and another group to cut the telegraph and telephone wires that connected with Maracay. Among the
active participants in the movement was General Contreras's own son, a student at the Military College.

So efficient was the spy system that Gómez had developed that, although the details of this plan were not
worked out until the afternoon of the day on which they
were to be carried through and in spite of the extreme
caution which the conspirators exerted, General Contreras was informed of them in time. The informant
was one Lieutenant Mariano Montilla.

Even then, the coup was nearly a success. At ten
o'clock on the night of the 7th, Albarado and Barrios
went to the room of the commandant of the barracks
and demanded his surrender.

There was a mild resistance, several officers were shot
dead and the barracks, with its store of arms, was in
the hands of the revolutionists. The doors were opened
and the civilians poured into the building and armed
themselves. Then the whole straggling, shouting band
flooded the streets of the city and headed for the palace

of Miraflores. Something of a battle took place there. The soldiers fired from the high walls and balconies and the civilians fired back at them, taking cover in doorways and behind lamp-posts, the rifles flashing in the darkness, the unrhythmic rattle and the shouting echoing against the buildings of the narrow streets.

It was all over soon. The palace fell into the hands of the revolutionists. Gómez wasn't there of course but some of the family were, among them his sister, Regina, who watched the battle from a high window. More arms were taken here and then the mob headed for San Carlos. They seized automobiles and piled on the runningboards, shouting and waving their rifles. They reached the square in front of the San Carlos barracks and drew up for a conference. There was no signal from Fernández but the building was in darkness and all seemed serene. Albarado gave the order and the mob advanced upon the barracks. Lights flashed on and a terrific burst of machine gun and rifle fire poured out from the windows and roof. The revolution of April 7th died in its tracks, with success only a few yards away.

General Contreras had gotten word before the detail arrived at his house to arrest him. He hurried to the barracks of San Carlos, arrested Lieutenant Fernández and several others, took command of the troops and stationed them at the windows to await the coming of the revolutionists.

Gómez's direct orders were to "chastise them severely." That was the kind of order that his "machetes" delighted in. The prisons were filled again. The Rotunda, which had been turned into a storehouse for the Department of Public Works and had been named for the site of a city park, was reopened and put to its old use. The Military College was closed, permanently, the students of the Central University were ordered to be arrested. Many of them hid in the homes of friends and some of them managed to get out of the country in disguise. The spies combed the city, searching them out. Thousands of students and clerks and merchants were thrown into prison, many of them, most of them probably, having had no part in the movement. They had no chance to defend themselves before a court.

In this general imprisonment there were a few individuals who were put through the mockery of a trial. One of the students who had been involved in the affair was a citizen of Chile and the Chilean Minister demanded of Gómez that he be given a hearing. So he, with a few Venezuelan students, some five or six out of the hundreds, were tried before a military court. It is significant that the Chileño, out of the thousands of those arrested, was the only one set free. Gómez was always very careful in dealing with foreigners.

The torturing began again. Albarado was hung up by his testicles. He lived through it but he died in prison later. The tortol, the cepo and the verga again began to function. Hundreds of the prisoners died within a few months of arsenic and dysentery. No medical aid was ever given in the prisons. Many of those who finally obtained their freedom died of tuberculosis.

The tortol was a knotted rope that was drawn about a prisoner's head above the eyebrows. A stick was put through the rope in the back and twisted, in the manner of a tourniquet, drawing up the slack and pressing the knots into the flesh and bone of the skull.

The cepo was an apparatus of torture developed in the Venezuelan prisons. It was so complicated and well-thought-out that it could only have been the product of a diseased imagination. It worked like this. The thumbs of the victim were tied together tightly. Then he was made to squat upon the floor and bend his elbows so that they came below his knees. A rope was fastened to his wrists and tied around his neck. Then a rifle was passed under the knees and over the elbows, the butt protruding on one side and the barrel on the other. Two of the torturers stood upon these protruding ends and jumped up and down until the victim "sang" or fainted. The strain of this weight on the upper vertebrae and the abdomen was terrific. It produced frightful rupturing of the abdominal walls, accompanied by bloody urinating and defecation and the vertebrae were sometimes so separated and injured that the victim was rendered insane, if he lived at all.

What could have been the type of men who could do these things to other men? It seems unbelievable that they could exist in numbers. One or two of them, perhaps, scattered over the earth, isolated cases, criminally insane, pathological freaks, sadists. But here were numbers of them. Twenty, fifty, a hundred of them, working in groups. At the Libertador, at San Carlos, at the Rotunda, at the Cuño, at La Guayra and at all the other minor prisons. Perpetrating the same atrocities, delighting in them. How could there be so many of them in the same place. Where did they all come from? Who were they?

Well, they were personal, life-long friends of the Benemérito, of the genial, child-loving old man whose soft voice "was like a caress," one American journalist said, whose ideals were peace and prosperity for his country.

The chief of the prison, Libertador, was General Paulino Camero, a red-headed, fat, sloppy Andino of sixty years. He had been an officer under Gómez since the days of the Restoration and had been made president of a state. He loved to assemble all the prisoners and have them look on while he demonstrated how much better he could administer a beating than the guards under him. He would swing his heavy verga with terrific force against the naked flesh, laughing, the blood spattering his red whiskers and hairy chest. Sometimes he would bring a phonograph into the courtyard and swing his lash to music. Gómez gave him a present of seven hundred thousand dollars, supposedly as payment for an hacienda but the hacienda wasn't worth five thousand dollars.

Rafael María Velasco was one of the principal executioners of Gómez. He had many different posts, all of them connected with activities of subjugation. He was Governor of Caracas, Prefect of Police, Director of Public Safety and so on. He, too, had come with Gómez from the mountains as one of the Restorers. He grew very wealthy and invested money in farm lands in Canada and when Gómez died he got away, taking his money with him. He is in Canada now, safe on his farm.

Pedro García was Velasco's right hand man. He had many important posts, as well, at different times—Prefect of Police, Chief of the Rotunda. He had been a procurer for a well-known prostitute, a Colombian, named Pura. His place of business was a botaquín at Puente de Hierro, the same place where Eustóquio Gómez killed Dr. Mata Illas.

There were hundreds of them, jefes and subordinates, all of the same cut, equally low, equally bloodthirsty. That was why they had their jobs. Elias Sayago, Nereo Pacheco, Jorge García, General Volcán, Colonel Cárdenas, Lorenzo Carvallo, Carlos Montaubán, hundreds of them.

Everyone went back to prison, all the "enemies of the Cause," the old ones and hundreds of new ones, boys of thirteen and old men of sixty-five, even women this time for some girl students had made some speeches, too. Twenty newspaper writers were arrested in one day when a copy of a clandestine paper called *El Imparcial* was found by a spy.

On February 25, immediately after the harmless demonstrations of the students during Student Week, before the uprising of April 7, Arévalo González sent this telegram to Gómez:

I have never begged anything of you nor of any governor, certainly not my own liberty on the thirteen occasions that it has been taken away from me.

Today I am going to beg for the liberty of the imprisoned students. I do not beg on bended knee nor with grace because that would be an offense to them. I beg it with due respect, but on my feet, as one exercising the right to demand justice.

What did the first four or five students do? Involve themselves, like the others, in youthful amusements.

Have they sinned in this?

To lament in ingenuous speeches that we have not known how to utilize the sacrifices and exertions of our Liberators.

Is it also a crime to sing of liberty?

Does it merit punishment to extol that goddess of all worthy and happy people?

Soon the rest of them found places in the prisons beside their comrades. Isn't that a beautiful thing? Doesn't it make you feel proud that the people whom you rule has a youth in whom shine such radiant virtues? Do they deserve to be punished, those who so demonstrate such qualities of companionship, solidarity and pride?

General: It is the duty of magistrates who rule the destinies of peoples to encourage the noble sentiments of those who later will be the leaders in the progress and betterment of the fatherland, and I promise myself, beforehand, the satisfaction of seeing, on this occasion, so pleasing a duty fulfilled.

Your attentive servant and compatriot,

ARÉVALO GONZÁLEZ.

González was arrested the next day and put into prison for the fourteenth and last time, for this time he died there.

In these later years Gómez had added a new means of punishing the "enemies of the Cause." The prisons would hold no more and there were more to be punished. He had embarked on his widely-publicized program of road-building so he sent the prisoners out to work on the carreteras. Into the swamps and jungles they went, young, city-raised boys, to work under the tropic sun from daybreak till nightfall, dragging their iron shackles. Out into the shadeless llanos of Gúarico, the mosquito-infested bogs of Anzoátegui. Starved, poorly clothed, no shelter against the sun and rains and insects, day or night. They died like flies under the lash of the guards and from starvation and pneumonia and dysentery. So many of them died and were buried along the carreteras that in certain places the superstitious peons were afraid to travel the roads at night for fear of ghosts. They called the road between Barcelona and Aragua in the state of Anzoátegui el camino de los huesos, the road of the bones.

Yet Gómez considered this mild punishment. These last disturbances in the capital had been so wide-spread and the news of them had traveled into the exterior to such an extent that he couldn't ignore them as he had similar disturbances before. He made a statement that was printed in the *Nuevo Diario* in which he said, among other things:

". . . I have opened the doors of the University to them and secured and paid magnificent professors that they might learn honorable professions; but they do not care to be anything but politicians. . . . since they do not wish to study, they can learn to work. I have treated them as a severe parent. I have sent them, temporarily, out to the carreteras. . . . There, they will reflect and understand their errors. I do not consider these boys my enemies. For the true enemies, for those who disturb the order and the social well-being, they know that I have methods of true severity."

He speaks always as the absolute owner of the country. "*I* pay the professors. *I* opened the doors of the University." He ignores the fact that the doors of the University were open centuries before he was born and that the professors were paid out of national revenues. He takes full credit for all the punishment meted out.

The slogan of the Rehabilitation which Gómez delighted in sticking up everywhere—on the walls of public buildings, on monuments and under his own picture —was: "Unión, Paz y Trabajo." "Union, Peace and Work."

The Caraqueños said, "Union, Peace and Work. Union in the prisons, Peace in the cemetery and Work on the carreteras."

Chapter XXVI

INVASIONS

❖

THE first of a new series of armed revolutionary movements against the Gómez government by the Venezuelan exiles in foreign countries was known as the *Angelita* Expedition and originated in Brooklyn, New York.

This expedition marked the farewell revolutionary gesture of quite a few of the old caudillos—the type that was disappearing fast, that was being replaced by the modern-thinking, idealistic crusaders.

Gómez did not destroy the caudillos as is claimed by his adulators. Quite the contrary, as a matter of fact. It was he who kept the old type alive. His whole system of maintenance of power was based upon the utilization of the very worst examples of the type. His reign was a representation of the caudillo type in complete and sustained victory, throughout its whole duration. It relied entirely upon the support by force of arms, obtained by money, of the worst of the Andean guerrillas—Félix Galaviz, Pérez Soto, León Jurado, Aristídes Tellería, Tobías Uribe, Guillermo Willet and the rest of them. In Venezuela the caudillos were not destroyed. They were simply quiet because they had what they wanted.

In exile the caudillo type died a natural death because modern times made its obsolete methods of warfare impotent. Machine-guns and airplanes and the disapproval of youth finished with it and the later revolutionary invasions were led by a new type of fighter.

The leader of the movement that culminated in the *Angelita* Expedition was Dr. Leopoldo Baptista who had been plotting and planning for years in Europe and the United States. Associated with him in the venture were many of those whom we have mentioned before—Dr. Ortega Martínez, General Rafael María Carabaño, General Régulo Olivares—and some of the new, youthful element, notably, Pedro Elías Aresteigueta. This group had for its object an armed invasion of Venezuela, the overthrow of Gómez and the establishment of Dr. Santos Dominici as provisional president until a popular election by the liberated people could be held. Dominici was a liberal who had been part of the Gómez régime for some time but had come to see the error of his ways. Still, he was not acceptable to many of the revolutionary groups because of his former political connections.

General Mario Terán arrived in New York, incognito, from Caracas, bringing a sum of money from revolutionary elements there. This money, together with other sums raised among the plotters and donated by Baptista, who was a wealthy man, was used for the purchase of an old tub of a boat called the *Angelita*. The boat was put into dry-dock in Brooklyn and reconditioned.

At that time Alvaro Obregón was president of Mexico. He was sympathetic to the plans of the Brooklyn conspirators and promised a park of arms and ammunition. However, it was necessary that the *Angelita* arrive at the designated Mexican port to receive it on one particular day—the last day of Obregón's term as president.

General Olivares, with a group of military men, was to proceed to Mexico by train and await the arrival of the *Angelita*, bringing the remainder of the revolutionists.

After many delays, the vessel sailed from Brooklyn. Within twenty-four hours she had developed engine trouble and was forced to put into Newport News for repairs. More lengthy delays, and then the *Angelita* got under way again. Soon she reported in distress off the Florida coast and an American vessel took her in tow to Key West. Meanwhile, Olivares and his group had arrived in Mexico and the date fixed for the delivery of the military park had gone by. Nevertheless, after more expensive repairs in Key West, the *Angelita* proceeded southward. She reached Cuba this time; but that was the end of her journey. The funds had given out and the vessel had to be sold in Havana for the dry-dock bills.

Gómez, of course, had been informed of the expedition's progress and vicissitudes from the first. Now, through his minister in Cuba, Rafael Angel Arraiz, he requested the Cuban government to seize the vessel, arrest all the conspirators and send them to him—a highly improper request, contrary to diplomatic procedure, and to comply with it would have been a violation of international law. This was before the dictatorship of Machado in Cuba. A liberal, Dr. Alfredo Zayas, was president, and he flatly refused to interfere with the liberty of the Venezuelan exiles.

That was the end of the *Angelita* Expedition and none of the conspirators mentioned above with the exception of the youth, Aresteigueta, and General Carabaño figured further in revolutionary movements against Gómez, although Dominici was afterward named for presidential honors by another group.

Early in 1929 another invasion was attempted, this time from the Dutch island of Curaçao, just off the Venezuelan coast. The group involved was composed entirely of the new element and the leader was Rafael

Simón Urbina, a youth in his twenties, a gallant, handsome lad, with no military experience but plenty of energy and imagination.

Urbina organized the exiles who had taken refuge on the Dutch island and formed a most audacious plan. They had purchased a few rifles somehow or other and one night, when the American steam vessel, *Maracaibo*, of the Red D Line, was in port, they went to the residence of the Dutch governor, took him prisoner and seized the arsenal at the barracks. They marched the governor aboard the American vessel and ordered the captain to put to sea and head for the Venezuelan coast. The governor was taken along as hostage to discourage any attempt of the Dutch officers to interfere with them.

Before daybreak the next morning the expedition disembarked at Le Vela del Coro, where so many such expeditions had landed during the time of Castro. The *Maracaibo* returned to Curaçao with the governor of the island aboard.

Gómez had been informed of what was going on, of course. He had telegraphed to León Jurado, the president of Falcón, and Jurado was prepared. In the advance upon the town of Coro, the young revolutionists were met by the government forces and the expedition came to an end right there. Most of the invaders were taken prisoner but Urbina managed to escape into the hills.

He made his way across the border into Colombia and finally arrived in Mexico where he planned another expedition of somewhat the same nature. Urbina was a native of the town of Coro and had a considerable following among the people there. He had lived under the tyranny of León Jurado and he had for him a violent, personal hatred.

Gómez no longer goes out at the head of his troops

to meet these invaders as he once did. He stays in his stronghold and delegates the task to others. The reason is that he is growing old and cannot be far away from his doctors. He has developed prostatitis. He has occasional attacks when the valve of the prostate gland becomes locked and a sound must be introduced into the urethra tract so that the urine may be drawn off. He has foreign doctors attending him. When word spreads throughout Venezuela that the Catfish is suffering from one of these attacks the people wait with bated breath and whisper, "Que se muera! Que se muera!" "May he die! May he die!"

About this time a revolutionary movement got under way in the state of Portuguesa under the leadership of a rancher of Barquisimeto, José Rafael Gabaldón.

Gabaldón was an educated man of liberal tendencies and great prestige in the Andean states of Trujillo, Lara and Portuguesa. He was not politically inclined. However, he watched the course of Gómez's despotism until he could no longer remain silent. He wrote Gómez a courteous, mildly worded letter in which he suggested that Gómez had had enough time in power and should retire. Gómez was infuriated. He ordered Gabaldón's arrest. Gabaldón took to the hills and rounded up his friends and declared himself in revolt.

On May 13, 1929, Gómez sent the following telegram to Dr. Juan Bautista Pérez who, at that time, was acting as the Catfish's dummy in the presidency:

Yesterday the Generals Eustóquio Gómez, Pedro María Cárdenas, León Jurado, Félix Galaviz and Juan Fernández set out for the states of Lara, Portuguesa and Trujillo with the authority and the forces necessary to finish with those evil sons of the fatherland who have risen up in some towns in those jurisdictions: an evil plague that must be destroyed by the roots to clean out those regions fallen victims to a group of malefactors who must be radically exterminated by the moral and material forces of the Government.

Lo saluda su amigo,

J. V. GÓMEZ.

Radically exterminated they were. Over two hundred were taken prisoner, among them Gabaldón himself, and these were sent to the Libertador where they suffered the tortol, cepo, verga and double grillos of seventy pounds. One boy of thirteen whose father was among the revolutionists was subjected to the tortol and it left him permanently deaf and mentally befuddled. Within a few months' time, twenty-four of the followers of Gabaldón were carried out of the Libertador, dead.

In August, 1929, there occurred a revolutionary invasion that was by far the most ambitious and best-equipped of all the movements made against the government of Juan Vicente Gómez. At the head of it was General Roman Delgado Chalbaud.

Chalbaud had been one of the Restorers under Castro. He had remained loyal to Castro and had held posts during his rule that made him wealthy. He had had a monopoly on coastal navigation and commerce, had been Commander of the Navy and owned the coastal salt rights. When Castro was overthrown by Gómez, Chalbaud stayed along with the new régime, though his money-making opportunities were trimmed down somewhat. He was a very ambitious and energetic man and he didn't remain satisfied long under Gómez. He initiated some furtive steps along the way of usurpation and the spies found him out. He was put into prison in the Rotunda and stayed there for fourteen years.

When he was released in the general amnesty of 1927, he went to Paris where his wife and son were living.

He began to make plans for an armed invasion of Venezuela at once.

Chalbaud was fanatically addicted to his cause. He was almost a mad man, so driven was he by the memories of his many years of torture, by his hatred of Gómez and his desire for revenge. He threw himself heart and soul into the project of which he dreamed. He turned everything he owned into cash to buy munitions—his wife's property in Paris and her jewels. He communicated with the exiles all over the world and pleaded with them to join him. He had some difficulty here, for his motives were suspected because of his former connections. Nevertheless, he did gain a large group of followers. He convinced most of them that his years in prison had reformed him and that he was converted to liberal views and others felt that motives should not be scrutinized too closely, that the foremost object was to overthrow Gómez and the other things could be taken care of later.

A conference was held at Geneva and Dr. Santos Dominici was named as candidate for the provisional presidency, Dr. Alfredo Smith for the vice-presidency.

Chalbaud succeeded in bringing in the outstanding anti-Gómez leaders from everywhere and many of them went to Europe from Mexico, New York, Curaçao, Colombia and Trinidad to lend their active aid.

His assistant, second chief of the expedition, was one of the new, young element, a student of the Central University, Armando Zuloaga Blanco. Pedro Aresteigueta, the young lad who had been with the *Angelita* fiasco, joined him. There was General Carabaño, also of the *Angelita*. There was Captain Luís Pimentel, the young officer who had been hung up four times by his testicles in Villa Zoila and still lived. He had spent five years in prison, absolutely incommunicado, and now he was ready to return to the fight. Then there was General

Francisco Alcántara, the West Pointer, the old candidate of the bastoneros under Castro. There was the writer, José Pocaterra, Dr. Carlos Rojas, General Doroteo Flores and some three hundred others, officers and men.

A coal-burning steam vessel of two-hundred-and-forty-foot length and thirty-four-foot beam was purchased in the city of Danzig. She was called the *Falke* and, since her construction in Bremen in 1909, had taken part in many revolutionary raids in the Caribbean under different names. Her German captain and German crew of thirty-five men were hired to carry the expedition to the coast of Venezuela.

A large quantity of rifles, machine-guns and ammunition was purchased and put aboard. The vessel was coaled and rationed and, in the late days of July, left Danzig for the voyage across the Atlantic, carrying the revolutionists. On August 10, the *Falke* arrived off the peninsula of Araya in the eastern part of Venezuela.

Gómez had been informed of the expedition through his agents in Europe but the revolutionists were counting on the fact that he wouldn't know at what point they would strike. They themselves didn't decide till the day they made their landfall in Venezuelan waters. They decided upon the town of Cumaná as the point of attack.

If we look at the map again, we shall see that the peninsula lies north and east of the town. At a remote spot on the peninsula, a considerable store of arms and ammunition was put ashore for Pedro Aresteigueta who, with some two hundred and fifty men that he recruited among the fishermen of the coast, was to attack the town by land from the east, marching his men around the Gulf of Cariaco. The attacks were to be made simultaneously by the land party and the party from the *Falke* at daybreak of the 11th.

The *Falke* weighed anchor and headed west and Aresteigueta set out with his men immediately.

At three the next morning the vessel anchored off the wharf at Puerto Sucre with all lights extinguished. The plan was to await the sound of firing that would announce the attack of the land party from the east before the troops should disembark. This plan of a simultaneous attack was necessary for the capture of the city because of the geographic features. The Manzanares River divides Puerto Sucre from Cumaná, the main part of the town and the site of the principal government barracks, and there is only one narrow bridge crossing it.

Chalbaud waited aboard the *Falke* from three until five. Then, still not hearing any sound of firing from the shore, he became impatient and ordered his men to disembark, believing that Aresteigueta would arrive any minute and would hurry when he heard the sound of Chalbaud's attack.

The men were put off in small boats and drew up on the wharf, just as the sun rose over the hills and poured its rays onto the calm water of the bay.

Chalbaud took the head of the column and gave the order to attack the customs house and its garrison. The alarm sounded as they advanced and the firing began. The column moved forward under punishing volleys. They drove out the defenders from the customs house and fought their way along the main street of the town till they reached the narrow bridge that crossed to Cumaná proper. Here they were forced to stop and take cover as best they could. Still no sound from the east.

Chalbaud attempted an assault across the bridge and he fell dead. Until nine o'clock in the morning the battle waged at the bridge, assaults being launched by both sides, always failing. The losses were heavy. Blanco was killed, Flores, Alcántara, Vegas, and Pacheco were wounded, of the revolutionist officers. Scarcely an officer remained. Of the government forces, the commander, General Emilio Fernández, was killed, besides many others.

Meanwhile the *Falke,* standing out in the harbor, was seen to weigh anchor and head to sea. Upon seeing this, the revolutionists gave up. It was nine-thirty and Aresteigueta had not appeared.

The *Falke* had been left in command of José Pocaterra. Not only did he order the German captain to abandon the scene and head for the sea, but, a little later, he ordered the remaining park, a considerable store of guns and ammunition, to be thrown overboard. The *Falke* continued on to the British island of Granada. Pocaterra has made some lengthy statements as to his reasons for these acts but the logic is rather difficult and most of the Venezuelans seem to be unconvinced.

Pedro Aresteigueta and his men had been marching the whole day and night of the 10th without rest. The night was very dark and the local guides had become lost. The company struggled among the mountainous paths and boggy salinas and tidal lagoons for eight hours, making no headway in the right direction at all. When daybreak came they found themselves and they were miles away from Cumaná, where they should have been at that hour. They hurried forward as fast as their tired legs would permit them. They took short cuts across swamps and streams that they had to swim. They approached the town at noon, eight hours too late.

As they advanced toward the pink-walled town, two airplanes appeared in the sky, coming from the west. The men broke ranks and took cover. The planes carried no bombs but they swooped down and emptied their machine guns at the revolutionists. These answered with rifle fire and disabled one machine-gun. They continued their advance, harassed by the one plane that continued firing, but, by taking cover at its approach, they suffered no casualties. The planes had been sent from Maracay and were manned by two Belgian fliers.

On arriving at the outskirts of the town they learned that their companions had attacked and been defeated. Nevertheless, they attacked the barracks themselves, tired, hungry and thirsty as they were. They fought for two days, intermittently, sometimes in the outskirts of the town, sometimes in the city streets, sometimes maneuvering about the hilly paths, making sudden sallies in the darkness. Aresteigueta was killed, Pimentel and Carabaño were wounded. On the third day reinforcements of one thousand men arrived for the government army and the revolutionists who were still able to stand on their feet attempted to flee. Most of them were taken prisoner.

That was the end of the *Falke* Expedition. If the town of Cumaná had been taken, as it would have been had the land force arrived in time, a considerable store of munitions would have fallen into the revolutionists' hands and thousands of easterners would have come to join them. The whole town of Cumaná favored the invaders and all of the people would have helped them had they had arms. They took the wounded into their homes and treated them like heroes. They tried to hide them from the Gómez agents after the defeat but they were all searched out and put into prison.

Nothing ever seemed to have a chance against Gómez. No matter how well-planned or well-equipped a movement was, the brujo always won out. The forces of chance always seemed to be on his side.

There was another period of quiet for two years. Then, in 1931, young Rafael Urbina invaded the coast of Falcón for the second time. This time he came from Vera Cruz, Mexico, in a vessel called the *Superior*. His

VICENTE GÓMEZ, JR., ONE OF THE TWO MUCHACHOS, IN THE CENTER

followers were a few Venezuelan ex-students and some two hundred Mexicans—rather radical-thinking young visionaries. This was the only armed movement against the Gómez government that even faintly merited the label "communistic," which the dictator had come, of late years, to apply to every demonstration, knowing that he could thus secure sympathy for his radical actions of suppression among the capitalistic nations. He even applied it to the demonstrations in front of the house of Bolívar in Caracas, when hundreds of Venezuelan women got down on their knees and prayed for the welfare of their sons and husbands inside the prison walls.

Urbina landed again at La Vela del Coro, and again, his old enemy, León Jurado, was waiting for him. He was defeated easily and most of the band was killed or taken prisoner. He, again, managed to escape.

Jurado sent a telegram to Gómez after the battle. "Today the buzzards of Falcón will eat Mexican flesh," he said.

That was the last armed insurrection ever attempted against the brujo. It was useless.

Chapter XXVII

JUAN BOBO

❖

JOHN BOOBY. That was the name of the President of Venezuela from 1929 to 1931. At least that was the name the Caraqueños gave him and it really fitted him better than his real name, Dr. Juan Bautista Pérez. Juan Vicente Gómez put him into the presidential chair, temporarily, in one of those gestures that he was always making to sustain the naïve fiction that he was not a dictator at all but a self-sacrificing patriot and the people's choice. However, these gestures did make fine copy for his ministers abroad to feed the foreign press with.

Pérez was also called the Cadaver because, they said, like a dead body, he was found to be rotten inside of twenty-four hours. He was a tall, thin, gray-haired man who was befuddled and considerably frightened by the sudden apotheosis.

Jorge Luciani describes him thus: "A native of Caracas, a mediocre, obscure lawyer; innocuity that passed for merit. Irreproachable in his private life, virgin in politics, always apart from the world, very gentlemanly, very serious, very gentle. One of those creatures who do the same things every day with chronometric punctuality, who eat, sleep, bathe and defecate at fixed hours, who keep the Sabbath, carry umbrellas and salute the most humble with a deep bow. Inheritors of a modest estate that endures and grows without assistance; much addicted to etiquette; very respectful of the government that imposes taxes and orders imprisonments; without intellectual curiosity and without spiritual unquiet of any kind; . . . who, on clear days, pronounce in magisterial tone, 'It is a fine day,' and on cloudy days, discover, very pompously, that 'It is going to rain'; who give alms publicly on Saturdays but who are incapable of inconveniencing themselves for anything or anybody. More than good-natured, they are egoists who will not permit their mode of life to be disturbed. And there, in the bosom of their tranquil homes, they are petty tyrants."

That was the man of straw, made to order for Juan Vicente's purposes.

The details of the process by which Gómez foisted this dummy upon the nation as its supreme magistrate is lo mas genial, most amusing.

The dictator's legal term of office expired in 1929 and the Congress met on April 19 to elect the next president. Naturally, the members were decided upon Gómez, for he had appointed them. However, in his message at the opening of Congress (it was read, for Gómez seldom appeared in the capital now), he declared that he was not a candidate for re-election.

Consternation among the senators and deputies. What did it mean? What were they expected to do? What was the significance of this succinct declaration? Was it a trap?

Highly agitated, a committee of Congress members hurried out to the mighty one's shrine in Maracay and requested an audience.

They waited nervously in an anteroom, tapping their canes, fingering their formal bow-ties. After considerable time the door opened and El Benemérito appeared. He was arrayed in his grand Bolívaresque uniform, a sword at his waist, the foreign orders blazing on his chest. The deputies and senators rose and Gómez stared at them sternly, without a word of greeting. There was a period of awkward silence. Gómez strode around the table and struck it a blow with his verga. Cayama Martínez, the leader of the Congress, coughed nervously, and began to recite the sugary oration which the committee had composed.

Gómez heard him through in silence, his eyes veiled, his mouth hard. Then he smote the table once more and left the room, slamming the door behind him.

The members of the committee were completely baffled. They trembled in their patent-leather boots. They scurried back to Caracas, half-expecting to be arrested by the soldiers stationed along the way, and recited to their colleagues what had taken place. There was excited argument, conjecture, examination of consciences. Finally it was decided, with the aid of some gentle hints from emissaries from Maracay, that the whole Congress should repair en masse to the shrine of El Benemérito, that that was the procedure which he considered propitious to the occasion.

So, out they went, the whole Sovereign Congress, frock-coated and perfumed and apprehensive.

But there was nothing to worry about this time. The General met them with a bland smile and warm words of greeting. He listened approvingly as Martínez recited once more the glowing sentiments of the Congress, the same speech he had delivered the day before with such an unappreciative audience, nodding his head and smiling benignly. Then he addressed the assembly and his words as reported in the *Nuevo Diario* of May 16, 1929, were these:

"You come surprising me. I really expected you to come to honor me, but also, you come, insisting upon something which I cannot do. (Meaning, reconsider his decision not to accept the presidency.)

"It is an affair which I explained in my Message and

in my telegram from El Trompillo, in which I said that I cannot see this need for I feel that the need of Venezuela now is to form men.

". . . I found this country, a house in ruins and I made it into a house of solid foundations.

"And what is needed to maintain such a house? An individual who can guard it and conserve it. My presence is no longer needed.

"The energies that I possess are not alone to work for the Fatherland and I have decided to devote them now to cultivate the soil.

"I am a farmer and a stock-raiser, for in these labors I was raised and I have done them well.

"In these works of farming and cattle-raising I have had much practice and for this reason, I wish that you would concur in my desires, although always I shall be concerned with the welfare of the Fatherland. (Great applause.)

". . . I must repeat that I will not accept the presidency.

". . . You must seek the solution of this matter.

"And now will you permit me to say what you can do? (Voices: Sí! Sí!)

"Well, then, many enemies have said, 'What he wants is that they go and beg him to be President.'

"I do not wish that you come to beg me, for I am not accustomed to be begged nor to beg. I must tell you how we can meet the situation.

"I will not accept the presidency, but I do wish that you name me General-in-Chief of the Army. (Great applause.) Because for me the Army is life itself. There are two things that I love very much: the Army and Work.

"So it is up to you to find a man who is in accord with me in everything and for everything, to exercise the functions of President.

"In respect to the Army, it was I who organized it and I am responsible to the country for the tranquillity and progress of Venezuela.

"With this Army commanded by me . . . the enemies will know better than to bring any action against the Republic.

"The individual whom you select must work in every instance in accord with me and in this way everything will go well.

"If you agree, then, you will organize the matter and make the nomination on the 23rd of May. (Great applause.)

"If you agree, I will give you a candidate whom I shall have to search for, for this candidate will have to act in accord with me.

"If you will authorize me, I shall find him for you. (Voices: Sí! Sí!)

"What we have resolved here should be published tonight so that all the world shall know, within and without the Fatherland, the action taken and the motives and reasons that I have in refusing the presidency and in accepting the command of the Army."

The man whom he looked for and found was John Booby. He was named President by the Congress on the 23rd of May.

All this, of course, was strictly contrary to the Constitution and the laws of the land. Gómez's ignoring of them, ignorance of them, rather, is typical. And his naïve belief that his arbitrary methods with the Congress of the nation would be considered justified by the public by his feeble explanation of motives, is ludicrous. It shows how primitive, still, his concept of democratic political government was, how steeped he was in the political traditions of the caudillos from Páez down to Castro, how imbued with the spirit of complete dominance of the caciques of his mountain tribe. He was completely primitive in everything political, his only concession to modern liberalism being his repeated phrases, "If you agree" and "If you will authorize me" and to paternalism, constant allusions to Work and Peace and Progress. And, as a matter of fact, it took no more than these few thin phrases to fool the world. Not his own country, of course, but most of the outside world.

He blandly ignored the legal questions which his demands involved and gave all the Congressmen fifteen thousand bolívars. The cabinet ministers and the members of the Supreme Court dug into their law volumes and racked their brains to make changes in the Constitution that would legalize the thing they had to do. They made a lot of changes, finally, that made a mess of contradictions out of the nation's basic code.

The two-year duration of Juan Bautista Pérez's administration was marked by the same methods of delegated power operations that had been characteristic of the earlier dictatorships of Páez and Guzmán Blanco. In this case the free action of the dummy President was even more closely curtailed, for Gómez maintained much closer contact with affairs than Páez had been able to from his hacienda at San Pablo or Blanco from Paris. It was a situation where the so-called President attended to all the minor details of governmental functioning and the dictator sat in his country paradise and made all the decisions.

With the naming of the new President, although it was against all probability, a faint glimmer of hope was born in the minds of the people that Pérez might prove to be more of a man than he appeared. Perhaps, with the opportunity at his hand, he might rise above his mediocrity and react against the dictator. He might, conceivably, find new strength in his sudden exaltation and strike a blow in the interest of democracy. In this hope they were disappointed. They were quickly disillusioned. The Cadaver was found, in truth, to be "rotten within twenty-four hours."

The same old methods, the same suppression of the press, of the airwaves, of free speech, of the right of assembly; methods of discrimination, of monopolies and favoritism. No liberation of political prisoners, not one gesture of sympathy toward the people.

On the 17th of December, the anniversary of the death of Bolívar, the Liberator, a day of general mourning throughout Venezuela, of Te Deums in the cathedrals, the women of Caracas organized a demonstration and petitioned Pérez to free the prisoners. A large body of citizens, composed mostly of the women relatives of the students and other "enemies of the Cause" who were incarcerated, appeared before the Bolívar House in the center of the city, the birthplace of the Liberator and something of a national shrine. They filled the streets in a solid mass. They knelt down on the asphalt and the cement sidewalks and prayed, asking the help of God for their men.

While the women were on their knees, a rumor spread among them, a wave of whispering filtered through the crowd and it grew into joyful shouting. "The prisoners have been liberated! The prisoners are leaving the Rotunda this very minute!"

The whole mass rose to its feet and moved in a body toward the Rotunda, going as fast as the narrow streets would permit, the women laughing hysterically, uttering thanks to God. They ran headlong to greet their sons and husbands.

As they approached the Rotunda their spirits fell. There was no sign of liberation there. The same grim walls, the same massive doors, iron-barred and silent. The solid mass of people pushed up to the entrance.

They saw that they had been misled and, in their misery and resentment, began to shout maledictions.

Suddenly, without warning, a roar of rifle fire burst from the prison walls, directly down upon the solid mass of people. There were four killed and forty wounded, mostly women. This was on the anniversary of the death of Bolívar, the Liberator, whom Juan Vicente revered so much.

The leaders of this demonstration were women of some of the best families of Caracas. Among them were Señora Dolores de Blanco, mother of the imprisoned poet, Andres Eloy Blanco, Señora Carmen de Lony, wife of General Mibely, Señora Adelina de Silva Pérez, Señoras de Ponte, de Vegas, de Arraiz, de Gabaldón and the young señoritas of these families.

Radically exterminate were the orders of the Catfish and John Booby was his man to any extreme.

On May 22, 1930, Gómez sent a letter to President Pérez pointing out that there was a balance of ninety million bolívars in the national treasury and asking that the external debt of nineteen million bolívars be paid off in full. Congress passed the bill authorizing the payment the very next day. In the great acclaim that was given this act by the press of Caracas and the ministers of Venezuela in foreign lands, all credit was given to Gómez and nothing odd was seen in the fact of such an act originating with one who was nominally only the Commander of the Army.

The John Booby farce came to an end in June, 1931, after Pérez had served only two years of the seven year term which the Venezuelan Constitution allowed.

The process by which Gómez accomplished the removal of the straw man and his own reinstatement was also somewhat "genial."

He let it become known to Pérez (his secretaries, José García and Rafael Requena were particularly adept at getting their little veiled interpretations of his desires over to the nominal lawmakers) that he rather felt the urge to be President again in name as well as fact. Pérez resigned at once and faded, probably gladly, back into obscurity.

Again the Sovereign Congress repaired en masse to Maracay. They came, pleading that the Well-Deserving sacrifice himself and respond to the great need of the country that was tottering on the brink of ruination and return to the presidency. He was the only one who could save the nation. The words of Martínez this time were to the effect that Gómez was needed ". . . to solve the serious political disturbances that have come to agitate the public opinion during your absence and to deal with the economic depression that is beginning to be felt with great intensity in the Republic."

Gómez had heard something of the criticism that his arbitrary juggling with the Constitution in his last shifting of the presidency had caused and he was more wary this time. He flatly refused to take office.

He said, "I cannot see clearly the legality of any means which could be taken for this procedure and under no conditions will I accept the presidency."

The Congress returned to the capital. The members knew what was expected of them this time. Gómez's words had hinted at it and their soft-footed contact men had suggested it. The changes in the Constitution were to be made beforehand, this time. Accordingly, the Congress elected the Minister of Foreign Affairs, Itriago Chacín, Provisional President, and immediately set about making the necessary reforms in the national laws. Then they elected Gómez President under the new provisions. They sent him a telegram which stated, "In the midst of scenes of wild enthusiasm, during which the public filled the halls of Congress, shouting, 'Viva Juan Vicente!' the deputies have today elected unanimously General Juan Vicente Gómez President of the Republic. The Constitution will be reformed, conferring upon the President extraordinary powers."

Gómez sent a telegram to Congress on June 20: "I have studied, patriotically, your letter of the 6th in which you insist in the demand that I assume the direction of the national destinies, accepting the presidency of the Republic, as the only remedy for the salvation of the country. You have invoked the Fatherland to persuade me. Never have I hesitated to work for its greatness and prosperity. . . . Continuing as Chief of the Army and assuming the duties, attributes and responsibilities of the administration and with complete authority to reorganize the Republic, I shall be disposed to attend your desires."

The two reasons which had been hit upon as the excuses for the need of the dictator's return to the presidency, the things that were causing the "ruination of the Republic," were political disturbances and the economic depression.

During the Pérez administration there had been no more such political disturbances than there had been when Gómez was President. Furthermore, Gómez had remained Commander of the Army during this period and as such was responsible for the suppression of these things just as he would have been had he been President. It was for this purpose, he had said, that he wanted to be named Chief of the Army. In his own words he had taken the responsibility of maintaining the peace and had promised to suppress any uprising. He had said, "In respect to the Army, it was I who organized it and I am responsible to the country for the tranquillity of Venezuela. With this Army, commanded by me . . . the enemies will know well not to bring any action against the Republic."

As for the economic depression, there was no nation

on earth that had felt the effects of the depression so little. From 1922 till 1930, through the early part of the depression, the nation's income and balance over expenditures had increased on a steady upward curve to reach a peak that made its financial condition perfectly secure for quite a few years to come, even if income should be almost wiped out. Petroleum production increased, though at a retarded rate, throughout the whole depression. Less than a year before, in May, 1930, Gómez had written to Pérez commenting on the prosperity of the country, mentioning the ninety million bolívars balance in the treasury and asking the payment of the foreign debt. Now, according to Congress, the nation faced economic ruin.

It is true that, after 1930, the national income fell off sharply and the bolívar dropped from the normal exchange rate of twenty cents of the American dollar to fourteen cents, but just the same, at the very lowest point, the end of 1931, the expenditures were only forty million bolívars over income and there was a balance of forty million bolívars in the treasury. And this was against an all-time peak in expenditures, no curtailments having yet been made.

The whole thing was ridiculous anyway, for Gómez had been President in reality all the time and John Booby hadn't made a single important move without consulting him.

After Gómez assumed office again, there was no apparent change in the course of things at all. He continued to stay in Maracay and the cabinet ministers continued to go there for their meetings. The only differences were that the decrees were now signed by their real author instead of by Juan Bautista Pérez and were dated Maracay, instead of Caracas.

The Caraqueños said that Pérez used to get the official papers from Maracay and sign them without

looking at them. On one afternoon, after he had signed
a whole sheaf of papers naming individuals to various
government posts, he called his secretary and asked him
to bring in the new copy of the *Official Gazette.*

"I want," he said, "to find out what appointments
the President made this morning."

Chapter XXVIII

THE OLD MAN OF THE SAMÁNES

❖

THE valley of the Aragua and the valley of Lake Valencia that it opens into are high, but the mountains rise still higher around them. The breezes are shut off and the valleys lie in still, burning heat. The sun is a blazing ball set in the turquoise dome and the light that floods the valleys is so brilliant that the shadows under the spreading samán trees seem black. All the shadows seem black. The shadows of the adobe walls in the towns, black, on the cobblestones and in the corners of arched courts; the shadow of a peon and his loaded donkeys, black, moving along the blazing white road; the coffee bushes living coolly in the black shadows of their mother-trees.

The samán trees dot the cultivated valleys, low and flat and wide-spreading, very dark green the thick foliage; and the old man who sits under them is dappled with black shadows.

The concrete road twists along the base of the hills. The flat valley stretches away, fields of cane and grassy meadows with cattle huddled against the fences, wandering streams of clear water. The road is wide and smooth. The turns are banked and wider still, the outside edges are lined with sturdy concrete rails, the fills are retained by stone masonry. The bridges over the little streams that come out of the tributary valleys are concrete and steel and freshly calcimined.

The road follows the valley of the Aragua till it joins

the valley of the lake and then it divides and circles the lake, twenty-five miles long and ten miles wide. It goes on to the city of Valencia and then turns north and follows another valley, through narrow mountain gorges, thirty miles to Puerto Cabello on the Caribbean coast. At Maracay, on the northern shore of the lake, two branches of it go north, the thirty miles to the coast, one to the collapsed boom-city of Turiamo, and at the eastern end of the lake a branch goes south over a range of hills, thirty miles to San Juan de los Moros.

In the dry season the valleys are still green with irrigation but the hills are parched and brown. Fires crackle on their slopes and billows of blue smoke hang over the meadows. At night the hilltops are ringed with thin halos of flickering, dull red. The trees are dry skeletons.

When the rains begin to come, before the new leaves uncurl, the apamate trees blaze out with brilliant yellow clusters, showering the brown hillsides and green valleys with fixed rocket fire. The yellow fades out and then the bucare bursts and the glowing masses are deep orange. The orange fades and the deep red of poinciana and flamboyant follow quickly like the finale of a celebration. The display is over then, the fireworks are drowned out by the increasing rains and all the hills are green again.

All along the road are fine haciendas. There are neat, rambling houses, brightly tinted, showing bits of themselves from shading samán trees, half-hidden in their rich fields that wander up the fissures between the hills.

All of these are of the Gómezs. All along the valley of the Aragua and in the valley of the lake and in the valleys that lead to the coast and that go south to San Juan de los Moros, the cultivated lands and the comfortable houses belong to the Gómezs. The straw-thatched and adobe huts that squat near them are of the farm laborers and vaqueros. The haciendas of Gonzalo, of José Vicente, of Servilia, of Belén, of Mísia Amelia, of Josefina, of Flor de María, of Hermenegilda, of Rosa, in the valleys and stretching over the rolling hills.

They all have their haciendas. They all have, as well, houses in the town of Maracay, houses in the residential section of Caracas, houses at San Juan de los Moros, where there are mineral springs, and houses on the sea-coast at Macuto.

Juan Vicente has his own haciendas and houses at all of these places and he lives a sort of migratory life among them. He lives mostly at his house at Las Delícias, up in the narrow, wooded valley of a small stream, a few miles out of Maracay.

He is getting old and he is thin, now, with the wrinkled thinness that follows stoutness. He rises at daybreak. He is so set on early rising that he has ordered military bands to march about the streets of Maracay at daybreak, playing loudly, so that no one will be able to sleep late. The Indian, Tarazona, brings him a cup of caldo, the hot, onion broth of the Andes. Tarazona tastes the liquid himself, first, and Gómez watches him. Then Tarazona helps the old man to dress.

He goes into his small office and his secretary, Requena, is there with his brief-case bulging. There are several hours of work. Gómez gives his orders and Requena takes notes and transcribes the words into grammatic Spanish. The old man still speaks in mountain vernacular.

After the paper work is finished, callers will be received—people of every sort, most of them asking for something.

Then, if it is Sunday, the old man's cronies will be there, dark-skinned men with short necks and glittering black eyes, and there will be cock-fights at the pit near by. After that, the cars will be driven up and the General will go for a paseo. Perhaps old Pimentel will go along or perhaps the muchachos, if they aren't away at one of the other establishments or carousing in Caracas. The motorcycle escort will lead the way and the cars will roll along the smooth, straight, paved road to Maracay. Shade trees line the road and the hills rise on both sides. On the way, there is a low, adobe house beside the road. Gómez had it built and it is supposed to be a replica of the house in which he was born, La Mulera. But it is a glorified version of the house at La Mulera and he wasn't born there anyway.

The party skirts the town of Maracay by the back streets and turns west along the road to Valencia. A few miles of this road, and then a left turn is made onto a broad boulevard that is lined with modern lighting standards. It is lost in uninhabited desolation and has the air of an abandoned Florida boom-town. On the right is a wide field and a hangar. This is the commercial flying field that belongs to the Venezuelan air line. The boulevard is short and ends at the lakeshore at a spot called Boca del Rio.

There is a park here, also lost in desolation. It is filled with concrete figures and monuments of Mayan and Incan motifs. It was built at the suggestion of Requena who is something of a student of archeology. There are flower gardens and fountains and masonry retaining walls. There is a pavilion of Modernistic-Mayan design with a dance-floor and flood-lighting. Near by are the straw huts of the peon caretakers and usually the goats and pigs and chickens root around among the lonely paths of the park. When Gómez is coming they are hurriedly shooed away.

Below the park stretches Lake Valencia—clear, green water, green hills rising across it, green islands scattered over its surface.

There is a cobbled wharf for the three steam ferry boats that are used to bring Gómez's cattle to the abattoir in Maracay, providing a short-cut from his great hacienda at Guigüe in the hills across the lake. Riding at anchor are seven or eight bright new speedboats that belong to the muchachos and the other boys of the Gómez clan.

Next, a stop will be made at one of the cattle farms on the road back to Maracay. Here the General will get out of the car and wander among the clean, modern barns and feeding sheds, looking over the animals with an expert eye, asking questions of the attendants, pointing with his walking-stick. He is dressed in loose-fitting khaki, as usual, wears high boots, a wide Panamá hat and tortoise-shell-rimmed glasses. The group that accompanies him trails along a few steps behind and all the attendants fall away ahead and stand, fixed, in an attitude of anxious servility like slaves before a maharajah. Nevertheless, the old man is very genial. He smiles constantly and addresses personal remarks to the workers, always using the intimate form, tu.

"How are things going? You are all happy, no? Good?"

He has become a little garrulous with old age. He talks in a musing sort of way, to himself rather than to anyone in particular, talks in his characteristic short phrases, reminiscing, giving bits of information about past events.

"When I came here there was nothing. I built all this. That is good, no? To build something where there was nothing. They used to starve here in the dry season. A man was killed by a tiger once, right over there. I have an electric plant there now.

"Mendoza came right down that road there. That was in the time of Castro. I caught him at Villa de Cura. I caught him asleep in his chinchorro in the plaza and he hadn't time to get his boots on. Diverting, eh?

"They didn't know what meat was in Caracas. They were eating carrion. I showed them what good meat was. They eat good meat in Caracas now.

"That little pump there. You see it? I found a spring there that the animals were polluting and I cleaned it out and put in a pump and now the water keeps the potrero green all year.

"I built the new road around the Samán and had the experts fix the tree up and I built the bronze fence around it. Bolívar sat under that tree and it should never die, don't you agree?

"I put everyone to work here, do you see? There are no vagabonds here. I sent word to Velasco, if there are any vagabonds there, send them to me that they may be put to work. He sent me many and Pérez Soto sent me many, too. There is no unemployment in Venezuela. Good, don't you agree?

"I went along the Sierra and I told the bad ones that if they wouldn't work I would burn their ranches. I burned many.

"I saw in a dream that Fernández would pass a place on the Sierra of Carabobo where there was a cross-roads and a little shrine. I called a vaquiano of the locality and asked him if there was a cross-roads and a shrine at that place and he said yes and I hurried there and defeated Fernández."

Passing through the narrow streets of Maracay the dark peons stand in the doorways of their one-story adobe huts. The houses are old and poorly-made like the houses of a small village. Maracay was never anything but a small village and is a small village still except for the things that Gómez has built. There are some buildings that have been remodeled and made into government department offices.

In a narrow, congested section beside the railway

station is the industrial center. There is a long, three-story, many-windowed building that extends for a block and the hum of machinery lies on the still air. That is the cotton mill. Near by is the abattoir. It is a new, concrete building with open courts, washed clean, long, covered corrals for the animals, frames for drying meat, white counters where aproned workers make sausages and spiced meat by-products. There is a plant where hides are tanned. There is an ice plant and a fleet of huge, stream-lined, aluminum-painted refrigerator trucks wait at the landing platforms to carry meat to Caracas. No other meat is sold in the capital.

Across the street is the dairy. There are long milking-sheds with mechanical milkers and a laboratory with foreign chemists at work.

Further up the street is the factory for making candles, soap, cooking oils and synthetic perfumes.

Everything is orderly and efficient-looking. Barbed wire fences with galvanized pipe framework surround the factories.

The quarters of the laborers extend in solid blocks over the level ground. They are one-storied adobe huts, much like the other houses of the town. There is no electric light nor plumbing and the people bathe and wash their clothes in the stream that runs by.

It is noon now and the cars pass through the old part of the town, the old, ill-kept plaza with its statues covered with white bird-droppings, and come to the wide, new paseo.

The paseo extends for some two miles. It is of concrete, extremely wide, with center gardens and statues along its length.

At this time on Sunday morning it is crowded with people walking or sitting on the benches and children roller-skating. Military bands play at various points, so many of them that their music overlaps. Automobiles overloaded with family parties and dressed-up, carousing young peons pass in an endless chain on both sides of the parkway. There are khaki uniforms everywhere. The direct rays of the sun draw a white glare from the concrete roadway and the buildings that line it. Everything, in spite of the tempering of green from the parkway, is washed in a white brilliance that brings water to the eyes. The dark natives don't seem to mind.

Along one side of the paseo extends the huge army barracks that houses fifteen thousand men. Behind it is a vast, level plain for cavalry and artillery maneuvers. Close by is the military aviation school with its hangars and sixteen planes. The new aviation school is well under way but is not yet finished—a fine concrete and stucco building of modern architecture. Across the paseo is the new Military College. The old one in Caracas has remained closed ever since the plot of 1928 and Gómez has built this new one so that he can keep the young cadets under his own eye.

On that side, too, is a club for the wealthy Gómez amigos. There is a swimming-pool and tennis courts. On the same side and next door to it, begins the vast length of the Hotel Jardín.

At the entrance, the motorcycle escort draws up, the white-jacketed attendants dash out under the canopy and open the doors of the cars as they come up. The General will lunch with his amigos at the hotel.

It is a two-story building that extends for two thousand feet along the paseo. There are four hundred rooms, all with large, modern, tiled bathrooms. Each has its balcony with double French doors. There are spacious patios and gardens, huge lounges, wide, mirrored corridors and a modern bar. It is not ornate. It is vast and cool and in simple taste. The manager is a Swiss and all the attendants are young Swiss. Except when Gómez is there or his amigos have collected in

Maracay for some festivity, it will be almost vacant. Frequently there are no guests at all and the great corridors are in deathly silence except for the echoing calls of the birds in the patios and the whistling of the Swiss lads in the kitchens.

The Jardín is one of four such hotels that Gómez built and foisted upon the nation. He built them in the out-of-the-way places that only he and his friends visited and where there was no earthly demand or need for them. All of them remained almost absolutely empty ninety per cent of the time. Besides the Jardín, there is the Miramar, at Macuto on the seacoast near La Guayra, the San Juan de Los Moros at the mineral springs near Maracay that Gómez developed and visited every few weeks for a day or so, and the Independencia on the beach at Ocumare near the site of the exploded-dream city, Turiamo. The Miramar gets a few luncheon customers from the tourist ships that spend a day in La Guayra but aside from that, like all the others, it has always been a place of morgue-like silence. Occasionally, when Gómez takes it into his head to visit one of these places, the horde of satellites flocks there and it becomes a scene of brilliant activity for one night.

The General built these hotels so that he would have a place of suitable comfort for his friends wherever he cared to go. He built them with government materials and government labor and everything that was used in them came into the country duty-free. He made a long-term contract with a business associate, a Swiss named Becker, for their operation. When they were completed, he sold them to the nation, along with the management contract, at an enormous profit. So he had his hotels for himself and to show to foreign visitors, made a nice sum of money, and left the nation to sustain the loss inevitable to their operation.

After lunch the old man would retire for a short siesta. Tarazona stood guard at the door.

In the late afternoon perhaps there would be a bull-fight. Gómez had built a new bull-ring, much superior to either of the two in the capital and said to be the finest in South America. He had a ranch where he kept fighting bulls, imported from Spain, and he brought matadors over especially to fight them in his own ring. When he died, he had contracted with Juan Belmonte to appear in Maracay.

Sometimes he would drive in to Caracas to see his horses run at the race-track he had built there.

If there were no bull-fights on that Sunday, the General would drive back to Las Delicías and spend the afternoon in his park there.

There is a zoo at Las Delicías, the personal property of Juan Vicente. There, in the narrow valley of the swift-flowing stream, shaded with great, tropical trees, he has his little Paradise. The animal cages are clean and devoid of the odor that seems to be an indispensable part of zoos everywhere else. The waters of the stream have been diverted and a swift, clear current flows in a narrow concrete trench through every one of the cages. There are wading pools for the birds and natural bits of screened-in jungle for the monkeys and other harmless animals. There are animals which have been sent as gifts for the Well-Deserving from all over the world.

The old man wanders along the paths among the cages, entranced by the animals. He knows every one of them, his habits and peculiarities. He stops before a fenced, concrete pool of water.

"Ven!" he says. "Ven, tu!" "Come! Come!"

The surface of the water ripples and slowly, the great, shiny bulk of the hippopotamus emerges from the pool and fixes his beady eyes on the old man.

Gómez turns to his friends and smiles. "Do you see?" he says.

"The hippopotamus," the Caraqueños say, "comes when he calls, like the Papal Nuncio."

When the sun goes down over the hill and the shadows in the valley grow long, he will go and sit on the balcony over the swimming-pool and watch his friends and his children playing about in the water.

Then he will go to the pavilion and listen to the orchestra play and watch the people dance. He sits, smiling, keeping time with his wide-spread fingers. He is seventy-two years old, but somewhere among the friends who have gathered, there will be a nicely dressed and pretty young girl who is accompanied by a nurse-maid who holds one of his infant children.

In the evening he will go to his theater and see the movies. Nothing but news-reels are shown. He has every news-reel that is issued sent out to Maracay and he goes to see them every night. He sees the same ones over again if there are not enough new ones. He watches them with silent intensity and afterwards he will ask questions of the "men of talent" about the subjects dealt with. For years he has learned everything he knows of the outside world from news-reels. He mutters to himself, "Que le parece! What do you think of that!" at the wonders which he sees.

He is building a new theater in Maracay. It is huge, modern in design, much finer than any other theater in the country. It is much too fine for this little isolated village, the whole adult population wouldn't fill it, but it isn't too fine for the mighty one.

All the artists of the world that come to Venezuela come out here to perform for the General. Opera companies, musicians, famous orchestras, dancers, performers of every sort, come out to appear before the dictator before their regular engagements begin in the nation's capital. The artists are put up at the Jardín and they are entertained by the General's officials. They are offered gifts of money and the old man pats the women and sometimes kisses their hands. Lydia de Rivera said, like the American journalist, that "his voice was like a caress."

Chapter XXIX

A MODICUM OF ESTIMATION AND CRITICISM

❖

HE maintained the peace. That is probably the greatest achievement of all the achievements attributed to him. And we must concede him credit for it, with reservations, if we do not consider the nature of the peace nor the methods used to maintain it.

The reservations have to do with all the revolutionary movements that actually did occur, all those that we have been recounting, the disturbances to the peace that began with his usurpation of power and continued almost without interruption during his whole reign. They were so quickly done with and news of them so well-suppressed that, for the outside world, the visiting traveler and the interests of foreign enterprises, their effects were minimized to the extent that the country did present the semblance of peace for the whole period. And that is something.

As for the cost of that peace to the Venezuelans, it was very, very high. It cost their political liberty. It cost their freedom of speech, of press, of right of assembly, of movement about the world, of private communication. It cost them their right to representation in Congress, to trial by jury and the right of selecting their executive. It nullified their Constitution as completely as though it had never been written. Of course a lot of people will say that they never deserved to have those things, that they weren't capable of self-government anyway, and we will not discuss the matter with those people at all for we have no common ground.

As for the nature of the peace, we have seen something of that. It was the peace of blind, unholy terror. It is significant that thousands were ready to face death and much worse rather than enjoy it.

He accomplished economic stability for the nation. That is true, without any reservations at all. He took over the power when the nation was burdened with a foreign debt of one hundred and thirty-five million bolívars and an internal debt of sixty-seven million and its income was four million bolívars under the expenditures for that year. When he died there was no foreign nor internal debt at all and there was a balance of some ninety-six million bolívars in the treasury. The nation had weathered the world-wide economic depression. From the low point of 1931 there was a sharp upward turn in income and the expenditures were curtailed so that by the end of 1932 and from then on, they were some fifteen million bolívars per year less than revenues. The exchange rate of the bolívar, normally twenty cents of the American dollar, after passing through the early depression years when the United States remained on the gold standard at a depreciation which reached a low of fourteen cents, rose to an all-time high of twenty-nine cents in the early months of 1936. Besides, there had been hundreds of millions of bolívars spent on public works. The nature of these public works from the standpoint of their benefit to the people at large, their excessive cost, and the fact that almost an equal amount was spent on the army by a nation that needed no defense whatever against foreign enemies are other matters.

In his economic accomplishments it is true that Gómez was extremely lucky in two things—the increased prices of raw materials that Venezuela produced, brought about by the World War and the discovery of petroleum and its rapid exploitation. But his handling of the petroleum development so that the nation would receive its just benefits against the cunning of avaricious foreign exploiters was not luck at all, it was sheer economic sagacity. And the fact remains that he had advanced well along the road to financial stability before the World War and before the discovery of petroleum.

Economically, he accomplished great things but those things were first and foremost for Juan Vicente Gómez. The nation benefited slightly, somewhat by accident, as in the case of the money spent in the land by the foreign oil workers, and somewhat because Gómez's egotism and his sometimes almost childish desire to be well thought of in foreign countries led him to spend money on public improvements. However, even these were usually planned so that his own business enterprises were the ones to receive the most benefit. His motives were personal, not patriotic. He owned the nation and it was up to him to make it pay him as he had made his hacienda at San Antonio pay him. If his accomplishments could be made to appear motivated by patriotism through a little inexpensive propaganda, the old man was doubly delighted.

The claim that was often made by his admirers that Venezuela was a nation without taxes levied upon its people is not true. There were no direct taxes and no income tax. The reasons for that is obvious. No one except those in the potrero would have been able to pay them. But there were indirect taxes, plenty of them. The tariff on imports was extremely high, there were stamp taxes and stamped paper taxes on every sort of transaction, on bank checks, on telegrams, on permits to move about the country, on permits to cross rivers and board vessels and disembark from vessels. There were taxes on cigarettes and liquors. And there were direct taxes, too, that did not appear on the law books, the arbitrary levies of the petty tyrants scattered all over the interior of the country—the jefe civiles. These were taxes imposed upon the small farmers and cattle-raisers, the fishermen along the coast, the village shop-keepers and the arrieros who transported local products by pack-train.

He is credited with freeing the country from banditry and making it safe for travelers in the interior. That is true only to a limited degree for the country always was largely free from banditry. By his disarming of the people and his summary dealing with criminals when they were caught, he did discourage robbery and violence so that it became practically non-existent. But there never was much of things of the sort. Long before his time people traveled into the remote regions along the lonely trails on foot or mounted. There were no banks, as we know them, where one can obtain funds by writing a check, and money had to be carried in large sums, sufficient to last the duration of the journey. Paper money was little used, not accepted in many places, and silver coins were carried in leather bags on a burro's back. Yet there were few robberies, even then.

To the claim that Gómez brought contentment and prosperity to the people we can only say that it is not true. How can a people be contented under the dominance of such sadistic tyrants as Eustóquio Gómez and Santos Matute and all the little, illiterate jefe civiles that were scattered over the whole country? It is true that in the seaports and the petroleum centers where the peons came in contact with the free-spending tourists and other foreigners, they had come to demand high wages and to present a false appearance of prosperity. But their pockets were usually empty and their earthly possessions still amounted to a hammock to sleep in, a mud hut, some discarded tin-cans for cooking utensils.

The streets of Caracas are still over-run with horribly diseased beggars.

The villages in the interior are as badly or even worse off than they were under Castro. There are a few newly-paved streets and a new fence around the plaza and a statue or two but that is all. All of them have diminished in population, the men going to the capital or to the petroleum centers in the hope of participating in this much-touted prosperity. The domestic servants and farm peons are still virtually slaves. The daily wage, when any is received, for women who work fourteen hours, is still one or two bolívars. In 1928 there was an old woman in the town of Barcelona who lived solely on the output of two hens. She sold the eggs for three cents apiece to the American oil men who lived there.

If the peons of the Venezuelan interior bear the look of contentment it is because of their natural dispositions; because they can always dig up a yucca root and pound it for casabe and pluck a plantain from a stalk; because they can go naked till they are eight or ten and then make a pair of pants out of a cement sack that will last, with an unbelievable amount of patching, the rest of their lives. It has nothing to do with the national prosperity accomplished by Juan Vicente Gómez. They don't know anything about that.

Next in importance to the maintenance of peace and the economic salvation of the nation among the achievements of Gómez comes his program of public works. Of this program, his road-building has been the most highly publicized.

We have spoken of the excessive cost of the roads he built, of the grafting that was involved on the part of the officials charged with their construction. Now let us look at the extent of road-building that was actually accomplished.

Foreign tourists who leave their ship at La Guayra

and take the one-day automobile trip to Caracas, to Maracay, to Valencia and rejoin their ship at Puerto Cabello have traveled over more than fifty per cent of the paved roads of Venezuela.

Let us look at the map of Venezuela again. If we draw a quadrilateral, beginning at the town of Puerto Cabello on the northern coast, go southwest to Tinaquillo, then due east to San Juan de Los Moros, then northeast to Macuto, east of La Guayra, to close the quadrilateral with the coast, we have inclosed an area of approximately two thousand, one hundred square miles. It is one two-hundredth part of the whole area of the country. And within that area are absolutely all of the paved roads of Venezuela. And practically all of the bridges as well.

That area is the field of activities, the scene of all the goings and comings of Juan Vicente Gómez for the last twenty-five years of his life. He never moved outside of that area. It is the area, too, that was visited by practically one hundred per cent of foreign travelers, exclusive of oil men, who came to the country. In it were all the places that Gómez visited for business or pleasure—Macuto, Los Teques, San Juan de Los Moros, Maracay, Ocumare, Turiamo, Guigüe—all his industries and homes. In it are all four of the huge hotels that he built. In it he spent ninety per cent of all the money spent on public works during his rule and in it lives only ten per cent of the nation's population.

He built paved roads and bridges everywhere where it was for his interest and comfort to do so. Their use to other people wasn't considered any more than in the cases of his parks lost in the wilderness around Maracay, his hotels, his zoo and his bull-ring and theater. He built paved roads that ended at his hacienda gates. He built seventy miles of paved road from Maracay to one of his haciendas near the coast and to Ocumare that were used by no one at all but himself, and forty-five miles around Lake Valencia to his farm at Guigüe, these alone comprising over one-third of the total mileage of the nation's paved roads. These figures are exclusive of the few miles of paved streets that exist in some of the larger towns.

He built roads so that he and his friends could travel quickly and comfortably, so that he could move his troops rapidly into Caracas and to a port of embarkation on the coast.

As for the rest of the country, the three hundred and eighty thousand square miles of the rest of it, one can imagine, when it is considered that only ten per cent of the funds for road building was spent on it. Even at that, the ten per cent was a lot of money for the work that was actually done. The roads in the interior are all dirt roads, or gravel, if the natural earth happened to be gravelly. They are mostly what is called "natural roads," roads made by the traffic of pack-trains and moving herds of cattle.

In the dry season it is possible to travel by car over the Great Eastern Highway the four hundred and fifty miles from Caracas to Ciudad Bolívar in four days. In the rainy season the road is practically impassable. The side-roads are impassable in any season. It is possible to travel over the Great Trans-Andean Highway along the Cordillera to San Cristóbal at any season but it is a rough and lengthy journey. The pack-train is still the only dependable means of travel and transportation in the interior of Venezuela.

If some hardy youth wants something in the way of back-breaking work—not romantic adventure, though, as writers are inclined to picture it—let him attempt to drive a car from Caracas, say to Barcelona on the eastern coast. In the rainy season he won't get far. He will be bogged down on an average of every two hundred yards

FOURTEEN TONS OF LEG-IRONS THROWN INTO THE SEA AT PUERTO CA
AFTER GÓMEZ DIED

GRILLO, OR LEG-IRON, OF SEVENTY POUNDS

THE OLD MAN OF THE SAMÁNES

HIS BODY GOES TO THE CEMETERY BUT
THE PEOPLE DON'T REMOVE THEIR
HATS

"THE PEOPLE DEMAND THE IMPRISON-
MENT OF THE ASSASSIN, VELASCO"

and will be stopped permanently at the first flooding stream he attempts to rush through. In the dry season he'll make it but he'll know he's been through something. He'll wonder, if he knows about it, if the work that was done on this road was worth all the thousands of bolívars spent as well as the lives of all the young "enemies of the Cause" who died on it.

In his road-building, Gómez was something of an innocent victim of his amigos. He really believed that a lot more was being done than there was. No one, of course, would ever give him any but good reports and he was deceived constantly. For instance, he was shown a photograph of a section of the Great Eastern Highway that pleased him so much that he had it published in the papers. It showed a straight stretch of broad, smooth road that disappeared at the horizon. Here is what had been done. The particular piece of road was over the sandy llanos of eastern Guárico. The road workers had cleared off the grass and smoothed the white sand to a beautiful, straight, sixty feet wide boulevard. But, when the photograph was taken, if the camera had been pointed just a little to the right, it would have taken in the deep, twisting ruts of the single-track, "natural" road that all the cars that passed that way followed. They didn't dare go onto the smooth highway. The first ones that tried it nearly buried themselves in the sand.

In the way of development of industry Gómez never did anything except for himself and his friends. He modernized and improved his own industries but he suppressed those of others by unfair competition. When he had created a monopoly by these means, he took advantage of it by boosting prices. He monopolized the meat business of Caracas and then put the price up to unreasonable levels. He produced the only butter in Venezuela and kept the price at well over a dollar a pound. Imported tinned butter was just a little lower and no one but the wealthy could afford either.

The city of Valencia had been the center of the cotton industry for many years. The existence of the city depended almost entirely on the industry. The methods used in the factories were old-fashioned and no efforts had been made at expansion. Nevertheless, the factories had produced good, cheap cotton goods in quantities sufficient for the nation's needs. Gómez decided to modernize the industry. He built a large factory at Maracay with government materials and labor, he hired foreign dye chemists and fabric experts, he imported modern machinery and dye-stuffs duty-free. When he had ruined the cotton industry of Valencia he raised his prices higher than those of the old, inefficient factories.

All of Gómez's methods, political and social, had precedents somewhere back along the line in Venezuelan history. He introduced nothing new. Like Páez he loved money and killed his enemies. Like Blanco he used arbitrary methods with Congress and delegated the presidential power to others. He knew no other methods than these and probably saw nothing wrong in them. They were the ways of his country, had been the ways of his country throughout its history. So long as they were successful and the country prospered, they were the right ways. There was no argument. He knew nothing about such ridiculous things as political liberty and he didn't want his people to know anything about them.

It is interesting to observe that, with all his pretenses to modernism, he made no efforts in the way of public instruction. Absolutely none. His paid writers would have us believe that he did but actually he did not. He passed laws making schooling compulsory and then provided no schools. When he came into power, the yearly expenditures of the Department of Public Instruction amounted to a mere six million bolívars. It continued at close to that figure till 1927, all through the first nineteen years of his reign, through the vastly increased national revenue years of the war and the petroleum development. Then the expenditures were increased, slowly, to reach the amount of ten million bolívars yearly when other national expenditures had increased to a total of two hundred and sixty-five million. While the nation's yearly income had increased over five hundred per cent, the amount spent on public instruction had increased only sixty-six and two-thirds per cent. This, in twenty-five years. Two and one-half times as much was spent on the spy system.

He had a kind of patriotism after his fashion. He loved his country, the material country, the earth and the things that grew in it and the animals that roamed it. He wanted to live in it and enjoy it. Nothing outside it ever tempted him. He wanted to own it. After he had it, he could afford to indulge in a little benevolence to the other people who lived in it. He did that so long as the other people behaved themselves and didn't dispute his ownership.

He had a strong sense of family and clan loyalty but that is simply a form of egotism. He had a measure of loyalty to friends, also, but that, too, depended upon the person's behavior. He had been a friend of Castro for years but he sold him out as thoroughly as anyone was ever sold out, to get what he was after.

There is a vast psychological difference, of course, between the ordering of an act of cruelty and the perpetration of it. The difference is not of degree of guilt, for the one who orders is more accountable than the one who acts, but of psychological traits. It is doubtful, for instance, that Gómez, personally, would have aided in or even witnessed—though his son, Vicentico, did—the emasculation of a young boy. There is no instance given anywhere of any act of cruelty that he himself executed. His nature, apparently, was averse to the commission of acts of cruelty. At least it took no delight in it. It was cold, avaricious and calculating and capable of ordering cruelty without a qualm when his will was crossed but it avoided it on all other occasions. When his will was crossed, Gómez became absolutely implacable. He may even have been capable of executing cruelty himself on those occasions had it been necessary. Apparently his nature derived satisfaction not from the witnessing of the suffering of his enemies but in the knowledge that they did suffer because he had ordered it. It is conceivable that certain cruel natures could derive more pleasure out of murder accomplished by the pushing of a button far removed from the scene than by the bloody process of bludgeoning a skull. The very ease of it might well have its allure. Or it may be that there was no sadism in him at all, not even this indirect kind, and that he was driven to ordering these cruelties by his terrific thirst for absolute authority, believing that only by thus putting the fear of God into the people could he maintain that authority.

There are those who believe that Gómez was not really responsible for the acts of cruelty that were perpetrated during his rule, that he did not give definite orders and that he was kept in ignorance of the methods that were being used. Unfortunately, logic doesn't bear that out. Gómez knew his men very well. He had known Eustóquio and Velasco and the rest of them from childhood. He knew their natures as well as he knew his own. And his orders to them were definite enough for anybody. He sent word to them, "You must chastise them severely." "You must exterminate them radically." "You must obtain confessions." He knew exactly what such orders to such men would mean. He had them in the positions they occupied precisely because they were capable of doing the things which they did when he gave them orders like that.

In judging Juan Vicente Gómez by what he accomplished for his country, we must compare his accomplishments with what could have been done with these same opportunities by a man of equal mental talents who was blessed with democratic ideals. What a country would have been made of Venezuela.

Chapter XXX

THE VULTURES GATHER

❖

HE lay in his bare room in his house at Las Delícias. A photograph of himself hung on the wall and he had written on it, "I shall live to be a hundred years old." Beside it was a photograph of his mother, Hermenegilda.

He must live to be a hundred at least. He had to live until the young boys grew up. He was seventy-eight now and the youngest of them was five and it would be twenty years before he would be able to tell much about him. He must live to see one of them grow up to be worthy. Surely one, out of all the sons he had produced, would be worthy. He would raise these young ones differently. He had the time now and he would raise them himself and not leave them to the women who would make boobies out of them. He would take them back to the mountains and raise them himself. He would make them work and teach them to rope and brand and castrate bulls and maybe some of the strength of the bulls and of the mountain crags would grow into them and some of the coldness of the snowy peaks. They would grow up to be cold and strong. Surely out of all the sons, one would grow up to be cold and strong and intelligent as well.

He had worked very hard to produce these last sons. Time was growing short and he had worked desperately these last few years with new, strong young girls.

Maybe that's why the attacks were coming more frequently and lasting longer.

They had all failed him. One after another. Not one of them had been worthy. Vicentico had been cold and strong but he couldn't be trusted. He hadn't the clan spirit. You had to work with the clan, that was one of the first principles. Vicentico couldn't understand that and he never learned to use other people. He hadn't the far-sightedness. He had had high hopes of Vicentico for a while, too.

Gonzalo was a booby. He was strong but he wasn't cold enough and he had no ambition. He only liked to play baseball and drive his speed-boats.

Alí had been the intelligent one but he had been soft. Much too soft. Maybe he would have outgrown that. It was too bad he had died.

All the others had been riff-raff. They had been produced of unworthy women. Some of them had served well enough as colonels and jefe civiles but not one of them would do for anything better. The women were the key to the whole thing. The women had to be strong and intelligent like Hermenegilda had been.

The muchachos were worse than boobies. They hung around together, furtively, whispering to each other, sucking on their cigarettes. They wouldn't look you in the eye. They had never learned to work.

Maybe out of the young ones growing up there would be one. He must live to see to it, he must keep them away from Amelia and all the silly women and keep them away from Caracas and raise them in the mountains where all strong men were raised.

The brilliant sunlight made a square patch on the white-plastered wall. The square marched slowly with the hours, became elongated and marched across the face of Hermenegilda Chacón. The leaves of the samán tree stirred at the window. From up the narrow valley the sounds of the animals came faintly—the braying of the zebras, the squawks and chortlings of birds and occasionally the descending rumble of a lion. A peon prodded his pack-animal along the road and his voice drifted on the heavy air. "Mu-u-*la!*" "Mu-u-*la!*"

The attacks had been coming more and more frequently and lasting longer until there was scarcely an interval between them at all. The prostatitis had become aggravated and the accumulated poisons had caused uremia and now there was a diabetic condition as well. During the attacks the old man lay in a half-conscious state for days at a time and only occasionally would he stir and speak a few words.

The whole clan had gathered at Maracay. They moved on tiptoe about the house, whispering together, conjecturing, planning. Tarazona stood at the door to the General's room and admitted the doctors and those of the clan who were permitted to see him during his lucid moments.

Mísia Amelia was in a fine state. She fluttered about, wringing her hands, wondering what was going to become of them all, imploring the doctors to let her go in to see the "poor, dear General." She did get in quite often and she devoted the minutes given her to hurried propaganda. She wanted Gómez to marry her. At first she used what she thought were very subtle methods, fussing over the old man, smothering him with endearing and sympathetic words, moaning over what was going to become of her and her children; but they had no effect at all. The General didn't seem to get the idea. Then she resorted to direct attack and asked him outright to marry her. Gómez didn't answer her. He simply ignored the question, staring at the ceiling with his half-closed eyes. She kept up the attack, imploring him, begging him, on every occasion that she was admitted to his room. He never let on that he heard her.

Mísia Amelia was really quite desperate. None of her children had been recognized as had been the children of Dionisia and they had no legal civil rights whatever to share in the Gómez estate. Juan Vicente had always intimated that his second family had been recognized but no documents had ever been found to prove it. Amelia knew that and the other family knew it. And the General refused to make a will.

So a family feud waged silently over the General's sick-bed. Regina, Juan Vicente's sister, had never married and had always been closer to him than the others. She had always been rather partial to Dionisia and the earlier family and realized, now, that it was to her greater interest that there be only one family to share the spoils. She took charge of the negative propaganda. She, too, demanded permission to see the General as often as possible. She used every argument she could think of to convince him that it would be wrong to marry Mísia Amelia.

Among the men, apart from the matter of inheritance, there developed a bitter controversy over who was to succeed to the General's power. Gonzalo, who had never interested himself much in politics, suddenly felt the surge of new ambitions. Eustóquio and Santos Matute became aggressive and even the muchachos, under the urgings of Mísia Amelia, began to assert themselves, feebly. There had been no Vice-President since Gómez had abolished the office after the murder of Juancho, so now it rested with him who was to be his successor. The men moved about the house in Maracay, eyeing each other, whispering to their followers, secretly making plans to consolidate their partisans in the various parts of the country.

The Andean vultures hovered about the nest of the stricken eagle.

Whenever the news that the Catfish had another attack spread throughout Venezuela, in the mysteriously rapid way in which news always spreads in primitive countries, the people heard it with apathy. They had been hearing such news for years. They were used to it. Nothing ever came of the attacks; the Catfish always came out of them as mean as ever. That one would never die. Never. He was brujo. Nothing could ever be done against him and he would never die. He would go on forever, producing more and more of his hateful breed till they would spread like a pestilence over the whole land and consume everything in it. Why, he was seventy-eight and he was still having children! They said that Maracay was full of his young children, some of them only a few weeks old. They said that he had taken a new girl only yesterday, that he had danced a joropo at the pavilion at Las Delícias. Didn't that prove that he was brujo and would never die? Ordinary human beings couldn't do things like that at seventy-eight, no, señor.

Early in December of 1935 the dictator had a severe attack of prostatitis, complicated with uremia and diabetes. He went into a state of coma that lasted for over a week, the longest time he had yet passed in that condition. The doctors were alarmed. They worked over him frantically and succeeded in reviving him for a few short periods but he always relapsed into a stupor again and the middle of the month came and he was still the same.

The seriousness of this attack began to raise a flicker of hope in the people and apprehension in the government officials. The cabinet ministers and most of the members of Congress went out to Maracay and took up quarters at the Hotel Jardín. In one of his moments of consciousness Gómez asked Congress to name General Eleázar López Contreras, the Minister of War, as Provisional President to serve until he should be able to reassume the presidential duties himself. The Congress complied with the request immediately.

Here was a situation for the Gómez clan. Should the old man die now, Contreras would be President.

The truth has never come out and probably never will come out about the plots and counter-plots that were hatched around the death-bed of Juan Vicente. All sorts of stories are told; Eustóquio had three regiments in the hills surrounding Maracay with artillery trained on the army barracks; someone was feeding the old man ground glass and that was the real cause of his sickness. It is known, however, that the Indian, Tarazona, Gómez's servant and body-guard, was arrested and when they searched him he was found to have twenty thousand bolívars in bills wrapped by a cloth around his body under his clothes. It is known, too, that Gonzalo stood at the door of his father's room with his pistols drawn, ready to shoot any priest who tried to enter or any civil officer who might come to perform a marriage ceremony. It is known that Maracay was a hot-bed of plots, of clashing ambitions, of personal jealousies and hatreds. The whole Gómez clan was involved —Regina, Gonzalo, Eustóquio, Santos Matute, Mísia Amelia, the muchachos and all the hundreds of in-laws and cousins and uncles and aunts.

On Sunday, December 15, a report that Gómez had died spread in Maracay and filtered rather weakly about Caracas. The report was quickly denied by the doctors. Then, two days later, Tuesday, December 17, at two o'clock in the afternoon, Dr. Requena called the Hotel Jardín from the house of the dictator and announced to the cabinet ministers that Gómez was dead.

December 17 is the date of the anniversary of the

death of Simón Bolívar. Gómez had falsified the date of his birth to make it fall on the birthday of the Liberator. And two days before there had been that rumor of his death. The brujo had always been concerned about dates.

They buried him in the family vault which he had built in the cemetery at Maracay beside Hermenegilda and Alí. His sons carried the coffin from the motor hearse and all the high government officials and the foreign diplomats followed behind it. The people lined the streets and stared, blankly, and the men didn't remove their hats. They couldn't believe it was true.

RENACIMIENTO

Chapter XXXI

NEW ORDER

❖

THEY couldn't believe it at first. It took them two days to believe that the brujo was really dead and then it was like coming out of a trance. Courage flowed back into the people and they rose and stretched and felt the spell leave them as numbness leaves a cramped body.

They had been under a spell, actually—as actually as a nightmare leaves one shaking in helpless terror. They had been paralyzed in a blind, unreasoning fear that had crept over them and taken possession of them completely during all the years of hopelessness. It was not a physical fear—fear of death or torture or imprisonment—it was a psychic fear, centering on only one man, a brujo, who was invulnerable to all human antagonisms, who survived, year after year, with magic ease, the bullets of assassins, the organized plans of enemies, the opposing will of the whole people. So long as the brujo breathed the spell hung over them and the moment he ceased to breath, or rather the moment they were convinced that he had ceased to breath, it lifted.

During the last years of Juan Vicente's life there had been many periods during which he lay unconscious, utterly helpless, dead, so far as his ability to act against his enemies was concerned. The people knew that. Yet, from 1931, all hope had died, the paralysis of fear had seized the pueblo and no action had been raised. The brujo still breathed and while he breathed he was a

menace. During those times the nation had been without a head. There had been no one to direct the brujo's
lightning, there was no one else whom the people
really feared, but he lived and that knowledge alone was
enough. The last attack had rendered Gómez completely
helpless for over two weeks before he died, yet the
people, knowing it, remained as utterly docile as they
had when he sat in Miraflores and directed his killers.

He died on December 17, at least he was officially
reported dead on that date, and it took the people two
days to believe it. On the 19th the spell lifted suddenly
and, oddly, it lifted simultaneously over the whole country. On the afternoon of that day, while they were bury-
ing the brujo in Maracay, the people rose up in Caracas, in Maracaibo, in Coro, in Táchira—everywhere, all
over the country.

In Caracas the people poured into the Plaza Bolívar,
shouting, laughing, demanding. "Se murió el Bagre!
Viva la Libertad!" "The Catfish is dead! Long live
Liberty!" They were answered by volleys of rifle fire
from the police of Rafael Velasco, the Governor of
Caracas. Many fell dead and wounded. In Maracaibo,
they were fired upon by the soldiers of Pérez Soto.
Once, that would have been enough. Once, they would
have fled and the rising spirits would have been
drowned in terror then and there. Not now, though.
It was the brujo they had feared and now the brujo was
dead. He wasn't a brujo after all, for he had died. They
hadn't feared his rifles nor his prisons nor his chácharos.[1]
They didn't fear Velasco nor Eustóquio nor Pérez Soto
nor García nor Jurado nor Tellería.

So they gathered up their dead and wounded, left the

[1] Literally, the mountain boors. In Caracas the term came to be applied to the Andean mounted troops under the command of Velasco
that patrolled the city streets and caused deep resentment among the
people.

plaza and marched through the city streets, shouting, waving hastily-lettered placards. They went to the office of the *Nuevo Diario,* the most servile of the Catfish's newspapers, and tore the building apart. They wrecked a theater belonging to old Pimentel and the club where the muchachos held their orgies. They tore down every picture of the General from the walls of offices and from store windows and burned them. They moved out to the boulevards of Paraiso and took the houses of the Gómezs apart, brick by brick. When the provisional president, López Contreras, learned that Velasco had fired on the people he removed him and put Félix Galaviz in his place and warned him that he wouldn't tolerate such action under any circumstances.

Contreras was an elderly man—tall, thin, bespectacled. He was a soldier by profession, had been an officer under Castro in the days of the Restoration, had studied military science in foreign countries, had risen to become Minister of War under Gómez. As a soldier, he had been loyal to the government he served and he had obeyed orders unquestioningly. He had arrested his own son during the student-army revolt of 1928 and saw him imprisoned in the Rotunda and beaten into a bloody mess by García. Nevertheless, he had a reputation for justice, however stern, and enjoyed considerable popularity in the army and among the civilian population. Everyone conceded his honesty. Goméz had sent him as the nation's representative in the arbitration of the Tacna-Arica dispute, giving him thirty thousand bolívars for expenses. When Contreras returned, he turned back fifteen thousand bolívars to the nation. An unheard-of procedure.

He had never betrayed the slightest antagonism to Gómez nor distaste for his methods. He had always been considered a steady, quiet, trustworthy man who was too interested in his job of soldiering to have time for social or political philosophies.

When Gómez died he left his organization intact. The army was loyal, the strong men still occupied the key positions in the body-politic and there was no reason to suspect that Contreras would not continue along the old lines, utilizing the same elements. In fact he was expected to do just that both by the Gómez followers and by the people. He was expected to attempt it, at least, for it was considered certain that there would be trouble and plenty of it, once the bonds of terror were struck from the people by the dictator's death.

So his immediate declaration for repudiation of the old system was a complete surprise. He announced a new order. He emptied the prisons of political offenders and invited all the exiles to return to the country. One of his first acts was to remove Eustóquio Gómez from the presidency of Táchira.

The old crowd was amazed. They looked at one another and muttered, "Traitor!" The pueblo was amazed, but skeptical. It was some kind of trick, surely.

The day after the demonstration in Caracas, the day after Gómez had been buried, Eustóquio came into the city with ten or twelve followers, armed to the teeth. They drove up to the new Government House facing the Plaza Bolívar and pushed their way into the offices of the Provisional President. The crowd, still bravo from yesterday, not at all cowed by the slaughter that Velasco's guns had wrought, learned that Eustóquio was in the Government House and formed in a clamoring mass outside the building. They wanted Eustóquio's head.

"Eustóquio's head!" the people shouted. "We want Eustóquio's head!"

Eustóquio appeared on the balcony with his handful of men, their guns ready.

"I have come to finish with the traitor who is inside!" he cried. "If you want my head, come and get it!"

The people were unarmed but that didn't matter, now. They surged toward the entrance to the building. Among them was a young, tall man, slender and handsome, with the best sort of dark handsomeness that the Venezuelan criollo type produces. His ankles bore the scars of grillos. This man raised his arms and calmed the crowd. "Let me go in alone," he said. "I have suffered more than any of you."

The people stayed where they were and the young man went into the building. He mounted the stairway to the second floor, met Eustóquio in the corridor and shot him dead.

The crowd went wild. They burned Eustóquio's car in front of the Government House and swarmed through the streets of the city looking for more houses to sack.

López Contreras informed the members of the Gómez family and the worst offenders against the people among the old régime that he would not be responsible for their safety, that he would not use arms against the pueblo in their protection. He advised them to leave the country at once and offered them a gunboat to transport them to Curaçao.

So nearly a hundred of the Gómez clan boarded the gunboat, *Zamora,* at the port of Ocumare, near Maracay. They left the back way, for they would never have gotten through Caracas alive. Mísia Amelia, the muchachos, Gonzalo, Velasco and all the in-laws and cousins and uncles and aunts, gathered up what articles of value they could, all the money they could lay their hands on and sailed to Curaçao. From there, they scattered to various countries. Velasco went to his ranch in Canada, Santos Matute went to Jamaica and the family of Mísia Amelia went to Santo Domingo where they were sure to find refuge and sympathy under the dictator, Trujillo. No one knows how much money they carried away with them but it was known to be considerable. One of the muchachos deposited two million dollars in gold in the Maduro Bank in Curaçao.

Many others left the country by other means. Some got away in airplanes and some, disguised, in steamships. The former Secretary of State, Itriago Chacín, tried that but he was caught at La Guayra. Pérez Soto got away to Trinidad in a private yacht. Some of them remained in hiding in the country. Regina Gómez, her leg broken during the excitement of the public demonstration, has stayed in hiding in Caracas ever since. For a prim old maid, Regina has seen a lot of excitement in her life. She saw the Sesenta leave for Caracas and watched the attack on the palace of Miraflores in 1918 from behind a balcony curtain.

The Caraqueños tell a story about the embarkation of the royal family on the *Zamora*. Unfortunately this story, too, has to be explained beforehand.

One of Mísia Amelia's daughters was married to a notorious homosexual. The Venezuelan slang word for his kind is pato which means duck and is the equivalent of our word, "fairy."

The *Zamora* was quite a tiny craft and the story has it that, when the crowd of refugees with all their belongings and heavy boxes of gold went aboard, the queer one and the two muchachos approached the captain and expressed the fear that the vessel would sink.

The captain, a lean Margariteño, delighting in the situation, replied, "Sink? What are you worrying about? You, my friend, are a duck and can fly and you, muchachos, are sons of the Catfish and ought to be able to swim."

After the killing of Eustóquio Gómez there were several months of quiet in Venezuela. Contreras was going about his reorganization slowly and the people, still skeptical, were impatient with his conservative progress but inclined to give him a chance. The press and radio were entirely free.

For the first time in thirty years, actually for the first time in Venezuelan history, there was complete freedom of speech, press and assembly. The exiles began to pour back into the country. They were met at the boat by delegations of citizens and greeted like heroes. There were meetings on every street corner, there was speech after speech. Everyone made speeches—the bootblacks, the taxi drivers, the city bums. The returning exiles and all the released prisoners told their stories and every edition of the newspapers screamed with them. The airwaves throbbed with them. Everything came out—all the stories of the years of suffering, all the details of the torturings and horrors, all the pent-up hate of years against the Gómez tribe. The streets were flooded with printed hate by day and the air with spoken hate by night.

The right to organize labor unions was granted and inside of two weeks' time every possible type of worker had organized, even domestic cooks, and some of them had exercised the right of strike just to see what it was like.

Contreras was proceeding too slowly. There were still many of the old régime among his appointees. True, he was putting into office some of the liberal element, some of the released prisoners and returned exiles, but Galaviz was Governor of Caracas, Jurado was president of Falcón, Pérez Soto, Tellería and many other state presidents still held their old jobs and the Gómez Congress was still intact. The public began to clamor more and more loudly against the delay, to demand the immediate liquidation of all Gómez accounts. "Liquidación!" the orators began to cry. "Liquidación!"

Chapter XXXII

LIQUIDACIÓN!

❖

WITH the sudden new freedom that came to the people and the influx of the young exiles, there developed a tendency to radicalism among some elements. The younger exiles, especially those who had taken refuge in Mexico, brought back communistic and anticlerical doctrines which they preached among the working classes with the proselyting zeal that always marks the radical thinker. The nature of their sojourn in foreign lands—that of political exiles—placed them at once in the rôle of crusaders and they were sought out by the radical organizations in those lands and had come to absorb their philosophies. So now the free press gave space to their propaganda and the free radio gave time to their speeches. Furthermore, all sorts of personal attacks, accusations of the most sensational kind, against the hated Gomecistas appeared in the newspapers every day. Félix Galaviz, Governor of Caracas, didn't like that at all.

On the 10th of February, 1936, the Minister of Fomento, Dr. Pedro París, announced a policy of strict censorship of the radio and the next day *El Heraldo* printed an editorial denouncing the action. On the 12th, Félix Galaviz replied with an order to all periodicals prohibiting publication of articles directed against public officials, articles of attack on individuals, articles of inflammatory nature which would have a tendency to arouse the public, articles wich reflected communistic principles, and commanding that all copy be submitted to the office of the Governor for approval before publication.

On the 13th the newspaper publishers met and issued a statement declaring the suspension of their periodicals until the order should be rescinded. The Federation of Students declared itself in sympathy with the newspapers. The directors of the Caracas radio station announced their co-operation in the protest and the leaders of the gremios, the labor unions, met hastily and declared a general strike which should go into effect the following morning. Heavy-type circulars were run off the presses and distributed over the city during the afternoon.

The evening of the 13th was fairly quiet, although there was speech-making in the plaza and restaurants and shops were forcibly closed and the crowd discovered one of Gómez's old spies on the street and hacked him to death.

On the morning of the 14th the city was in the grip of the general strike. All shops were closed, their heavy doors padlocked, no street cars nor taxis moved. The streets were filled with citizens moving toward the plaza on foot. By eight o'clock the plaza and all the four streets around it were dense with people. The same plaza where the Indians from the Andes had camped when the Restorers had come into the city, the same four streets that the carriages of the Caraqueños had circled when Juan Vicente Gómez had stood by the statue of Bolívar and watched the moving lights. The center was strangely quiet without the accustomed noise of traffic. The sun was very bright and the hum of human voices hung on the warm air like the drone of bees.

There was great talking and moving of arms and hands. Everyone talked at once. The crowd was split up into hundreds of little groups, each group surrounding an impassioned orator. At first the composite sound was low in the open expanse of the square, like the drone of bees, and then, as the morning went on, it grew louder, occasional voices rose in shouts till it was almost a roar.

At ten-thirty the doors of the balconies on the second floor of the Government House opened and soldiers came out and rested their rifles on the iron-grilled railings. There was the rattle of snapping bolts, an instant's silence, and then the roar of three volleys fired down into the mass of people in the plaza.

The screams of the victims rose with the roar of the guns and kept on when the roar was over. The people scattered, dropped to the ground, crouched below the plaza wall, crowded into shop doorways, got behind trees. There was some confusion among the soldiers on the balconies, wild gesticulations, and then they disappeared into the building. There was no more firing, no more "throwing of lead." The people poured back into the plaza to look after the victims.

Bodies lay everywhere, on the walks of the plaza, along the streets, leaning against the buildings, some of them crawling, some of them still. All of them seemed to be screaming.

They got them away rapidly. They carried them on their shoulders to the abulances and private cars that hurried to the center from all parts of the city. There were eight dead and two hundred wounded, many of whom died later.

There was blood everywhere. The asphalt streets were slippery with it and great puddles of it lay shining on the plaza walks.

The people soaked their handkerchiefs in it and wrote with it on the walls of the buildings, on the Casa Amarilla and the Government House, huge red letters as high up on the walls as they could reach. Great, red, scrawling letters, "Assassins!" "Death to Galaviz!"

L BENEMÉRITO

Forty-eight Hours
His Death, Pictures
Like This—

EL BAGRE

—Were Replaced by Pictures
Like This

"Death to the assassins!" They soaked their handkerchiefs and wrote until the blood in the pools had
thickened in the heat, till it had clotted up and wouldn't
write any more. Then they took the bloody handkerchiefs and draped them on the statue of Bolívar and
left them there. The red pennants hung there for many
days, till they were black and stiff and the breezes carried them off.

"Liquidación! Liquidación!" The people were aroused
now. They pillaged and sacked and burned. They
roamed the streets, demolishing offices and factories and
homes and burning motorcars. Liquidation of everything that smelled of Gómez. They broke into the
homes of everyone who had been connected with the
Gómez régime. They paraded through the streets, carrying the spoils. They sold silver platters and statuary and
champagne to anyone who offered a few bolívars. They
carried chairs and chinaware and water-closets to their
homes. They moved out into the suburbs and sacked
the quintas there, the houses of the Pimentels and Santanas and Pachecos and Tinocos and Llamosas and
Cárdenases and Garcías. Not only in Caracas, but all
over the country, the sacking went on as soon as word
got around. In the interior the Gómez haciendas were
burned and the cattle driven off or hamstrung.

A crowd, bearing the coffin of a little girl who had
been killed, paraded through the streets. They caried
placards lettered with blood and held aloft a picture of
the Liberator taken from the house of Pérez Soto.

Two drunken peons, their white drill suits and straw
hats covered with blood, reeled along, crying, "We are
the true sons of Liberty! We have bathed in the sacred
blood of the Martyrs!"

In the afternoon a great procession formed and
marched to the president's palace at Miraflores. It was
composed of all the elements of the city's population—

the merchants and lawyers and clerks and students and laborers and all their women. Everyone was dressed in his Sunday best and there was great calm and order. They massed in the streets around the palace for blocks. The spokesmen were granted an audience with the President and presented their demands. Contreras spoke over the radio and promised the people everything—absolute freedom of press and radio and speech. He ordered the arrest of Félix Galaviz and his trial on the charge of murder. He named new state presidents, cabinet members and other government officials, appointing for the most part, the old exiles and the new, progressive, youthful patriots—General Mibely, Régulo Olivares, Gabaldón, Néstor Luís Pérez, Félix Montes, Jorge Luciani, Ramon Gallegos, Gil Borges and so on —all liberals and old "enemies of the Cause." Most of them had suffered years of prison and exile. Many of them we have known as plotters against Gómez in New York and Europe.

The general strike was declared raised and the city returned to comparative normal, although the sacking continued in sudden spurts for four or five days, mostly at night and mostly in the suburbs. The mounted chácharos still patroled the streets at night and truckloads of soldiers rumbled about but no one was disturbed, not even the mobs in the act of looting houses.

The day after the shooting the people wandered through the plaza, staring at the bloody mementos, examining the nicks that the bullets had made in the concrete and in the tree trunks. A small crowd stood, laughing, about a bootblack who was carving letters in an acacia tree with his penknife. The tree was slender but no more slender than the boy for it had protected him from the bullets the day before. On the opposite side were the marks of two bullets, buried deep. The boy laughed as he carved and the people who watched

LIQUIDACIÓN!   307

him laughed. The words he cut into the tree were, "Dios bendiga este árbol." "God bless this tree." The letters will be there for many years. Gómez had never been able to understand the Caraqueños, not even the boot-blacks.

There were still some Gomecistas in public office and the people were not satisfied but they decided to be patient. Contreras initiated a series of radio talks in which he discussed frankly all the problems of the government. He cautioned the people to patience and asked them to help him in the suppression of the looting, pointing out that all the property of the Gómez estates now belonged to the nation and they were to be liquidated to settle the law-suits that were being brought in the courts against the Gómez heirs.

During the turmoil following the death of Gómez the element that wielded the greatest influence among the people was the F.E.V., Federación Estudiantil Venezolana. The president of the organization, young Jóvito Villalba, had been imprisoned in the Rotunda and the Libertador since 1928. He is a stirring speaker and his power in the new Venezuela that is forming is amazing. The Federation has the total sympathy of all the people and, so far, it has acted as go-between among the various elements and has exerted its influence for calmness and moderation. It did more than any other agent toward the discouraging of sacking.

An inventory was ordered of all property belonging to the Gómez family. These properties are so vast that it will be a long time before their value can become known. Many estimates have been made of the value of Juan Vicente's possessions and they range from two hundred million dollars to several billions, but such estimates are really vain. Gómez was not a man to let money lie idle and he was always putting it into new enterprises. Consequently it is doubtful that there will be much cash found among his possessions. The value of his complicated industrial and agricultural holdings is impossible to estimate and their realization at forced sale would be only a tiny part of their actual worth as based upon their income-producing power when in operation. The members of his family of course had large amounts of cash and easily liquidated assets such as jewelry but it is not known how much of this they carried away nor how much they had deposited or invested in foreign countries.

Meanwhile, all the thousands of victims of the Gómez reign of terror are bringing suits for damages against the estate in the Venezuelan courts. The widows and children of those who died in prison and on the carreteras, those who spent years in exile, suffering the loss of their businesses and suspension of their professional activities for the time, and those who lost their health or minds under Gómez's torturings, are filling the columns of the papers daily with their demands on the courts.

The one solid Gómez element that remained in the Venezuelan governmental structure was the Congress. The people clamored constantly that Contreras dissolve this body and appoint new members but he replied that as Provisional President he was not able to do that legally. He cautioned the people to be patient and await the election of April 19. On that date the old Gómez Congress met and, in the face of the great pressure of public opinion, elected López Contreras Constitutional President.

That is the situation in Venezuela today. Contreras has reacted against the old régime and is proceeding slowly toward complete eradication of all Gómez elements but he is criticized somewhat on two sides. The more conservative faction is impatient of his tolerance of certain radical tendencies in the people and criticize him for not suppressing drastically the looting and street demonstrations. The new liberal-to-the-limit faction is impatient with his caution. They still are a little skeptical. They point to his long connection with the Gómez régime, his personal friendships with some of the worst of the Gómez tribe. They make much of the fact that he aided the Gómez family to get away with their money instead of arresting them all, that he let Velasco and Pérez Soto get away, that he appointed Galaviz Governor of Caracas. They have distinct communistic leanings and recently have raised demonstrations demanding the expulsion of the priests.

The oil companies view this latter element with apprehension. The radicals are working their propaganda upon a very volatile laboring class that is still in the intoxication of emergence from political impotence, that is composed entirely of illiterates. And it is so very easy to destroy a whole oil field by the tossing of a match.

López Contreras heads a nation that is without any debt whatever. There are ninety-six million bolívars in the national treasury. The income from oil alone is enough to defray all ordinary expenses of the government and that income is constantly increasing and should continue to increase.

He has initiated a good program of public works and is reorganizing the educational system under the direction of the writer, Romulo Gallegos. He has taken off his military uniform. He has finished with the system of jefe civil cutthroats in the villages of the interior and now, instead of coroneles and tenientes and generales, the officials are Citizen Fulano, Citizen Fulanito.

He has cleaned out the old crowd almost completely, both within the country and among the officials who serve abroad.

He always had great prestige with the army and he

has consolidated it into complete loyalty by naming young Colonel Isaías Medina Minister of War and Marine.

He opened the Rotunda to the public so that everyone could go inside and see its horrors and read the words that were scratched on the walls of the cells and then he ordered it demolished.

Unfortunately he is an elderly man and his tuberculosis is said to have become aggravated.

The Castillo del Libertador squats on the rocks in the harbor of Puerto Cabello. The sun is always on the moldy walls and the waves of the Caribbean always beat about their foundations.

The people crowded down to the water's edge by the seawall, under the shade of the coconut palms that nodded their plumes to the breeze, and looked toward the Castillo.

The heavy doors of the prison swung open and a group of citizens pushed out a small flat-car that was piled high with iron that looked like scrap-iron in the distance. There were fourteen tons of iron on the flat-car.

They pushed the car along to the water's edge and halted it beside a barge that was tied up to the wharf. The citizens threw the iron pieces one at a time into the barge and the dull thumps came over the water like the sound of saluting cannon.

When the last piece had been tossed into the barge, the citizens cast off and a tug towed them out into the harbor. They stopped a few hundred yards from shore. The barge lay in the sunlight on the dancing water and the citizens tossed the iron, piece by piece, and the little white jets of spray leapt up to take them.

On the shore a young man spoke to the people. He was young but he looked old. He was thin and dark-

skinned with hollow cheeks and high forehead and he
had the sunken, burning eyes of a poet and zealot. His
ankles were scarred and his lungs were partly eaten
away.

Andres Eloy Blanco finished speaking to the people.
". . . We have thrown the grillos into the sea," he
said. "And curse the man who ever comes to make new
ones and to put a ring of iron about the flesh of a son
of Venezuela."

GRAPHS OF THE FINANCES
OF
VENEZUELA

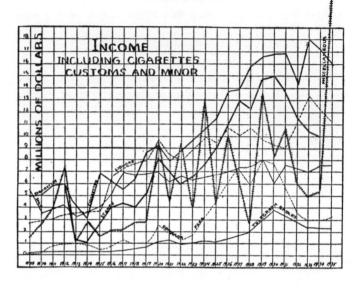

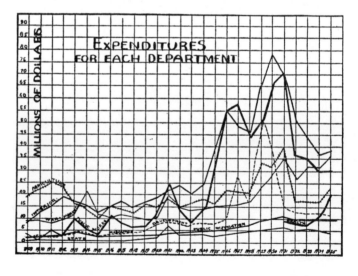

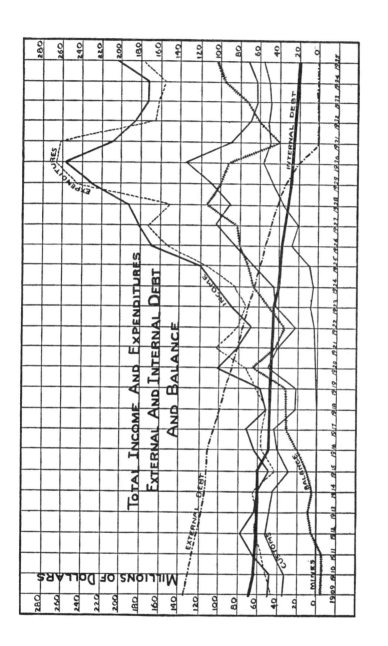

TOTAL INCOME AND EXPENDITURES
EXTERNAL AND INTERNAL DEBT
AND BALANCE

MILLIONS OF DOLLARS

EXPENDITURES

INCOME

EXTERNAL DEBT

INTERNAL DEBT

CUSTOMS

BALANCE

MEXES

280 260 240 220 200 180 160 140 120 100 80 60 40 20 0

1909 1910 1911 1912 1913 1914 1915 1916 1917 1918 1919 1920 1921 1922 1923 1924 1925 1926 1927 1928 1929 1930 1931 1931 1931 1934 1935

BIBLIOGRAPHY

❖

Angell, Hildegarde, *Simón Bolívar, South American Liberator.* New York, 1930.

Arcaya, Pedro Manuel, *Venezuela y su Actual Régimen.* Washington, 1935.

Bustillos, V. Márquez, *Semblanza de General Juan Vicente Gómez.* Caracas, 1919.

Catorce de Febrero, El. Caracas, 1936.

Contreras, Eleázar López, *Cualidades Militares de General J. V. Gómez.* Caracas, 1917.

Cournos, John, *Simón Bolívar, Liberator.* Indianapolis, 1928.

Cuentos Gregorianos. Caracas, 1936.

Flórez, Carlos M. y Otros, *Tiranias Gomecistas.* Caracas, 1936.

García, Antonio y Otros, *Presidios de Venezuela.* Bogotá, 1936.

Gil, Pio (Pedro María Morántes), *Personalismo y Verdades.* Caracas, 1936.

González, Fernándo, *Mi Compadre.* Barcelona, 1934.

González-Ruano, Cesar, *El Terror en América.* Caracas, 1936.

Juliac, J. M., *El General J. V. Gómez.* Caracas, 1936.

López, José Heriberto, *Veinte Anos sin Patria.* Habana, 1933.

Luciani, Jorge, *La Dictatura Perpetua de Gómez y sus Adversarios.* Caracas, 1936.

Mendoza, R. Tello, *Ligeros Rasgos de Juan Vicente Gómez.* Caracas, 1904.

Naranjo, Nemesio García, *Venezuela y su Gobernante.* Caracas, 1931.

Parra, Pedro María, *Venezuela Oprimada.* Curaçao, 1913.

Vaucaire, Michel, *Bolivar the Liberator.* New York, 1929.

Vivanco y Villegas, Aurelio de, *Venezuela al Dia.* Caracas, 1925.

Ybarra, T. R., *Bolívar: The Passionate Warrior.* New York, 1929.

INDEX

❖

320   INDEX

Restorers, 71, 77-78, 80, 94, 110,
243, 303
Revolutions against Gómez, 1928,
227-231, 269, 297; *Angelita* Expedition, 238-240; later, 241-
249, 274
Riera, General Gregorio, 92, 96,
98, 102, 124, 206
Rojas, Dr. Pedro José, 124, 226
Rolando, General Nicholas, 90,
92, 96-98, 100-106, 109, 124
Roosevelt, Theodore, 86, 97, 137,
139
Rotunda, 16, 30, 147, 153-154,
157, 182-184, 197, 199, 227, 231,
233-234, 243, 256, 297, 307, 310
Royal Dutch Shell (Caribbean
Petroleum Company), 166

San Carlos, prison, 147-149, 152-
153, 156, 184, 197, 230, 233
Santander, General, 17, 19, 21
Santos Matute, *see* Gómez, Santos
Matute
Sinclair Oil Company, 167
Slaves, liberated, 24
Soto, Pérez, 73, 175, 185, 206, 238,
267, 296, 300, 309, 301, 305
Soublette, General, 23
Spy system, 133, 158-159, 161, 179,
186, 190, 195-197, 230-231, 243,
283, 303
Spaniards, coming of, 13-16, 167
Standard of California, 166
Standard Oil Company, 164

Standard of Indiana (Lago Petro-
leum Company), 166
Standard of New Jersey, 166-167
"Student Week," 228, 235
Sucre, General, 17, 21
Sun Oil Company, 164, 166

Tarazona, 140, 143, 181, 215, 222,
264, 271, 288, 291
Taxes, 276-277
Tellería, General Arístides, 96,
124, 127, 158, 206, 238, 296, 301
Terán, General Mario, 239
Texas Oil Company, 166
Tocuyito, 74, 77, 91, 95, 113
Trinidad, 91, 104, 158, 244, 300

United States, 22, 25, 163, 165,
184
Urbina, Rafael Simón, 240-241,
248-249

Velasco, Rafael María, 159, 199,
204, 234, 296-298, 309
Venezuelan Oil Law, 1818, 168
Venezuelan Post Office Depart-
ment, 195
Vidal, General Zoilo, 92, 96-97,
124, 184
Villalba, Jóvito, 307

Wilhelm II, Kaiser, 86, 137, 140,
161

Zoila, Mísia, 118-120, 145, 160